MW00953429

A NEW AND CONCISE HISTORY OF THE PRESIDENTS OF THE UNITED STATES OF AMERICA

Andrew W. Martin

Copyright © 2024 Andrew W. Martin

All rights reserved

No part of this book may be reproduced, or stored in a retrieval system, or
transmitted in any form or by any means, electronic, mechanical, photocopying,
recording, or otherwise, without express written permission of the publisher.

ISBN: 9798874201937

Cover design by: Art Painter
Library of Congress Control Number: 2018675309
Printed in the United States of America

CONTENTS

FOREWORD

This book about the history of the Presidents of the United States will be of enormous interest to both the general reader that would like to know more about the subject as well as students at school or college who may need it for their studies. It tells the story about all the Presidents since George Washington was elected as the first one in 1789 right up to the present day. For each President there is a detailed summary of their lives and careers, including their background, their entry and progress in politics, their election campaigns and results, their terms in office and their lives after the presidency. The principal events of each presidential term are described along with a description of their key decisions, policies and legislation. Readers will be able to see how they all shaped their times, and how they were shaped by them, and contributed towards the growth and development of America. The reader will also be able to see how the role of the President has evolved and changed since it was first created in the Constitution of the United States. Dates of birth and death, and details of marriages and children are made immediately available at the head of each chapter. Tables in the text provide the details of every result in the presidential elections since 1789. A useful series of appendices provide further interesting information about the Presidents and their achievements, as well their First Ladies.

The history of the Presidents of the United States is a subject that people want to know about and this interesting book will be of appeal to everyone with an interest in history or politics.

INTRODUCTION

The President of the United States is the nation's chief executive, head of state and head of government. The office is the most important in America and the most powerful in the world. Under the Constitution of the United States, the President has many duties. As the head of the executive branch of government, he is responsible for making sure that all the federal laws are faithfully executed (put into effect). As Commander-in-Chief, he is responsible for leading the nation's armed forces and directing the nation's defense in peace and war. He sets a legislative agenda for Congress by making an annual *State of the Union* address and can influence the legislature by threatening to veto any bills that they pass. He directs America's domestic and foreign policies. He nominates members of the Supreme Court as well as Cabinet ministers, ambassadors, and other important officials. He controls the nation's powerful arsenal of nuclear weapons and can decide if they are used.

To become President, a politician must first be nominated by his party at a national convention. He must then win an election which takes place every four years. The voters of America each cast one ballot to elect an Electoral College that will select the new President. The presidential election takes place at the start of November and then the President is inaugurated in Washington D.C. on the following 20th January. If the serving President dies, resigns, or is removed from office then the Vice-President will become President. If the Electoral College fails to give any candidate a majority, then the U.S. House of Representatives will choose a President from the top three candidates. Unless a President dies in office or resigns, then the only way he can be removed from office is by impeachment. Impeachment requires a majority vote in the U.S. House of Representatives and a two-thirds majority vote in the U.S Senate.

A total of 45 men have served as President of the United States since George Washington was elected as the first one in 1789. One President, Grover Cleveland, served two non-consecutive spells in office and is considered as both the 22nd and the 24th President. There have therefore been 46 presidencies in 234 years with Joe Biden currently serving as the 46th President. All the Presidents have had a great impact on the development of America and the history of the world. This book will tell you something of their story.

BACKGROUND

After the thirteen British colonies won their independence from Great Britain in the *Revolutionary War* (1775 – 1783) they had to decide how they would be governed. At first, the thirteen new states attempted to establish a single government under what were known as the *Articles of Confederation*. However, under the terms of the Articles, each state behaved like a separate independent country. For instance, they continued to use twelve different currencies and to tax each other's goods. Some states also attempted to avoid paying for the debts that they had built up during the war. There was a risk of conflict and bloodshed between them. Far-sighted statesmen like George Washington and Alexander Hamiton called for a far stronger national government under a new or revised constitution.

In 1787, Hamilton helped to establish a national convention to which each state could send representatives to discuss and revise the Articles. On 14th May 1787, representatives of every state except Rhode Island met at the *Constitutional Convention* in Philadelphia. It soon became apparent that the delegates did not just want to revise the Articles of Confederation, they wanted to create an entirely new constitution that would set out a different and better way for the country to be governed. Although the task was challenging and difficult, the delegates succeeded in creating the *Constitution of the United States* that set up a new government that would directly exercise its authority over all the citizens of the United States of America.

The architects of the new constitution created a *federal* government where powers were divided between the national and state governments. They attempted to achieve a balanced national government by dividing authority between three separate independent branches – the Legislative, the Executive and the Judiciary. Under this arrangement, the Legislative branch would create the laws, the Executive branch would put the laws into effect and the Judicial Branch would evaluate and determine the meaning of the laws.

The delegates at the Constitutional Convention believed that the Legislative Branch was the most important part of the new Constitution and so the organization and powers of the new Congress were set out in Article I. The role and powers of the President were set out in Article II. It was in this part of the new Constitution that the office of President was created and his term was set at four years. Article II also created the office of Vice-President and said that he would be elected at the same time as the President and for the same term. The new Constitution stated that power would pass to the Vice-President in the event of the death or removal of the President. Further sections of the Article said that the President must be a citizen of the United States, must be at least 35 years old and must have been a resident in the country for at least 14 years. The Article stated that salary was to be provided to the President and that he would be the Commander-in-Chief of the U.S. Army and Navy, could make treaties, and appoint Ministers and Ambassadors.

Another important section of the 2nd Article of the Constitution said that before a President could take office, he must swear the following oath:

"I do solemnly swear (or affirm), that I will faithfully execute the Office of President of the United States, and will to the best of my Ability, preserve, protect and defend the Constitution of the United States."

The second Article also created the Electoral College, a group of people chosen by the voters of each state to elect the President and Vice-President.

The Constitution was signed by the delegates on the 17th September 1787 and sent to each state for ratification. Three months later, Delaware became the first state to ratify the Constitution. By early 1789, eleven states had ratified the Constitution and all them except New York then selected the presidential electors either in their legislatures or by the direct vote of the people. America's first presidential election then took place between 15th December 1788 and 7th January 1789, and on 4th February 1789 it was announced that George Washington would be the first President of the United States. He was inaugurated in New York on the 30th April 1789.

Since the Constitution was originally signed, there have been 27 Amendments made under the rules set by the Constitution. Four of these have directly impacted on the role of the President.

1 – In 1804, the *12th Amendment* stated that the electors in the Electoral College would could cast one vote for the President and one for the Vice-President. Up until then the electors would cast two votes and whoever got the most would be the President and whoever got the second-most would be the Vice-President. This change was made after Thomas Jefferson and Aaron Burr received the same number of votes and the House of Representatives then took a long time to decide which one should be the President.

2 – In 1933, the *20th Amendment* moved the day of inauguration from the 4th March to the 20th January. This change was made after President Herbert Hoover lost the election in 1932 and was then a "Lame Duck" President for four months until the 4th March 1933. A "Lame Duck" is an official that continues to serve in office but has not been elected. What is called the *Lame Duck Amendment* reduced the time that such Presidents served.

3 – In 1951, the *22nd Amendment* limited each President to two terms providing that they had not already served more than two years of another President's term. The maximum length of time that a President can serve is therefore ten years. This change was made because some people thought that President Franklin D. Roosevelt should not have served four terms between 1933 and 1945.

4 – In 1967, the *25th Amendment* stated that a Vice-President shall replace the President in the event of the Chief Executive's death, disability or removal from office. Also, it also stated whenever there is a vacancy in the office of Vice-President then the President should then nominate a new Vice-President who will then take office upon confirmation by a majority vote of both houses of Congress. In 1973, six years after this Amendment was ratified, Gerald R. Ford was the

first Vice-President chosen under this amendment when he replaced
Spiro   Agnew.

CHAPTER 1 - GEORGE WASHINGTON

1st President of the United States 1789 – 1797

Born: 22ⁿᵈ February 1732, Popes Creek, Virginia

Married: Martha Dandridge Custis (1731 – 1802), 6ᵗʰ January 1759

Number of Children: None

Died: 14ᵗʰ December 1799, Mount Vernon, Virginia

Final Resting Place: Mount Vernon, Virginia

Introduction

George Washington was a hero of the American Revolution who was unanimously elected as the nation's first President. He had already long held a reputation as a man of brave and noble character whose heroic and courageous leadership could unite people behind him. He was elected as a representative of Virginia at the First Continental Congress in 1774. He was then appointed Commander-in-Chief of the Continental Army by the Second Continental Congress which also approved the Declaration of Independence from Great Britain in 1776. As commander he won a series of stirring victories over the British including Trenton (1776), Saratoga (1777) and Yorktown (1781). In 1783 the British recognized the Independence of the United States of America. Washington then presided over the Constitutional Convention (1787 – 1788) which created the U.S. Constitution. In 1789 he was unanimously elected as the first President. During his first term he set many new precedents and appointed the architect Pierre L'Enfant to design a new capital city for the nation. In 1792 he was once again unanimously elected and used his second term to restore relations with Great Britain and to remain neutral in a wide-ranging and destructive European war. His death in 1799 was followed by great national mourning and the new federal capital was later named after him. Today he is remembered as one of America's greatest ever Presidents.

Background

George Washington was born at Pope's Creek, in the British colony of Virginia, on 22nd February 1732. He was the eldest of six children of Augustus Washington and his second wife, Mary Ball. Augustus also had four children from his first marriage. George's great-grandfather, John Washington, had sailed from England in the seventeenth century and decided to settle in America after being shipwrecked in the Potomac River. John's son Lawrence was George's grandfather.

George grew up on a farm near Fredericksburg and received only irregular schooling. However, by the age of fourteen he could read, write and perform arithmetic. He then did two years further studying to prepare for a career as a surveyor on the frontier. George's elder half-brother, Lawrence, was a former soldier in the British army that had fought against the Spanish in Central America. His war stories inspired George to join the British army and when he was twenty years old, he was commissioned as a major in the Virginia militia.

In 1754 a conflict broke out in North America between the British and the French known as the French and Indian War. George became aide-de-camp to Britain's General Braddock and advised him on the methods of warfare used by Native Americans on the frontier. On 9th July 1755, French and Native American forces ambushed Braddock and Washington on what became known as the Battle of Monongahela. Braddock was killed and his forces defeated, but Washington survived even though he had two horses shot from underneath him. Later in the war he was commissioned as a Colonel and became Commander-in-Chief of all the Virginia forces.

The French and Indian War became part of a wider global conflict known as the Seven Years War. The war ended very successfully for Britain and George returned to life on his plantation where he became a successful farmer. He did own slaves but historians say that they were always well cared for. On the 6th January 1759 he married Martha Dandridge Custis, a widow whose husband had left a fortune in land and money. They had no children together but George became the step-father of the two children from her first marriage, John and Martha.

The American Revolution

In the 1770's relations between Britain and her colonies deteriorated. The colonists were angered when the British imposed taxes to help pay for the colonists' defense. This included an unpopular new tax that was introduced on imported tea. The colonists said that they should not have to pay taxes unless they were represented in the British parliament. In the Boston Tea Party of December 1773, protestors dressed as Native Americans boarded three British ships in Boston Harbor and threw their cargoes overboard. In 1774, Washington was one of seven delegates elected to represent Virginia at the First Continental Congress in Philadelphia where a boycott of British goods was approved. In 1775 he was elected to attend the Second Continental Congress but by the time he arrived in Philadelphia the war with Britain had already broken out and the battles at Lexington and Concord had been fought in Massachusetts.

Most delegates of the Congress still wanted to avoid war but feared that this may not be possible. Washington advised them on how to build and supply an army to defend their cities. On 14th June the delegates called on Pennsylvania, Maryland and Virginia to send troops to the assistance of Boston, which had fallen under British occupation. Washington was unanimously elected Commander-in-Chief following a proposal made by John Adams and he accepted the command on 16th June 1775. Eight years of warfare now followed between the colonists and Great Britain. In March 1776 Washington succeeded in driving the British out of Boston. On 4th

July 1776, the Congress approved the Declaration of Independence from Great Britain. At this time the colonies were bitterly divided. Many colonists wanted neither war nor independence and it was only Washington's leadership that kept them united.

After the colonists' early victories, the war started to move in Britain's favor and they drove the rebels from Long Island and New York. Washington's army suffered from shortages in pay and supplies, mutinies and desertion, and it was a great achievement for him to hold it together. Most of his men were amateur volunteers and many were not properly fit or reliable. By December 1776, Washington was down to his last three thousand men and it seemed that the war would soon be over. However, on 20th December he was reinforced with further troops from Pennsylvania which gave him a total of 7,600 men. On Christmas Night, Washington led his army across the Delaware River where they made a surprise attack on Britain's unsuspecting Hessian mercenaries camping at Trenton. In the short battle that followed, Washington's troops won an overwhelming victory for the loss of only two men.

The effect of this small battle was enormous and some historians believe that it changed the history of the world. The colonists then realized that their cause was not lost and united behind Washington. In 1777 he defeated the British at the Battle of Saratoga and as a result France entered the war on the colonists' side. On 28th September 1781, Washington surrounded Lord Cornwallis's army of 8,000 troops at Yorktown and forced them to surrender. The war was now effectively over and two years of peace negotiations led to the Treaty of Paris in September 1783 in which Britain agreed to recognize the independence of the United States of America.

The Presidential Election of 1789

After the war, Washington returned to his estate at Mount Vernon. As a newly independent country, America now needed to determine how she was to be governed. When the Articles of Confederation proved too weak, the states agreed to call a meeting to revise them. On 25th May 1787, the Constitutional Convention opened in Philadelphia and the delegates elected Washington as President of the convention. He held the convention together as the debates about the constitution went on throughout the summer and agreement was reached in September.

Throughout 1788 the states of America began to prepare to adopt the new constitution and in February 1789 the members of the first Electoral College met in their own states and voted. At that time each elector voted for two persons. The person with the most votes became President and the runner-up became Vice-President. There were 69 electors in total and Washington was elected President with 69 votes, the highest number possible. John Adam was elected Vice-President with 34 votes.

Presidential Election of 1789	
Candidate	Electoral Votes
George Washington	69
John Adams	34
John Jay	9
Robert H. Harrison	6
John Rutledge	6
John Hancock	4
George Clinton	3
Samuel Huntingdon	2
John Milton	2
James Armstrong	1
Benjamin Lincoln	1
Edward Telfair	1
Not Voted	8

Washington's First Administration 1789 – 1793

On 30th April 1789 Washington was sworn in as the first President of the United States in a ceremony at Federal Hall in New York City.

He was very conscious that he was serving in an important new office and that everything he did would constitute a precedent to be followed by those that came after him. Indeed, every President elected since Washington has publicly taken the oath of office outdoors, made an inaugural address, and delivered an annual State of the Union speech to Congress. However, Washington was not the first President to live in either the White House or Washington D.C. as neither existed at that time. The first Executive Mansion was a house belonging to Samuel Osgood on Cherry Street, New York. In 1790 Washington moved to a larger house in Broadway. In 1790, Congress made Philadelphia the capital and Washington moved into a grand house in the city belonging to the financier Robert Morris. Washington also made many trips to Mount Vernon during his time in office and would stay there for up to three months when Congress was not in session.

Washington believed that the three branches of the government should be kept as separate as possible and he tried not to influence the laws being passed by Congress. However, he believed that he should veto any bill that they passed that he disagreed with. On 4th July 1789 he approved without comment the first important bill to be passed by Congress, which set a tax on imports to raise money to fund the government.

By September 1789, Congress had created three new departments to help run the government, namely the Treasury, the Department of Foreign Affairs, and the Department of War. They also created the post of Attorney General. Washington appointed men he knew and trusted to the run them. Thomas Jefferson, who had served with Washington in the Virginia legislature, was appointed Secretary of State. Henry Knox, who had been Washington's chief of artillery in the Revolutionary War, became Secretary of War. Alexander Hamilton, who had been one of Washington's military aides, became Secretary of the Treasury. Edmund Randolph, an old friend who had served as a governor of Virginia and a member of the Constitutional Convention, became Attorney General. In addition, Washington appointed John Jay as the first Chief Justice of the United States. A Congressman from Virginia, James Madison, became an important adviser to Washington. Washington called the group together for their first meeting in 1791 and from 1793 the term *Cabinet* was used to describe them.

When Washington became President there were only eleven states in the Union. Then North Carolina became a state in 1789, Rhode Island in 1791, Kentucky in 1792 and Tennessee in 1796. The First National Census began in 1790 and it took more than 200 census-takers 18 months to complete it. The population of the United States was recorded as being 3,923,214 including 697,000 slaves. As a result, Congress passed a bill to raise the number of US representatives from 67 to 120. However, in April 1792, Washington made his first veto of Congressional legislation and rejected it. He thought it was unconstitutional for some states to have more representatives in proportion to their population than others. Many people thought that the bill favored the northern states over the southern ones. Congress then revised the bill to provide for a house with 103 members.

In July 1790 Congress approved a bill to transfer the government to Philadelphia until 1800. After that the capital would be transferred to a new capital city to be located on the Potomac River. Washington appointed the architect Pierre L'Enfant to design the new city. When it was built it would bear Washington's name and be independent from the other states in its own separate administrative area known as the District of Columbia. In 1791, Congress passed the Bill of Rights, which became law on 15th December. The Bill created the first ten amendments to the US Constitution and guaranteed basic liberties to the American people.

When Washington became President, the government had millions of dollars of debt. The new Secretary of the Treasury, Alexander Hamilton, proposed a plan to put the finances straight. The plan was finally passed after much debate in July 1790 and the new national government assumed the wartime debts of the states. The following year, Hamilton sought the passage of a bill to create the First Bank of the United States. Jefferson and Randolph opposed the bill, arguing that there were no such powers to create such a bank given in the Constitution. Hamilton argued that the government could use all powers except those denied by the Constitution. Washington had to decide whether the Constitution gave the government the power to charter such a corporation. He believed in a strong central government and so signed the law.

It was during Washington's first term in office that America's first political parties began to develop. Those that supported Hamilton's views of a stronger national government began to call themselves *Federalists*. They found strong support in the Northern states as well as from bankers and manufacturers. Those who favored Jefferson's idea that the Constitution should be strictly interpreted to defend states' rights called themselves *Anti-Federalists* or *Democratic-Republicans*. They found strong support among the Southern states and the farmers. Washington tried to discourage the growth of the political parties and to bring the different sides into agreement.

The Presidential Election of December 1792

In 1792, Washington began to prepare for retirement and asked James Madison to help prepare his farewell address. Although Madison did so, he also urged Washington to accept re-election. Washington was also separately asked to continue as President by each of the members of his cabinet. Jefferson persuaded him that he could act a focus of unity that would bring all parts of the country together.

In December 1792, the 132 members of the Electoral College cast their votes in the country's second election. When the votes were counted in February 1793, Washington was once again unanimously elected. Adams was once again the runner-up with 77 votes and continued as Vice-President.

Presidential Election of 1792		
Candidate	Party	Electoral Votes
George Washington	Federalist	132
John Adams	Federalist	77
George Clinton	Democratic Republican	50

Thomas Jefferson	Democratic Republican	4
Aaron Burr	Democratic Republican	1
Not Voted	*	6

Washington's Second Administration 1793 – 1797

Washington was 61 years old when his second inauguration took place in the Congress Hall in Philadelphia on March 4th 1793. He had to face greater problems during his second term than during his first. The biggest problems concerned foreign policy. In 1793 a war broke out in Europe between Britain, Prussia, Austria and Spain on one side and the new French Republic on the other. The USA had signed an alliance with the King Louis XVI of France in 1778 but Washington wanted to remain neutral and signed a Neutrality Proclamation on 22nd April. This promised impartiality to all sides and prohibited American ships from carrying war supplies to the countries fighting. The French were angry that the USA had not stood by them. However, they had just beheaded the king who had made the treaty.

The French appointed a new ambassador, Edmond Genet, to the United States and he was formally received by Washington. Genet was determined to draw America into the war on the side of France and he secretly tried to win the support of the Democratic-Republicans to the French cause. In the summer of 1793, he tried to outfit French warships in American ports and send them to sea to fight the British. This angered Washington and he asked France to recall Genet because he endangered American neutrality. Genet was stripped of his power but was allowed to remain in the United States.

At the same time as relations with France went downhill, relations with Britain also deteriorated. British warships prevented American ships from carrying food supplies to France and seized their cargoes. They sometimes took sailors off American ships and forced them to serve in the Royal Navy. British troops refused to give up the western frontier forts which they were supposed to have surrendered under the terms of the treaty 1783. The British also stirred up the native Americans fighting on the frontier.

To settle the problems with Britain, Washington sent Chief Justice John Jay to London in 1794. On 19th November Jay signed a treaty with Britain by which British troops would give up the frontier forts and trade between the countries would be regulated. However, there was no requirement for the British to put an end to their stopping of American ships and taking off their crewmen. The Senate was under the control of Federalists who supported the treaty because it ensured continuing trade with Britain and ratified all but one section by 20 votes to 10. The section that they did not ratify concerned restrictions on trade between the United States and the West Indies.

The *Jay Treaty* was not popular with Americans and there were riots in New York and Philadelphia. Washington returned to Mount Vernon to consider whether to sign the treaty. Soon afterwards he learned that the British had intercepted a coded dispatch which indicated that Edmund Randolph was a traitor who had sold secrets to the French. Without saying anything about his suspicions, Washington then called a Cabinet meeting to discuss the treaty where Randolph argued that it should not be signed so long as the British continued to seize American ships. Washington became convinced that Randolph was in the pay of the French and so signed the treaty.

When Washington later confronted him about the message, Randolph protested his innocence and resigned from the Cabinet. Washington then faced the bitterest criticism of his career. The Democratic-Republicans accused him of falling victim to a Federalist plot and it was even suggested he should be impeached for overdrawing his salary. However, public opinion began to move in Washington's favor when he agreed a treaty with Spain opening the Mississippi to trade. Treaties were also agreed with Native Americans on the frontier as well as the pirates of the Barbary states, who released American prisoners and let American ships alone in return for a ransom of $800,000 and an annual tribute of $24,000.

Washington was by now growing old and had tired of public office. In 1796 he delivered his farewell address as President. In the election that year he supported John Adams, the Federalist candidate, but did not take an active part in the campaigning. Adams defeated the Democratic-Republican candidate, Thomas Jefferson, by 71 electoral votes to 68.

Later Years

Washington retired happily to Mount Vernon where he managed his farms. He made frequent trips to see the construction of the new capital, Washington D.C., which was then still called the Federal City. In 1798 President Adams asked Washington to plan a new army in case worsening relations with France led to a war. However, when Federalist leaders later asked him if he would be prepared to serve a third term, he refused. On December 14th 1799 he fell ill at his home and was attended to by several doctors. However, at about 10pm that day he died. He was given a full military funeral four days later amidst great national mourning. His body was laid to rest in the family tomb at Mount Vernon.

Summary

In a eulogy presented to Congress by Washington's friend, Henry "Light Horse Harry" Lee, the revered President was described as "first in war, first in peace, and first in the hearts of his countrymen." However, George Washington's most important contribution to the United States was to be as the nation's first President. With no precedents to follow, he had to create a new office and unite the young nation together behind it. He did this so well that by the time of his retirement both the Union and the Constitution had been established and accepted. He ranks alongside Abraham Lincoln as America's greatest ever President. Today he is remembered with one of the four faces on Mount Rushmore and a tall monument opposite the White House, and his portrait appears on banknotes, coins and postage stamps. He has been honored more than any other American and the nation's capital city is named for him as well as the state of

Washington and many counties, towns, streets, bridges, parks, universities, schools and hospitals.

CHAPTER 2 – JOHN ADAMS

2ⁿᵈ President of the United States 1797 – 1801

Born: 19ᵗʰ October 1735, Braintree (now Quincy), Massachusetts

Married: Abigail Smith (1744 – 1818), October 25ᵗʰ 1764

Number of Children: Six

Died: 4ᵗʰ July 1826, Quincy, Massachusetts

Final Resting Place: United First Parish Church, Quincy, Massachusetts

Introduction

John Adams was elected as the second President of the United States at a time when the growing country had fifteen states and nearly five million people. Prior to becoming President, Adams had been a successful lawyer and had played a key role in the American Revolution. At the First Continental Congress he had been one of the first delegates to urge independence from Britain. At the Second Continental Congress it was he that proposed George Washington as Commander-in-Chief of the Continental Army. He helped to negotiate the Treaty of Paris of 1783 by which Great Britain recognized the independence of the United States and later served as his country's first minister to Great Britain. He served two terms as George Washington's Vice-President and was regarded as an expert on foreign policy. When Adams became President in 1797, he had to guide the young country through some serious problems. The Napoleonic War between Britain and France threatened to engulf America and the nation was fiercely divided between feuding political parties.   During his term of office, the U.S. government moved from Philadelphia to Washington and he became the first President to live in the White House. His son also later served as the sixth President of the United States.

Background

John Adams was born the son of a farmer in Braintree (now called Quincy), Massachusetts on the 19th October 1735. His great-great-grandfather, Henry Adams, was a puritan who had sailed from Somerset, England, to America in the 1640's so that he could freely practice his religion. In 1755 John graduated from Harvard College and then studied to become a lawyer. He began to practice law in Braintree in 1758 but moved to Boston ten years later and became one of the leading attorneys in Massachusetts. On October 25th 1764, he married Abigail Smith (1744 – 1818), the daughter of a minister in Weymouth, Massachusetts. They had four children one of whom, John Quincy Adams, became the sixth President of the United States.

Entry into Politics

In the 1760's relations between the colonies and Great Britain began to deteriorate. In 1765, the British Parliament passed the Stamp Act which imposed a tax on legal papers, newspapers and other documents. As a lawyer, Adams was badly affected by the introduction of this tax. He began to organize opposition against the British and was one of three committee members appointed by the citizens of Boston to present a petition against the tax to the British governor. Adams argued that Parliament could not tax the colonies unless the people living in them had consented to it. In 1766 Parliament repealed the Act.

Tensions between the colonists and Great Britain remained high, however, and in 1770 a group of citizens in Boston attacked British soldiers stationed in the city. When the soldiers fired into the crowd, they killed three people and wounded eight others, two of whom later died. The incident became known as the "Boston Massacre" and the soldiers were put on trial for murder. Although Adams opposed British colonial policies, he defended the soldiers in court saying that they had only obeyed orders and should be freed. The British officer in charge of the soldiers, Captain Preston, was acquitted although two soldiers were later found guilty of manslaughter.

Adams prestige rose because of the trial and in 1771 he was elected as one of the representatives for Boston in the colonial legislature. There he led the fight against British colonial policies, supporting the action of patriots in the Boston Tea Party in December 1773. In 1774, the British responded by passing what became known as the Intolerable Acts. In response, the Virginia assembly called representatives from each colony to a meeting in Philadelphia. Adams was one of four delegates from Massachusetts that attended what was later called the First Continental Congress. There he became one of the first delegates to urge that the colonies seek independence from Britain.

When the Second Continental Congress met in 1775, Adams once again argued the colonies should become independent from Britain. He persuaded the Congress to create the Continental Army and proposed that George Washington be appointed as its Commander-in-Chief. During the Revolutionary War, Adams served as the chairman of the Continental Board of War and Ordnance. He also served on a committee that planned treaties with other European powers, particularly France. In June 1776 he seconded a resolution presented by Richard Henry Lee of Virginia that "these United Colonies are, and of right ought to be, free and independent States." The Congress appointed him to a committee to prepare the Declaration of Independence and he urged Thomas Jefferson to draft it. He then defended the Declaration in a stormy debate in the Congress.

In 1778 he was sent to France to help Benjamin Franklin strengthen America's ties with the nations of Europe. When he returned the following year, the people of Braintree elected him to a convention to frame a new constitution for the state of Massachusetts. He played a very important role in drafting it and it was adopted in 1780. Many other states also adopted its features when they drafted their own constitutions. Congress then asked him to negotiate peace and trade treaties with Great Britain and he once again sailed to Europe. There he helped to negotiate the Treaty of Paris in 1783 whereby Britain agreed to recognize American independence. Adams was also successful at gaining recognition for the new country from other European powers as well negotiating trade treaties. In 1785, Congress appointed him the first U.S. minister to Great Britain.

After nearly ten years overseas, Adams returned to the United States in 1788. Under the new U.S. Constitution, the first presidential election was held that year. At the time, every elector would vote for two men for the presidency. The candidate with the most votes would be President and the runner-up would become Vice-President. All the 69 electors voted for George Washington, who became the nation's first President. Adams received 34 votes and became Vice-President. He presided over the Senate with dignity and always sided with Washington in tie-breaking votes. In 1792, he was re-elected Vice President.

The Election of 1796

Two political groups began to form during Washington's term as President. The *Federalists* favored a strong central government whereas the *Democratic Republicans* (called Republicans at the time but later to become the Democratic Party) favored stronger states' rights. Adams was a leader of the Federalists and when Washington refused to run for a third term in 1796, they supported him for President. The Democratic-Republicans nominated Thomas Jefferson. In the election Adams received three more votes than Jefferson and became President. His political opponent became Vice-President.

Presidential Election of 1796		
Candidate	Party	Electoral Votes

26

John Adams	Federalist	71
Thomas Jefferson	Democratic-Republican	68
Thomas Pinckney	Federalist	59
Aaron Burr	Democratic-Republican	30
Samuel Adams	Federalist	15
Oliver Ellsworth	Federalist	11
George Clinton	Democratic-Republican	7
John Jay	Federalist	5
James Iredell	Federalist	3
John Henry	Democratic-Republican	2
Samuel Johnston	Federalist	2
George Washington	Federalist	2
Charles C. Pinckney	Federalist	1

Adams' Administration 1797 – 1801

Adams faced many severe problems during his term as President, both at home and abroad. Many of these problems were caused by the French Revolution which began in 1789 and led to a long European-wide war between the new French Republic and a coalition of countries led by Great Britain. Adams was determined that America should remain neutral in this conflict but her ships were attacked and seized by the navies of both sides. An important Federalist, Alexander Hamilton, led a faction of the party that demanded that America go to war against France. When Adams insisted on strict neutrality, the Federalist party split into two with the President leading one group and Hamilton the other. This made Adams' task as President more difficult as he could not count on the support of all the members of his cabinet or his party.

Adams sent ministers to France to negotiate a treaty but when they arrived three French diplomats (known as X, Y and Z rather than by their names) told them that a pact would only be possible if a bribe was paid to the French foreign minister, Charles Maurice de Talleyrand-Perigord. This was unacceptable and the U.S. broke off negotiations in late 1797. What was called the *XYZ Affair* caused great anger in America and Congress began to prepare for a war with France. A new Department of the Navy was established and more warships were constructed. Although neither side declared war, there were many battles between American and French warships. Adams later sent a second delegation to France to try and negotiate a treaty. This action cost him the support of his own party but war was avoided.

Adams' government faced much criticism for its opposition to France. Some of the criticism came from American citizens but some of the criticism was from French citizens that lived in America. In 1798, the Federalists attempted to deal with this criticism by passing new laws. The *Alien Acts* gave Adams the authority to banish or imprison foreigners by a simple order. The *Sedition Act* made it a crime to criticize the President, Congress or the government. Although Adams never used the Alien Acts, several journalists were arrested under the Sedition Act for supporting the Democratic-Republicans. The laws were criticized as unconstitutional as they violated the guarantees of freedom of speech and the press.

The Election of 1800

Before the election of 1800, Hamilton influenced many Federalist voters by criticizing Adams' policy towards France. The Democratic-Republican candidates, Thomas Jefferson and Aaron Burr, denounced Adams for the Alien and Sedition Acts and for hostility towards France. They believed that the French Revolution was a people's movement like the Revolutionary War in America and so wanted to provide assistance to France. In the election, Jefferson and Burr each received 73 votes while Adams received 65. The House of Representatives then chose Jefferson as President.

Late in 1800, the government moved from Philadelphia to its new home in Washington D.C. The President and First Lady moved into the unfinished White House, which still stood among swampy ground. Only six rooms had been completed and the laundry had to be dried in the East Room (which is the largest room in the White House, and is now used for entertaining guests after formal dinners). Adams made political appointments until his last day in office. One of his last appointments was John Marshall as Chief Justice of the United States.

Adams was so disappointed by his defeat that he refused to stay in Washington for Jefferson's inauguration. He left for his home in Quincy on 4th March 1801.

Later Years

Adams was 66 years old when he left the White House. He later mended his differences with Jefferson. They both forgot their political quarrels when they retired from public life. Coincidentally, both men died on the same day, the 4th of July 1826 – America's fiftieth birthday. Adams died just four months before his 91st birthday and for many years was America's longest-living President. He was buried in Quincy, Massachusetts.

Summary

John Adams served the United States well as both Vice-President and then President. He had earlier been a signatory of the Declaration of Independence and played a key role in the American Revolution. Although he was seldom popular, he provided decisive leadership and good judgement that guided the new country though some serious troubles. For these reasons, he is usually ranked highly among   the   Presidents.

CHAPTER 3 – THOMAS JEFFERSON

3ʳᵈ President of the United States 1801 – 1809

Born: 13ᵗʰ April 1743, Shadwell, Virginia

Married: Martha Wayles Skelton (1748 – 1782), January 1ˢᵗ 1772

Number of Children: Six

Died: 4ᵗʰ July 1826, Monticello, Virginia

Final Resting Place: Family graveyard, Monticello, Charlottesville

Introduction

Thomas Jefferson became President after defeating John Adams in the election of 1800. It was the first time that there had been a peaceful handover of power after a democratic election. Jefferson was already famous as the author of the Declaration of Independence and the Bill of Rights, and an important member of the cabinet in the governments of Washington and Adams. During his time as President the country doubled in size due to the Louisiana Purchase of 1803. He sent two explorers, Lewis and Clark, on an expedition to explore the new territory as far as the Pacific. Jefferson believed that Americans should live with as little government as possible and he became one of the founders of the Democratic Party. During in his two terms as President, America remained neutral in the Napoleonic War and Congress passed a law outlawing the slave trade.

Background

Thomas Jefferson was born on April 13th 1743 at Shadwell, the family farm in Albemarle County in Virginia. His father, Peter Jefferson, served in the house of Burgesses and was a surveyor, sheriff and colonel of the militia. His mother, Jane Randolph Jefferson, came from one of the oldest families in Virginia. Jefferson learned to read and write from his father and to play the violin. He later studied in local schools and learned French, Latin and Greek from a nearby clergyman. When he was 14 years old his father died and he became head of the family, inheriting Shadwell along with 30 slaves and 2,500 acres of land. In 1760, at the age of 16, he entered the College of William and Mary at Williamsburg. He spent two years there and formed many of his basic ideas about humanity and God. He graduated in 1762 and studied to become a lawyer, being admitted to the bar in 1767. In 1772 he married a widow, Martha Wayles Skelton, the daughter of a prominent lawyer. They had one son and five daughters but only two lived to maturity. After ten years of marriage, Martha died in 1782 and he never remarried.

In 1769 Jefferson was elected to the House of Burgesses and served there until 1775. At that time relations between the colonies and Great Britain were deteriorating and he took the lead in organizing protests against the import duties set up by the Townshend Acts. In 1774, he called for a meeting of all the colonies to consider their grievances. He was chosen to represent the Albemarle County at the first Virginia Convention. This in turn elected the Virginian candidates to the First Continental Congress. Jefferson could not attend due to illness but set out his views in a paper saying that the British Parliament had no right to govern America. Jefferson also attended the Second Virginia Convention in 1775 and was chosen as one the delegates to the Second Continental Congress.

Jefferson then took a leading part in the Second Continental Congress. Once the Revolutionary War began, he was asked to draft a "Declaration of the Causes and Necessity of Taking up Arms." In the spring of 1776 sentiment grew in favor of independence. On June 7th, Richard Henry Lee of Virginia introduced a famous resolution that "these United Colonies are, and of right ought to be, free and independent States." Congress appointed a committee to draw up a declaration of independence. The committee unanimously asked Jefferson to prepare the draft and then approved it with few changes. Congress began debating the declaration on June 28th and adopted it on July 4th with only a few minor changes. The Declaration of Independence remains Jefferson's best-known work. It affirmed the belief of the American Revolutionaries in representative government under a constitution.

In September 1776 Jefferson resigned from Congress and returned to the Virginia House of Delegates where he passed laws to reform land ownership and promote freedom of religion. The Virginia Assembly elected Jefferson governor for one-year terms in 1779 and 1780. During this time the state suffered severely from the effects of the Revolutionary War. In 1781 British troops invaded Virginia under Benedict Arnold and Lord Cornwallis. The state put up little resistance and Jefferson only narrowly avoided capture. He was criticized for the state's lack of resistance but an official investigation cleared him of blame. He left public office and Thomas Nelson was appointed to replace him as governor

Jefferson returned to his home at Monticello a bitter man. In 1782 his wife died, leaving him stunned and distraught. In 1783 he returned to politics and was elected to Congress. There he devised a new decimal system of currency that was approved by Congress. He also piloted through Congress the Treaty of Paris, which ended the Revolutionary War. He worked on the Ordinance of 1784 and the Land Ordinance of 1785 that formed the basis for all later American land policies. In 1784 it was proposed that the *Northwest Territory* would be divided into several states which would eventually enter the Union on a basis of complete equality with the original thirteen states. It never went into effect but became the basis for the *Northwest Ordinance* of 1787.

In May 1784 he was sent to France to negotiate commercial agreements. In 1785 he succeeded Franklin as minister to France and served there until October 1789. He was in Paris at the beginning of the French Revolution, which he sympathized with it, believing it was similar in purpose to the American Revolution. While he was in

France his fellow countrymen drew up a new constitution at a convention in 1787. James Maddison sent him a draft, which he approved. However, he argued that there should be a bill of rights. As a result, Maddison introduced the ten amendments that became the Bill of Rights.

In November 1789 Jefferson arrived back in the US. George Washington invited him to be the Secretary of State in his new government and he reluctantly agreed. Sharp differences arose between him and Secretary of the Treasury, Alexander Hamilton. Hamilton felt the country would be governed by the rich aristocracy whereas Jefferson had faith in the people. Hamilton also wanted to encourage shipping and manufacturing whereas Jefferson believed that the United States should remain a nation of farmers. Jefferson also opposed Hamilton's proposal for a state bank as he felt it would give too much power to the federal government. Their differences grew into a bitter personal feud and led to the development of the first political parties, the Federalists who supported Hamilton, and the *Democratic-Republicans* who supported Jefferson (called *Republicans* at the time but later to be called the *Democratic Party*). In Foreign Affairs, Jefferson urged recognition of the new revolutionary government of France. He also tried to persuade the British to abandon their forts in the Northwest Territory and worked for a free navigation of the Mississippi River.

By 1794 he had grown weary of office and resigned from the government. He returned to his farm at Monticello hoping to lead a quiet life but it did not last long. In 1796, concerned by the centralizing tendencies of the government, he accepted the Democratic-Republican nomination for President. He ran against John Adams, the Federalist candidate. Adams won 71 electoral votes while Jefferson won 68 votes. By the law at that time, Adams therefore became President and Jefferson became Vice-President. However, Jefferson took little part in the Federalist government and became leader of the opposition. His relations with Adams became steadily worse until they broke completely in 1800. In 1798, the XYZ Affair aroused great hostility towards France and war hysteria led the Federalist government to pass the Alien and Sedition Acts.

These laws limited freedom of speech and of the press and were greatly opposed by Jefferson.

Election of 1800

In 1800 Jefferson was once again nominated for President by the Democratic-Republicans. Former Senator Aaron Burr of New York was nominated for Vice President. The Federalists nominated John Adams with Charles C. Pinckney of South Carolina as his running mate. However, the Federalists were bitterly divided over foreign policy and a faction under Alexander Hamilton refused to support Adams. In addition, the Alien and Sedition Acts had made Adams and his administration unpopular. Jefferson won the election with 73 electoral votes with 65 for Adams. However. Burr also received 73 votes and, under the rules of the time, the House of Representatives had to settle the election. This led to the 12th Amendment to the U.S. Constitution whereby each elector in the college casts one vote for President and one for Vice-President.

Presidential Election of 1800		
Candidate	**Party**	**Electoral Votes**
Thomas Jefferson	Democratic-Republican	73
Aaron Burr	Democratic-Republican	73
John Adams	Federalist	65
Charles C. Pinckney	Federalist	64
John Jay	Federalist	1

Jefferson's First Administration 1801 – 1805

Jefferson was the first President to be inaugurated in Washington. The White House was only partly built when he moved in but he felt lonely in such a large house. His wife had been dead for over 18 years and his two daughters, Martha Randolph and Mary Eppes, served as hostesses from time to time. His grandson, James Randolph, was the first person to be born in the White House.

Jefferson believed that the government should play the smallest possible role in national life and he reversed many Federalist policies. The Naturalization Acts was repealed and Alien and Sedition Acts were allowed to lapse. Those people that had been fined under these Acts had their money refunded. He repealed the Judiciary Act of 1801, which had allowed President Adams to appoint two hundred new judges just before he left office, and the judges had their appointments cancelled. Jefferson replaced those Federalists in federal offices with Democratic-Republicans, reduced department expenditures and repealed excise taxes.

In his foreign policy, Jefferson urged action against the Barbary pirates of North Africa. The pirates demanded tribute and ransom from all countries and had received two million dollars from the United States over the previous ten years. The unruliest barbary state was Tripoli and in 1801 they opened war on American shipping to try and secure the payment of more tribute. Jefferson sent the navy to blockade Tripoli's ports and bombard their fortresses, and they succeeded in forcing the pirates to respect the American flag.

In 1803 Jefferson produced the greatest achievement of his presidency when his government made the *Louisiana Purchase* from France. The Louisiana Territory was a vast region between the Mississippi River and the Rocky Mountains. The region had been transferred from France to Spain in 1762 but in 1801 Jefferson learned that the Spanish planned to return it to the French. He sent James Monroe to Paris hoping to negotiate the acquisition of New Orleans and a guarantee of freedom of navigation along the Mississippi. However, the French offered the American minister, Robert Livingstone, the opportunity to buy the whole of the Louisiana Territory and for $15 million dollars the size of the nation was doubled and control was gained of the Mississippi River. The Senate then ratified the treaty by twenty-six votes to five.

In 1803 Jefferson obtained approval from Congress for the exploration of the West as far as the Pacific Ocean. He sent

Meriwether Lewis and William Clark on an expedition up the Missouri, across the Rockies and to the Pacific. Following this expedition, the population of the Northwest Territory grew rapidly. The government encouraged settlement of the West by selling farms cheaply to new settlers. The Union expanded when Ohio became the seventeenth state in 1803.

Election of 1804

Jefferson was renominated for President in 1804 with Governor George Clinton of New York nominated as his Vice-President. Support for Jefferson was high because the country was growing in size and prosperity. The Federalists nominated Charles C. Pinckney, a lawyer from South Carolina. Support for the Federalists had been poorly affected by a plot to remove New York and New England from the Union to preserve their influence after the Louisiana Purchase. Jefferson won the election by 162 votes to only 14 for Pinckney.

Presidential Election of 1804		
Candidate	**Party**	**Electoral Votes**
Thomas Jefferson	Democratic-Republican	162
Charles C. Pinckney	Federalist	14

Jefferson's Second Administration 1805 – 1809

Jefferson's second term began as he put it, "without a cloud on the horizon." But a storm soon began to gather. In July 1804, Aaron Burr killed Alexander Hamilton in a duel. Burr was already discredited in politics due to his support for New York's secession and this damaged his reputation further. Burr's name was then linked to a plot to overthrow his government by force. He was put on trial for treason but acquitted.

In May 1803 war once again broke out between Britain and France. Jefferson tried to keep America out of the war and uphold her rights as a neutral country but Britain had a desperate need for sailors and began to stop American ships to take off British deserters. However, as it was difficult to tell Americans and British apart, thousands of Americans were seized and forced into the British navy. The war became so intense that soon neither side cared about the rights of neutral nations. The French attempted to seize all ships sailing to a British port while the British blockaded all the ports in the hands of the French and their allies. In June 1807 the British frigate *Leopard* launched an unprovoked attack on the America ship *Chesapeake*. The Leopard had wanted to search the Chesapeake and opened fire after this was refused. Jefferson's attempt to resolve the crisis proved ineffective and was the greatest failure of his presidency. The *Embargo Act* of 1807 prohibited the export of any produce from an American port or the sailing of any American vessel to a foreign port. However, this hurt the U.S. far more than either Britain of France as American goods could not be exported overseas and many sailors lost their jobs. In March 1809 Congress repealed the act after the nation's economy had been ruined and it was clear it would not bring concessions from either Britain or France. It was replaced by the milder *Non-Intercourse Act*, which only prohibited American ships sailing to ports in Britain and France.

In March 1807 an Act of Congress came into force that prohibited the importation of slaves. No more slaves could be transported from Africa but it was still possible for Americans to buy and sell slaves already in the United States. Towards the end of his administration many people urged Jefferson to run for a third term but he declined and decided to retire after his second. However, he made it clear he wanted James Madison to be the next President and Madison easily won the election of 1808.

Later Years

In 1809, Jefferson retired from the Presidency aged 65. He felt relieved at leaving office and spent his remaining years pursuing his many interests. During this time, he invented a copying machine known as the polygraph and founded the University of Virginia in 1825. He remained interested in politics and his advice was sought by his successors as President. His sold his library of 6,400 books to Congress. He was reconciled with John Adams and the two men died the same day, the 4th July 1826. Jefferson was buried next to his wife in Monticello.

Summary

Thomas Jefferson was one of the most talented and inspirational men ever to become President. He was a farmer, an architect, an inventor, a writer, and a musician. As a politician he was the author of the Declaration of Independence and a founder of the Democratic Party. His key achievement in the White House was to double the size of the country with the Louisiana Purchase. For this reason, he is remembered as a great President and is one of the four faces carved on   Mount   Rushmore.

CHAPTER 4 – JAMES MADISON

4ᵗʰ President of the United States 1809 – 1817

Born: 16ᵗʰ March 1751, Belle Grove Plantation, Port Conway, Virginia

Married: Dolley Todd (1768 – 1849), 15ᵗʰ September 1794

Number of Children: None

Died: 28ᵗʰ June 1836, Montpelier, Virginia

Final Resting Place: Montpelier, Virginia

Introduction

James Madison, the fourth President of the United States, took office at a time when the country was expanding rapidly. Louisiana became a state in 1812 and Indiana in 1816, while Missouri was organized as a Territory in 1812 and Alabama in 1817. The total population by that time was nearly nine million people. Before he became President, Madison served in Virginia's state assembly, the Continental Congress, the Constitutional Convention and the U.S. House of Representatives. He played an important role in drafting the U.S. Constitution and the Bill of Rights. He was appointed Secretary of State by Thomas Jefferson and played a significant role in the Louisiana Purchase. After he entered the White House, he led the country into a war with Great Britain during which time the nation's capital was occupied by a foreign power for the only time in its history. Madison's term of office is also known as a period of strong growth in the economy and American national feeling.

Background

James Madison was born the eldest of twelve children on 16th March 1751 in Port Conway, Virginia. His ancestors had settled in Virginia in the 1600's and his parents owned a large plantation called Montpelier, worked by many slaves. Sometimes described as a frail and sickly child, he received private tuition before attending Donald Robertson School in King and Queen County. At the age of 18 he entered the College of New Jersey (now called Princeton University), where he took an active interest in politics and was an early member of the American Whig Society. He graduated in 1771 after only two years of study and, being deeply interested in religious subjects, showed an interest in pursuing a career as a minister.

Entry into Politics

Madison decided on a career in politics and entered local government when he was elected to the Committee of Safety in Orange County, Virginia, in 1774. Two years later he sat on the committee that drafted Virginia's constitution and the Virginia Declaration of Rights. These were later much copied by other colonies. He was elected to Virginia's first legislative assembly in 1776 and there first met Thomas Jefferson with whom he shared a lifetime friendship. However, he was defeated for re-election in 1777. In 1778 the Virginia Assembly elected him to sit on an advisory group, the Governor's Council. He served in this post until he was elected to the Continental Congress in December 1779. After taking his seat in March 1780 he advocated increasing the financial powers of the Congress so that it could raise taxes to pay national debts.

He returned to Virginia in 1783 and was elected for three consecutive one-year terms in the state assembly by the people of Orange County. There he played an important role in the passing of the Statute of Religious Freedom, separating the church and state in Virginia. In 1787 he represented Virginia at the Constitutional Convention where he played a leading role in drafting the new U.S. Constitution and obtaining its acceptance by each state. Because of his role he is sometimes called "the Father of the Constitution." However, his support for a strong central government displeased many Virginians who supported states' rights and they united in the Virginia legislature to prevent him winning a seat in the first United States Senate.

In 1789 he defeated James Monroe for a seat in the U.S. House of Representatives. There he proposed resolutions for organizing the departments of the State, Treasury and War as well as drafting the first tariff act. He was also responsible for drafting the first ten amendments to the U.S. Constitution, the Bill of Rights. Initially he supported many policies of the new Federalist party. However, he felt Alexander Hamilton's plans favored Eastern merchants at the expense of Southern and Western farmers and began to turn against them. When Jefferson returned from France in 1789, the two men joined in organizing the Democratic-Republican party, the forerunner of today's Democratic Party. During this period in Philadelphia, he met a young widow, Dolley Payne Todd, and they married on September 15th 1794. They had no children together.

In 1797 he retired to his estate having become weary of politics. However, when Congress passed the Alien and Sedition Acts, he was outraged and proposed joint action by the states in declaring these acts unconstitutional. In 1799 and 1800 he was elected to the Virginia legislature and fought against what he considered Federalist efforts to undermine basic human rights.

When Thomas Jefferson became President in 1801, he appointed Madison the Secretary of State. He then played a significant role in the Louisiana Purchase of 1803. Less successful was a war fought between 1801-05 against the Barbary pirates that preyed on American shipping. Although both sides agreed a peace treaty, the pirates soon resumed their attacks on American ships. Madison also attempted to prevent Britain and France from blockading American ships and seizing their crews. The Embargo Act of 1807 tried to protect American ships by stopping all commerce with foreign countries. However, the loss of trade caused widespread economic distress in the U.S. and the act was repealed in 1809. Congress replaced it with the Non-Intercourse Act which opened trade to all countries except Britain and France.

The Election of 1808

When Jefferson left office, he said that he would like Madison to succeed him as President. Madison was then nominated for President by the Democratic-Republicans with George Clinton nominated for Vice-President. The Federalists nominated the former minister to France, Charles C. Pinckney. In the election, Madison received 122 electoral votes while Pinckney received 47 votes. George Clinton received six votes for President but 113 for in the election for Vice-President.

Presidential Election of 1808		
Candidate	Party	Electoral Votes
James Madison	Democratic-Republican	122
Charles C. Pinckney	Federalist	47
George Clinton	Independent	6
Not Voted	*	1

Madison's Administration First Term 1809 – 1813

When Madison became President the most important problem he had to deal with was foreign relations with Great Britain. British and French warships continued to stop American shipping despite the Non-Intercourse Act. In 1810 Congress passed a new act that reopened trade with the two countries. It tried to stop violations of American shipping by applying economic pressure. The act provided that if Britain stopped its attacks on American shipping, then the United States would stop trade with France. Conversely, the act also said that if the French stopped their attacks, then the U.S. would stop trade with Britain. However, the act proved unworkable. When

42

Napoleon announced that the French would revoke their blockade of neutral shipping, the U.S. stopped all trade with Britain. However, Napoleon then issued secret orders for the blockade to continue and the French navy continued to stop American ships.

The Election of 1812

Relations with Britain continued to deteriorate. When tribes of native Americans on the Western frontier formed an alliance to defend their lands, many settlers accused the British of stirring them up. There were many people in America that wanted a war with Britain so that their territory in Canada could be annexed. With a Presidential election looming, Madison recommended war and on 18th June 1812 it was approved by Congress. The Federalists opposed the war, particularly as it would affect trade, and called it "Mr. Madison's War." When the election was held, Madison was re-elected with 128 electoral votes while his rival, Mayor DeWitt Clinton of New York City, polled 89. Madison's running mate, Governor Elbridge Gerry of Massachusetts, won 131 votes for Vice-President against 86 for his rival, Jared Ingersoll, the Attorney General of Pennsylvania.

Presidential Election of 1812		
Candidate	Party	Electoral Votes
James Madison	Democratic-Republican	128
DeWitt Clinton	Federalist	89
Not Voted	*	1

Madison's Second Term 1813 – 1817

What became known as the *War of 1812* did not go entirely well for the United States. American land forces invaded Canada but were defeated. In addition, the small American navy could not break the Royal Navy's blockade. In 1814, the British were able to send reinforcements to Canada after the defeat of Napoleon Bonaparte in

43

Europe. This made it impossible for American forces to conquer territory there. That summer the British became the only foreign power ever to occupy Washington D.C. and on the 24th August their troops set fire to public buildings in the city including the U.S. Capitol and the White House. Madison was very nearly captured and the troops ate a hot meal that had just been prepared for him. The British were then able to largely dictate the terms of the *Treaty of Ghent*, whereby the United States gave up all her claims to Canada. Congress approved the treaty in February 1815.

When the Madisons returned to Washington it was not possible for them to live in the burned-out White House. They took up residence in a private home nearby called Octagon House. In 1815 they moved to another house on the corner of Pennsylvania Avenue and 19th Street. The White House was slowly reconstructed but was not ready for occupancy until Madison left office in 1817. One other effect of the war was that it led to the growth of American national feeling. People increasingly thought and acted as Americans. "The Star-Spangled Banner," America's national anthem, dates from this time. Francis Scott Key was inspired to write it when stubborn resistance at Fort McHenry prevented the British from capturing Baltimore in 1814.

The war was not popular in New England, however. In 1814, the Federalists there had held a secret meeting known as the *Hartford Convention*. A rumor then circulated that the states of New England were planning to secede from the Union. The Federalist party was subsequently branded as unpatriotic and fell apart after James Monroe was elected President in 1816.

Later Years

The last two years of Madison's term was a period of strong economic growth. Improved roads and canals hastened the settlement of the west and a new system made it easier to claim land there. American industries were protected by a new tariff that was introduced in 1816. When Madison left office after forty years of public service he retired to his estate in Montpelier. He became president of the University of Virginia in 1826 and served as a member of the Virginia Constitutional Convention in 1829. He died on 28th June 1836 and was buried at Montpelier. His wife returned to Washington and lived there until she died in 1849.

Summary

James Madison served the United States in various offices for forty years and was a founder of the Democratic party along with Thomas Jefferson. As President he built a strong federal government and kept America out of the Napoleonic War. However, he did lead the nation into a disastrous war with Britain because of which Washington D.C. was occupied and burned. For this reason, he is usually ranked low among   the   Presidents.

CHAPTER 5 – JAMES MONROE

5th President of the United States 1817 – 1825

Born: 28th April 1758, Westmoreland County, Virginia

Married: Elizabeth Kortright (1768 – 1830), 16th February 1786

Number of Children: Three

Died: 4th July 1831, New York City

Final Resting Place: Hollywood Cemetery, Richmond, Virginia

Introduction

James Monroewas elected as the fifth President of the United States after already serving as a U.S. Senator, as the U.S. minister to France, Spain and Great Britain, and as Governor of Virginia. He had fought in the Revolutionary War and then simultaneously as the Secretary of State and Secretary for War in the War of 1812. As President he was best known for the Monroe Doctrine which prevented European countries interfering in the affairs of the Americas. Monroe served as President at a time known as "the era of good feeling." Peace had returned to America after the War of 1812 and prosperity grew as industries expanded and the frontier moved rapidly westwards. Five new states joined the union: Mississippi in 1817, Illinois in 1818, Alabama in 1819, Maine in 1820 and Missouri in 1821. Arkansas Territory was organized in 1821 and Florida, acquired from Spain, became a territory in 1823. By that time the nation's population had grown to more than eleven million people. As the frontiers expanded, Americans began to consider whether slavery should be allowed in the new territories. The Missouri Compromise settled this question for thirty years by setting definite limits on the extension of slavery into the lands acquired by the Louisiana Purchase.

Background

James Madison was born in Westmoreland County, Virginia, on April 28th 1758. The eldest of five children, his father's ancestors had settled in Virginia from Scotland in the 1600's and his mother's had come from Wales. He was a tutored at home and then at the school of Parson Archibald Campbell. At the age of 16 he entered the College of William and Mary. When the Revolutionary War broke out, he was commissioned into the army as a lieutenant and took part in the fighting at Harlem Heights and White Plains in the fall of 1776. He then took part in some of the most famous battles of the war at Trenton, Brandywine, Germantown and Monmouth. In 1778 he was promoted to lieutenant colonel and sent to Virginia to raise troops. There he first met Thomas Jefferson and began to study law under his guidance. He later moved to a home near to Jefferson's estate in Monticello. On February 16th 1786, he married Elizabeth Kortright, the daughter of a New York City merchant. They had two daughters and a son but the boy died at the age of two.

Entry into Politics

Monroe began his political career in 1782 when he was elected to the Viginia Assembly. In 1783 he was elected to the Congress of the Confederation where he served three years. In 1786, he was once again elected to the Virginia Assembly where he served a further four years. In 1788 he sat in the convention called by Virginia to ratify the U.S. Constitution. Monroe ran against James Madison for a seat in the first U.S. House of Representatives but lost. In 1790 the Virginia legislature elected him to the U.S. Senate. There he aligned himself with Jefferson and Madison against the Federalist program

47

of Alexander Hamilton. Together the three men founded the *Democratic-Republican Party* which would be become one of the two great parties in American politics.

In 1794 President Washington appointed Monroe the minister to France. However, he was recalled two years later after criticizing the Jay Treaty between the United States and Great Britain. In 1799 he was elected governor of Virginia. In 1803, President Jefferson sent him back to France to help Robert R. Livingston negotiate the purchase of New Orleans. By the time he arrived, Napoleon Bonaparte had offered Livingston the entire Louisiana Territory. Monroe urged Livingston to accept the offer without waiting to consult Jefferson and the two men made arrangements for the purchase. Madison was later appointed minister to Great Britain where he negotiated a trade treaty that Jefferson deemed too unsatisfactory to present to the Senate.

In 1807 Monroe returned to the United States where became a candidate for the nomination to succeed Jefferson as President. However, he was defeated by James Madison who also won the presidency. Monroe then served in the Virginia Assembly until 1811 when he was once again elected governor.

Three months later Madison appointed him Secretary of State. During his time in office, the United States fought the War of 1812 against Britain. In 1814 British troops burned down Washington D.C. leading to the resignation of the Secretary of War, John Armstrong. Madison asked Monroe to fill the vacant position as well as remaining Secretary of State. Monroe held both offices for the rest of the war.

Election of 1816

In 1816 Monroe won the nomination for President and stood against the Federalist candidate, Senator Rufus King of New York. His running mate was the governor of New York, Daniel T. Tompkins. In the election, Monroe received 183 electoral votes to 34 for King.

Presidential Election of 1816		
Candidate	Party	Electoral Votes
James Monroe	Democratic-Republican	183
Rufus King	Federalist	34
Not Voted	*	4

Monroe's First Administration 1817 – 1820

The years of Monroe's term of office are generally known as "the era of good feeling." Industries and prosperity grew quickly as the West was settled. The Federalist party disappeared and politics was dominated by the Democratic-Republican party. The British had burned down the White House in 1814 and it had still not been rebuilt by the time Monroe took office. For nine months he lived in a residence on I Street near 20th Street. On New Year's Day 1818, the President and First Lady held a public reception to mark the reopening of the White House.

The main issue of Monroe's first term concerned what was called the *American System*. This was a plan advanced by the House Speaker Henry Clay of Kentucky to strengthen national feeling by enacting a protective tariff to encourage manufacturing and develop the home market, and constructing new roads and canals to open the West. Monroe thought that the federal government did not have the power to carry out these activities. However, in 1824 he signed the *Survey Act* which planned for future improvements. That same year, Congress raised tariffs.

In 1818, Missouri applied for admission to the Union as a slave state. The House of Representatives passed a bill to admit Missouri but with the provision that no more slaves were to be bought or sold within the state. The Senate defeated this provision and after much debate Congress eventually agreed a bill known as the *Missouri Compromise*. This law permitted slavery in Missouri but banned it from all the other territories acquired in the Louisiana Purchase north of the southern boundary of Missouri. Monroe refused to interfere in these debates but henceforth slavery would become an important issue in American politics.

In 1817 fighting broke out between the Seminole Indians of Florida and settlers in Georgia. Monroe responded by ordering Major General Andrew Jackson to raise a force of militia and put down the Indians. Jackson's troops chased the Indians into the Everglades of Florida and captured Pensacola, the Spanish capital. The ease of Jackson's victory convinced the Spaniards that they could not defend Florida and in 1819 they agreed to cede their territory to the United States in return for cancellation of five million dollars in American claims against Spain.

There were some notable diplomatic achievements during Monroe's term in office. In 1817, the *Rush-Bagot Agreement,* signed with Great Britain, prohibited fortifications on the Great Lakes. In 1818, Great Britain agreed to the 49th parallel as the boundary between the United States and Canada from the Lake of the Woods, on the Ontario-Minnesota border, as far west as the Rocky Mountains. Great Britain also agreed to the joint occupation of the Oregon region. In 1819 Spain gave up her claims to Oregon as did the Russians in 1824.

Election of 1820

Monroe was unopposed for the Presidency in the election of 1820. He won all but one vote in the electoral college. William Plumer, an elector from New Hampshire, cast his vote for John Quincy Adams.

Presidential Election of 1820		
Candidate	**Party**	**Electoral Votes**
James Monroe	Democratic-Republican	231
John Quincy Adams	Independent	1
Not Voted	*	3

The Monroe Doctrine

During the Napoleonic Wars, the Spanish took little interest in their colonies in the Americas as they were so deeply involved in European affairs. Their colonies in South America took advantage of this situation and declared their independence from Spain. In 1817 Henry Clay advocated for U.S. recognition of these new countries. In March 1822, Monroe recommended that their independence be recognized. In December 1823, the President proclaimed the historic *Monroe Doctrine* in a message to Congress. The doctrine guaranteed the independence of the Americas against any European interference and has remained a basic American policy ever since.

Later Years

After he left office, Monroe retired to his estate near Leesburg, Virginia. In 1829 he became presiding officer of the Virginia Constitutional Convention. His wife died in 1830 and was buried in Oak Hill. He moved to New York City to live with his daughter and her husband and died there on 4th July 1831. In 1858 his remains were moved to Hollywood Cemetery in Richmond, Virginia.

Summary

James Monroe presided over the "era of good feeling" and delivered some noteworthy achievements. During his administration, the frontier moved rapidly westwards while in the south Florida was acquired from Spain. He is also known for the Monroe Doctrine, which protected the Americas from further European colonialism, as well the Missouri Compromise, which postponed settlement of the slavery question for thirty years. For these reasons, he is usually highly ranked among the Presidents.

CHAPTER 6 – JOHN QUINCY ADAMS

6ᵗʰ President of the United States 1825 – 1829

Born: 11ᵗʰ July 1867, Braintree (now Quincy), Massachusetts

Married: Louisa Johnson (1775 – 1852), 26ᵗʰ July 1797

Number of Children: Four

Died: 23ʳᵈ February 1848, Washington D.C.

Final Resting Place: United First Parish Church, Quincy, Massachusetts

Introduction

John Quincy Adams, the sixth President of the United States, was the first son of a President to also become President. His father was the second President, John Adams. Like his father, he failed to win a second term. Adams became President at a time when the country was developing rapidly. Although no new states joined the Union during his term, the Erie Canal linking New York City and the Great Lakes was opened in 1825, speeding settlement of the Midwest, and construction started on America's first passenger railroad, between Baltimore and Ohio, in 1828. Before he entered the White House, Adams served as the U.S. minister to Netherlands, Prussia, Russia and Great Britain, as a U.S. Senator, and as Secretary of State. He negotiated the Treaty of Ghent, which ended the War of 1812, and authored the Monroe Doctrine. As President he led the nation through a period of peace and prosperity but was defeated in the election of 1828. He subsequently served seventeen years in the U.S. House of Representatives.

Background

John Quincy Adams was born In Braintree (now called Quincy), Massachusetts, on 11th July 1767. He was the second of four children of John Adams who served as second President of the USA between 1799 and 1803. He grew up on a large farm but from 1788 accompanied his father on his postings abroad. He was educated in Paris, Amsterdam and Leyden as his father moved from one diplomatic assignment to another. He became the most learned President and fluent in several languages. At the age of 14 he went to St Petersburg and became the private secretary to Francis Dana, the first American diplomat in Russia. In 1783, he rejoined his father and served as his private secretary. In 1785 he returned to the United States where he entered Harvard University graduating two years later. He then studied to become a lawyer and set up his own practice in 1790. However, it was not very successful and he changed his career to become a political journalist.

Entry into Politics

In 1794 he entered politics when he was appointed minister to the Netherlands by George Washington. However, three days after he arrived there, Napoleon Bonaparte's French army invaded and occupied the country. Adams then moved to London on a diplomatic assignment and met his future English-born wife, Louisa Catherine Johnson, the daughter of the American consul general. They married on 26th July 1797 and she later became the first foreign-born First Lady of the United States. She was in fact the only one until Slovenian-born Melania Trump became the First Lady in 2017. John and Louisa later had four children. In 1796 Washington appointed Adams minister to Portugal. However, before he left for Lisbon his father was elected President and appointed him minister to Prussia where he served for four years.

In 1801 Thomas Jefferson became President and Adams soon returned home. In 1802 he was elected to the Massachusetts Senate and then to the United States Senate the following year. He was a Federalist but often voted with the Democratic-Republicans. 1807 he broke with his party when Congress passed the Embargo Act. The Federalists had wanted to trade with Britain but Adams felt an embargo would benefit the country. The Federalists thought that Adams had betrayed them and elected another man to his Senate seat in 1808. He immediately resigned.

Adams intended to permanently stay out of public life but President Madison appointed him as the minister to Russia in 1809. From 1814 to 1815 he helped to negotiate the Treaty of Ghent, which ended the War of 1812 with Great Britain. Madison then appointed him as minister to Great Britain and Adams began discussions that led to improved relations between the two countries. Both countries agreed to stop using forts and warships in the Great Lakes region and the border between the United States and Canada was left open and unguarded.

In 1817, President Monroe recalled Adams to serve as Secretary of State. In 1823, the Holy Alliance of Russia, Austria and Prussia helped King Ferdinand VII to regain the Spanish throne and Adams feared that they would also help Spain to regain her former South American colonies. He therefore authored the Monroe Doctrine which prevented any future European colonization of the Americas. His other achievements in this office included acquiring Florida for the United States and also making an agreement with Great Britain for the joint occupation of the Oregon region.

Election of 1824

Like Adams, James Monroe had served as Secretary of State before being elected President. Many people in America now thought that Adams should follow Monroe into the White House. In the election of 1824, he was opposed by Four Democratic-Republicans, Andrew Jackson, Henry Clay, William H. Crawford and John C. Calhoun. Calhoun withdrew and was elected Vice-President. In the election Jackson received 99 electoral votes, Adams 84, Crawford 41 and Clay 37. As none of the candidates had a majority, the House of Representatives had to choose one of the first three men to be President. This removed Clay from the race and he then threw his support behind Adams. As a result, Adams was elected President even though Jackson had won more popular votes.

Presidential Election of 1824		
Candidate	Popular Vote	Electoral College
Andrew Jackson	151,271	99
John Quincy Adams	113,122	84
William H. Crawford	40,856	41
Henry Clay	47,531	37

Adams' Administration 1825 – 1829

Jackson's powerful supporters in Congress immediately accused Adams of promising Clay a cabinet post in return for his support. When Clay was then appointed Secretary of State, they claimed that the two men had made "a corrupt bargain." The Democratic-Republican Party was split into two by this issue and Adams' group became known as the *National Republicans*. For the next four years Jackson's supporters opposed everything that Adams did.

Adams delivered his inaugural address in the Senate chamber of the unfinished U.S. Capitol. He recommended an ambitious program of national improvements including the construction of highways, canals, weather stations and plans for a national university. He hoped for a partnership between government and science. However, many Congressmen, including Jackson's supporters, opposed his plans and prevented them from reaching fruition.

By the time of Adam's administration, manufacturing had replaced farming as the chief activity in most New England states. These states favored high tariffs on imported goods. However, high tariffs would make the farmers of the South pay more for imported products and therefore Southern politicians wanted either low tariffs or free trade. In 1828, Congress passed a bill that put high duties on both manufactured goods and raw materials. The bill aroused bitter anger in the South and became known as the *Tariff of Abominations*.

Election of 1828

Adams was not a popular President at any time during his term of office. He felt that it was below the dignity of the President to engage in political debate and therefore did not defend himself against the attacks of Jackson and his supporters. He further alienated voters with his aloof manner. In the meantime, Jackson had become extremely popular. In the election of 1828 Adams received only 83 electoral votes to 178 for Jackson. Jackson received a popular vote proportionally larger than that received by any other candidate in the nineteenth century.

Later Years

After he left the White House, Adams initially planned to retire but widespread public support prompted him to run for the U.S. House of Representatives in 1830. This time he was successful and he subsequently served there for seventeen years. He recorded that he found his service there to be far more fulfilling than being President. During this period, he served for a time as the Chairman of the House Foreign Affairs Committee and as the Chairman of the Committee on Manufactures. In 1839, Adams supported the action of African slaves that had seized control of the *Amistad* and sought to return to Africa.

Another of Adams achievements as a U.S. Representative was to succeed in having the *Gag Rules* abolished in 1844. These rules had been introduced in 1836 to prevent the reading in the House of petitions regarding the abolition of slavery in Washington D.C. and the new territories of the West. Adams claimed that the rules violated the constitutional rights of free speech and petition. Adams also said that the government had the right to free slaves in a time of war. Abraham Lincoln later based the Emancipation Proclamation upon this argument.

In 1846 Adams suffered his first paralytic stroke but recovered and returned to Congress. On February 21st 1848 he suffered another stroke while working at desk in the House. He was too ill to be removed from the building and was carried to the Speaker's room where he died two days later. He was buried in the churchyard of First Unitarian Church in Quincy, Massachusetts. When his wife died in 1852, she was buried next to him. Their remains were later moved to the church crypt.

Summary

John Quincy Adams was the first son of a President to also become President and is usually ranked highly among them all. He led the nation through a period of peace and prosperity although he enjoyed only a few positive achievements while in office. Unusually among the Presidents, he was more successful both before and after he entered the White House. During his younger years he had been an accomplished diplomat and Secretary of State while in later life he served a productive period in the U.S. House of Representatives.

CHAPTER 7 – ANDREW JACKSON

7ᵗʰ President of the United States 1829 – 1837

Born: 15ᵗʰ March 1767, Waxhaw Settlement, border region of North and South Carolina

Married: Rachel Donelson Robards (1767 – 1828), originally August 1791, remarried: January 17ᵗʰ 1794

Number of Children: Three

Died: 8ᵗʰ June 1845, Nashville, Tennessee

Final Resting Place: The Hermitage, Nashville, Tennessee

Introduction

Andrew Jackson was a hero of the War of 1812 that was elected as the seventh President of the United States. During his presidency, the population of America reached nearly sixteen million people and the frontier moved rapidly westwards. Arkansas became a state in 1836, the same year that Wisconsin was organized as a territory, while Michigan became a state in 1837. Jackson was the first President to be born in humble circumstances but his victories as a soldier made him a popular candidate for President. Prior to entering the White House, Jackson had been a lawyer and a judge and had served in both the U.S. House of Representatives and the U.S. Senate. In 1828 he won the presidential election after one of the most bitter and negative campaigns in history. As President he introduced the *spoils system* into American politics and was responsible for one of the most tragic episodes in the entire history of the United States when he approved the enforced removal of Native Americans from their ancient tribal lands in the eastern states to reservations in the west. Many people died along what became known as "the trail of tears." However, he remained a popular President in his own day and his influence was still felt in American politics long after he died.

Background

Andrew Jackson was born on March 15th 1767 in the Waxhaw Settlement on the border between North and South Carolina. His parents were poor farmers who had settled in America from Ireland in 1765. His father died shortly before he was born. He was the youngest of three boys and attended school in the Waxhaw Presbyterian Church. In the Revolutionary War he joined the mounted militia of South Carolina. One of his brothers was killed in action while he and the other brother were taken prisoners of war by the British. While in captivity he was struck and wounded by a British officer for refusing to clean his boots. He was a left with a lifelong hatred of the British as well scars to his face and hand. The two brothers contracted smallpox in the prison camp and while Andrew survived, his brother died. Shortly afterwards his mother also died and he became an orphan at the age of 14.

After the end of the war, he briefly taught in a school. However, in 1784 he began to study to become a lawyer and in 1787 he was admitted to the bar. He loved gambling on horse-racing and cock-fighting and wasted an inheritance of three hundred pounds that had been left to him by his uncle. He would later own race horses and keep them in the White House stables. He was a hard drinker and also fought several duels. However, he was a very good lawyer and in 1788 was appointed attorney general of the area that is now Tennessee. His success as a lawyer enabled him to acquire a large law practice. In August 1791 he married Mrs. Rachel Donelson Robards. However, she was not properly divorced from her first husband and they had to re-perform their marriage on 17th January 1794. They had no children of their own but did adopt a son.

Entry into Politics

In 1796 Jackson was elected to the U.S. House of Representatives for the new state of Tennessee. In 1797 he was appointed to the U.S. Senate but resigned the following year as he felt the pace of life in Philadelphia was too slow. Six months later Tennessee legislators elected him justice of the state supreme court. In 1804, after six years in office, he resigned the judgeship to devote all his time to his private affairs. At this time, he was making money from speculating in land and from managing his two plantations. He continued to fight duels and in 1806 shot dead a lawyer.

Since 1802 he had served as a major general in the Tennessee militia. He was a successful leader and on March 27th 1814 defeated the Creek Indians in the Battle of Horseshoe Bend and forced them to give up their land in present-day Georgia and Alabama. In the War of 1812, he captured Pensacola which the British had been using as a military base. He was then sent to reinforce the American garrison in New Orleans. However, the war with Britain did not go well for America and in the Treaty of Ghent they had to give up all their claims to Canada. However, slow communications meant that news of the treaty did not reach New Orleans in time to prevent a British column of 8,000 troops from marching on the city. Jackson had built a force of only 5,000 men but they opened fire on the British from prepared positions. The British were forced to retreat having lost 300 dead while the Americans only lost 14 dead. In 1817 Jackson led his troops into Florida where they defeated the Seminole Indians. The apparent ease of this victory convinced Spain that they would not be able to defend Florida from America. In 1821 they ceded Florida to the U.S. and Jackson became the first governor of the new territory.

Election of 1824

Jackson's victories on the battlefield made him a national hero. Mant politicians called for him to be nominated for President. In 1823 the Tennessee legislature elected him to the U.S. Senate and then nominated him for President the following year. However, there was a strong field of candidates that included the Secretary of State, John Quincy Adams, Representative Henry Clay of Kentucky, and Secretary of the Treasury, William H. Crawford. In the election Jackson won 99 electoral votes, Adams won 84 and the others 78 between them. As no candidate had won an overall majority, the election would be decided by the House of Representatives, which voted by states. Clay threw his support behind Adams and, as a result, he received 13 votes to Jackson's seven. Five days later, President Adams named Henry Clay as Secretary of State. Jackson was furious and charged that the two men had made a "corrupt bargain." He never forgave either man and for the next four years he and his supporters did all they could to embarrass Adams, which they did quite successfully.

Election of 1828

Presidential Election of 1828		
Candidate	Popular Vote	Electoral College
Andrew Jackson	647,286	178
John Quincy Adams	503,064	83

The campaign of 1828 was one of the most bitter in American history. Adams sought re-election with Secretary of the Treasury, Richard Rush, as his candidate for Vice-President. Adams' opponents nominated Jackson with Adams' former Vice-President, John Calhoun, as his running mate. Adams' supporters attacked Jackson's marriage to Mrs. Robards calling her a "convicted adulteress." They distributed the "coffin handbill" which criticized Jackson for executing six Tennessee militia men who had mutinied in the War of 1812. Jackson continued to criticize the "corrupt bargain" and accused Adams of procuring a prostitute for the Czar of Russia. In the election Jackson won a sweeping victory by 178 electoral votes to 83. However, shortly after the election, on 28th

December 1828, his wife died of a heart attack. After the bitter campaign, Adams did not stay in Washington for Jackson's inauguration.

Jackson's First Administration 1829 – 1833

Jackson was inaugurated on 4th March 1829. During his term of office, the White House was managed by Emily Donelson. Her husband, Andrew Jackson Donelson, became the President's private secretary. Their four children were born in the White House.

One of his first priorities was to destroy what seemed to him to be a monopoly of federal offices by wealthy individuals. He also intended to clear incompetents out of these offices. He introduced the *spoils system* into national politics. Appointment to jobs was based on loyalty to Jackson. He rewarded his more deserving supporters by giving them good jobs. He dismissed about 2,000 of the government's employees. This was similar in proportion to Thomas Jefferson but was for political reasons. Jackson also formed a "kitchen cabinet," a group of unofficial advisers that met in the rear of the White House.

An important issue during his first term of office concerned the tariff. When the tariffs were increased on foreign manufactured goods, Vice-President Calhoun complained that it hurt his home state of South Carolina. He secretly wrote the *South Carolina Exposition* which said that the state could nullify (reject) any law passed by Congress which the state believed violated the constitution. In 1832 Congress passed another high tariff act. South Carolina declared the tariff laws of 1828 and 1832 null and void. The threatened to leave the Union if the government tried to collect duties in Charleston. Jackson responded by concentrating troops and warships near Charleston. Upon his demand, Congress passed a force bill which authorized him to use armed forces to collect tariffs. South Carolina withdrew the nullification of the tariff laws after Senator Henry Clay pushed through a compromise tariff bill that reduced them for ten years. During the crisis, Calhoun resigned as Vice-President and took a vacant seat in the Senate.

Another major issue of his administration concerned the Bank of the United States. In 1816, Congress had created the bank with a charter for twenty years. It had authority over the U.S. currency. Jackson felt that the creation of the bank violated the constitution. He criticized the bank for failing to establish a "uniform and sound" currency. He favored a "hard money" policy whereby paper money was based on gold and silver ("specie"). He felt the vast powers of the bank threatened democratic government and it meddled in politics. Its political supporters opposed Jackson and included Henry Clay. In 1832, Jackson vetoed a bill re-chartering the bank. This veto was upheld by Congress.

Election of 1832

The election of 1832 was the first one in American political history where the candidates were chosen by national political conventions. The Democratic-Republicans broke into two groups during the campaign for Jackson's re-election. His opponents took the name *National Republicans* and in 1831 they nominated Henry Clay for President with John Sargeant, the head of the legal staff at the Bank of the United States, for Vice-President. Jackson's supporters called themselves Republicans or *Democratic-Republicans*. In 1832 the nominated Jackson with Martin Van Buren for Vice-President. Historians trace the modern *Democratic Party* to the Democratic-Republican party of this period. The main issue of the election was the fight to re-charter that Bank of the United States. Jackson won an overwhelming victory with 219 electoral votes with 49 for Clay.

Presidential Election of 1832		
Candidate	Popular Vote	Electoral College
Andrew Jackson (Dem-Rep.)	701,780	219
Henry Clay	484,205	49

Jackson's Second Administration 1833 – 1837

Jackson interpreted his re-election as a sign that the public supported his bank policy. He ordered the Secretary of the Treasury, Louis McLane, to remove the government's deposits from the Bank of the United States and place them in state banks. Both McLane and his successor, William J. Duane, refused. Jackson then named Roger B. Toney to the office. Although Toney moved the deposits as Jackson requested, the Senate rejected Jackson's nomination of Toney for Secretary. This was the first time a cabinet nominee had been rejected. The withdrawal of funds reduced the bank's power.

The increase in tariffs and the sale of public land led to the government receiving more money than it was spending. On January 8th 1835 Jackson paid off the final instalment of the national debt, the only President ever to do so. Inflation became a serious problem due to all the money in circulation. On July 11th 1835, Jackson issued the *specie circular* which directed that government agents should only accept gold and silver for the sale of government lands.

In May 1830 Jackson approved the *Indian Removal Act* which aimed to force the Native Americans from the good land in the eastern states and move them to reservations west of the Mississippi. In 1828, Georgia had passed a law that gave the Cherokee Indians no protection if the state seized their lands. The Cherokees said that the federal government had guaranteed them this land by treaty. They said that a state could not nullify a federal contract. However, this time Jackson took the side of the states and Alabama and Mississippi seized the lands of the Cherokee and Chickasaw Indians. In 1831 the Supreme Court dismissed the Cherokee's case against the state of Georgia and many of them subsequently died in the forced migration off their land in what became known as *the trail of tears*. By the end of Jackson's administration, many of the Native Americans of the East had moved west of the Mississippi. The Seminole refused to be moved and fought on in Florida for seven years until they were almost wiped out.

Jackson's government did have some successes in foreign affairs. In 1830, America agreed to open her ports to the British in return for equal access to markets in the West Indies. In 1831, France agreed to pay off in six instalments America's long-standing claim for compensation for the plundering or "spoilation" of the Napoleonic War. In 1833 France failed to make a payment leading the U.S. to increase defense expenditure. The French then broke off diplomatic relations. However, in 1836, Jackson announced that France had paid four instalments with interest and diplomatic relations were resumed.

In 1831 William Lloyd Garrison began publishing the *Liberator*, an antislavery newspaper. In 1835, Texas revolted against Mexico. Antislavery forces did not want Texas admitted into the Union or even recognized as independent as it would upset the balance between North and South. On Jackson's last day in office, he established diplomatic relations with the Republic of Texas.

Later Years

After he left the White House, Jackson made it clear that he wanted Vice-President Martin Van Buren to be the next President. Van Buren subsequently won both the nomination and the presidential election. Jackson attended Van Buren's inauguration and then returned to the Hermitage. He became sick with TB and dropsy. On 8th June 1845 he fell unconscious and died in the evening. He was buried next to his wife in the garden of the Hermitage.

Summary

Andrew Jackson was a courageous war hero who believed that the President of the United States should provide the country was strong leadership. During his presidency, he vetoed more bills from Congress than all his predecessors put together. He believed that power should be exercised by the people and inspired reform movements that lasted until well after he left office. However. Some modern historians are critical of Jackson because of the way that

Native Americans were somewhat brutally removed from their ancient tribal lands to make way for settlement by people of European descent. For this reason, he is now ranked in the worse twenty   Presidents.

CHAPTER 8 – MARTIN VAN BUREN

8th President of the United States 1837 – 1841

Born: 5th December 1782, Kinderhook, New York

Married: Hannah Hoes (1783 – 1819), 21st February 1807

Number of Children: Five

Died: 24th July 1862, Kinderhook, New York

Final Resting Place: Kinderhook Reformed Church Cemetery, New York

Introduction

Martin Van Buren was elected the eighth President of the United States at a time when America was growing rapidly. The population by now exceeded seventeen and half million people and the first railroads were being built between the cities of the East. Van Buren's inauguration in 1837 was attended by people from New York City and Philadelphia who arrived on the first railroad into Washington D.C. In the West, the frontier town of Chicago was incorporated as a city and Iowa was organized as a territory. Before he entered the White House, Van Buren had served as a U.S. Senator, as Governor of New York, as Secretary of State and as Vice-President. When he became President, Van Buren believed that the government should play the smallest possible role in the life of the country. However, when he refused to help those affected by America's first great depression, known as the Panic of 1837, it led to his defeat in the presidential election of 1840. He later ran for President as the candidate of the Free Soil party in 1848 but was unsuccessful.

Background

Van Buren was born in the Dutch community of Kinderhook, New York, on 5th December 1782, the third of five children of a farmer and taverner. His ancestors had arrived in America from the Netherlands and he learned to speak Dutch as a child. He attended the village school in Kinderhook and then trained as an attorney. He moved to New York City in 1801 and was admitted to the bar in 1803. He then opened a law practice in his home town. On February 21st 1807 he married his childhood sweetheart, Hannah Hoes, and they had five children before her death in 1819, eighteen years before he became President.

Entry into Politics

Inspired by Thomas Jefferson, he entered politics as a Democratic-Republican and was elected to the New York senate in 1812, being re-elected four years later. Shortly afterwards, he was appointed Attorney General of New York. In 1821 he was elected to the U.S. Senate where he opposed the extension of the slave trade. He also fought hard against imprisonment for debt, and Congress passed a law abolishing such imprisonment in 1828. That same year he resigned from the Senate to become Governor of New York. However, he was only in office for two months before the newly-elected President, Andrew Jackson, appointed him Secretary of State. During his spell in office, he re-established trade with the British West Indies after the British had closed West Indian ports to American shipping in 1826 in retaliation for the high import tariffs imposed on British goods. He also successfully pressed claims for damages to American shipping by the French and Dutch during the Napoleonic Wars.

In 1831, Jackson tried to appoint Van Buren as Minister to Great Britain. However, the Senate refused to confirm the appointment by one vote. The following year, Jackson appointed Van Buren Vice-President and made it clear that he regarded him as his successor. Van Buren supported Jackson's decision to withdraw federal deposits from the bank of the United States. Debates in the Senate over the issue became so bitter that Van Buren had to carry loaded pistols into the chamber to protect himself against assassination.

The Election of 1836

With Jackson's support, Van Buren comfortably won the Democratic nomination for President in 1836. He then defeated the main Whig candidate, William Henry Harrison, by 97 electoral votes. However, he only received a slim majority of the popular vote. Van Buren ran for the Presidency without selecting a running mate. This was because no candidate for the vice-presidency received a majority of the electoral votes. The Senate then chose Van Buren's running mate, Representative Richard M. Johnson of Kentucky. He is the only Vice-President in history to have been selected by the Senate. Van Buren's inauguration was attended by visitors from New York and Philadelphia who arrived on the newly opened railroad into Washington, the capital's first.

Presidential Election of 1836		
Candidate	Popular Vote	Electoral College
Martin Van Buren (Democrat)	764,176	170
William Henry Harrison (Whig)	739,795	73

Van Buren's Administration 1837 – 1841

Van Buren entered the White House having inherited Jackson's popularity. However, his presidency soon ran into problems. On the 10th May 1837, the banks in New York faced a shortage of hard currency and so refused to convert paper money into gold or silver leading to a financial crash. Van Buren presented a bill before Congress to deal with the issue but it was rejected and the situation was made worse, causing a depression which brought financial ruin and misery to millions of people.

Americans looked to their government for help but Van Buren refused all public aid. Like Thomas Jefferson before him, he believed that government should play the smallest possible role in American life. As a result of his deeply held convictions, he became known as "Martin Van Ruin" and was blamed for all the economic hardship caused. He cut government expenditure by twenty percent and cancelled projects, such as naval construction, that could have reduced unemployment. He then made the unwise decision to expensively redecorate the White House at this time, which created a poor impression with those affected by the depression and left him vulnerable to criticism.

Van Buren was concerned, however, that the depression put in danger the federal funds held in private banks. He therefore attempted to create an independent treasury to hold the government's money and in July 1840 Congress passed a bill putting this into effect. The independent treasury was abolished after he left office in 1841 but later restored by President Polk in 1846.

Van Buren also had other important issues to deal with in his term of office. He had grown up in a household that had six slaves and in his inaugural address he pledged to defend slavery in those states where it already existed. However, he did not wish to extend slavery into the new territories in the West. When Texas offered to join the Union in 1837, he refused as he feared it would become a new slave state. This led to severe criticism from proslavery leaders in the South. On the other hand, antislavery leaders in the north criticized him for the Second Seminole War, fought to drive the Seminole Indians from Florida. They feared that he wanted to create a new slave state there.

Expansionists in his cabinet also wanted to extend America's borders into Canada. However, he refused and peacefully resolved a boundary dispute between Maine and New Brunswick that had been openly fought over. He continued President Andrew Jackson's hardline policy of removing Native Americans from their land in favor of white settlers. One quarter of all the Cherokee Indians died along the *Trail of Tears* when he attempted to remove them from Georgia to Indian Territory.

The Election of 1840

Although Van Buren was unpopular, the Democrats nominated as their candidate for re-election in 1840. However, he had to stand without a running mate as Vice-President Johnson failed to regain nomination and the Democrats could not agree on an alternative candidate. Van Buren thus became the only President in American history to seek re-election without a running mate.

His Whig opponent, William Henry Harrison, fought an effective campaign that played upon his status as a war hero and successfully portrayed Van Buren as an aristocrat who had no interest in resolving the unemployment caused by the depression. Although the result of the popular vote was close, Van Buren lost the electoral vote by 234 to 60.

Later Years

After the election, Van Buren remained active in politics, failing to win the Democrat's nomination in 1844. In 1848 he once again ran for President, this time as a member of the Free Soil party, which did not want to abolish slavery in those states where it already existed but opposed its extension into the new territories of the West. His bid was once again unsuccessful but he took so many votes in New York from the Democrat candidate Lewis Cass that the Whig candidate, Zachary Taylor, was elected. In his later years he remained a loyal Democrat but was opposed to slavery. He died on his estate at Lindenwald in 1862 and was buried beside his wife in Kinderhook.

Summary

Martin Van Buren was a man of dignified appearance and courteous manners. He was also a man of deep convictions and courage. However, his failure to bring relief to people suffering from America's first great depression, as well as his removal of Native Americans from their lands, means that he ranks very low among the Presidents.

CHAPTER 9 – WILLIAM HENRY HARRISON

9th President of the United States 1841

Born: 9th February 1773, Charles City County, Virginia

Married: Anna Symmes (1775 – 1864), November 25th 1795

Number of Children: Ten

Died: 4th April 1841, Washington D.C.

Final Resting Place: North Bend, Ohio

Introduction

William H. Harrison served the shortest term of any U.S. President and was the first President to die in office. He was the only President whose grandson, Benjamin Harrison, also became President. Harrison was a hero of the War of 1812 who was elected as the ninth President of the United States. As a young man he had served as a soldier and as the governor of Indiana Territory. He later served in the U.S. House of Representatives, the U.S. Senate and as the first U.S. Minister to Colombia before he became President. He spent only one month in the White House before dying of pneumonia.

Background

William Henry Harrison was born the youngest of seven children on 9th February 1773 on his father's plantation in Charles City County, Virginia. The family were a rich and prominent one and he enjoyed a comfortable upbringing. His father, a friend of George Washington, had served at both the Continental Congresses and had signed the Declaration of Independence. William was educated at home and then at Hampden-Sydney College, which he left before graduating to study medicine.

In 1791, however, he dropped medicine in favor of joining the army. He served in a war against the Indians in the Northwest Territory where he took part in the Battle of Fallen Timbers in 1794.

He was promoted to the rank of captain and given command of Fort Washington, Ohio. While there he met and married Anna Symmes, the daughter of a wealthy land investor. They had ten children, six of whom died before he became President. In 1798 he entered politics and served as secretary of the Northwest Territory. In 1800, President John Adams appointed him Governor of the Indiana Territory, a post he held for twelve years. He attempted to look after the Indians' welfare by inoculating them against smallpox and banning the sale of liquor to them.

In 1809 he negotiated a treaty with the Indian leaders which transferred nearly three million acres of their territory to settlers. Many Indians denounced the treaty and united under the Shawnee chief, Tecumseh, and his brother, known as the Shawnee Prophet. Harrison took command of the territorial militia and set out to drive the Indians from the lands submitted under the treaty. On November 7th 1811, Harrison's troops defeated the Indians at the Battle of Tippecanoe after overcoming a surprise nighttime attack.

Entry into Politics

When the War of 1812 began, President Madison promoted Harrison to Brigadier General and put him in command of the Army in the Northwest. They secured the region and then pursued the British and their Indian allies into Ontario where they defeated them at the Thames River on October 5th 1813, a battle in which Tecumseh was killed.

Harrison was now a national hero and in 1816 he was elected to the U.S. House of Representatives as a congressman for Ohio. There he was falsely accused of misusing public money while in the army but a House investigating committee cleared his name. In 1819 he was elected to the state senate from where he was elected to the U.S. Senate in 1825. In 1828, President John Quincy Adams appointed him as the first U.S. Minister to Colombia. However, a year later the President of Colombia, Simon Bolivar, requested his removal after being offended when Harrison urged him not to become a dictator, and he was recalled after Andrew Jackson became President.

Election of 1840

Harrison joined the new *Whig Party*, which was a coalition of people with different ideas about government that were united in their opposition to Jackson and Van Buren. In 1836, he was one of three candidates put forward by the party for the presidency but he was defeated by Martin Van Buren. In 1840, the Whigs again nominated him as their candidate and with John Tyler from Virginia as his running mate. Tyler, a Democrat from Virginia, was selected to broaden the appeal of the Whigs. Using the catchy slogan *"Tippecanoe and Tyler too,"* Harrison then fought the first modern election campaign in history, creating an image of himself as an "ordinary" man of the people while claiming that Martin Van Buren was "elitist." In this he was helped by an error made by his Democrat opponents who said that Taylor would rather be in his log cabin drinking hard cider than running the country. Harrison seized on this and run the *"log cabin and hard cider"* campaign that portrayed himself as a simple cider-drinking woodsman that was in fact far removed from his upbringing as Virginian aristocrat. They successfully portrayed Van Buren as a rich aristocrat who did little to resolve the hard times many people were experiencing during the depression. It was the first election where the candidates made speeches and addressed large rallies. Harrison won the election by only 147,000 votes but had a huge majority in the electoral college.

Presidential Election of 1840		
Candidate	Popular Vote	Electoral College
William H. Harrison (Whig)	1,274,624	234
Martin Van Buren (Dem.)	1,127,781	60

Harrison's Administration 1841

At his inauguration in 1841, Harrison spoke in the icy wind and rain for nearly two hours without an overcoat and caught a cold which was to lead to his death within a month. During his brief term in office, he spent much of his time deciding on appointments. However, just one week after taking office, the United States faced a crisis with Great Britain. Just over three years earlier, a U.S. steamboat, the *Caroline*, had been intercepted by the British while carrying supplies to Canadian rebels and three of her crew members killed. Later, the police in Buffalo, New York, had arrested a Canadian visitor that had been one of the party that attacked the Caroline. As soon as Van Buren had left office, the British demanded his release on threat of war. Harrison appointed Daniel Webster to resolve the issue. Webster apologized and subsequently negotiated the Webster-Ashburton Treaty in 1842 which eased tensions.

In March 1841, Harrison caught a chill while going out to buy some vegetables. The cold that he had caught on his inauguration day now developed into pneumonia and he died on the 4th April after just 30 days in office. He was buried in North Bend, Ohio.

Summary

Harrison was in office for too short a time for his presidency to be ranked. However, he did run the first modern election campaign in history.

Harrison was the first of seven consecutive Presidents elected in a year ending with "0" to die in office. The others were Abraham

Lincoln (1860), James Garfield (1880), William McKinley (1900), Warren Harding (1920), Franklin D. Roosevelt (1940) and John F. Kennedy (1960). Ronald Reagan was elected in 1980 but survived an   assassination   attempt.

CHAPTER 10 – JOHN TYLER

10ᵗʰ President of the United States 1841 – 1845

Born: 29ᵗʰ March 1790, Charles City, Virgina

Married: (1) March 29ᵗʰ 1813 – Letitia Christian (1790 – 1842) (2) 26ᵗʰ June 1844 – Julia Gardiner (1820 – 89)

Number of Children: (1) Eight with Letitia Christian (2) Seven with Julia Gardiner

Died: 18ᵗʰ January 1862, Richmond, Virgina

Final Resting Place: Hollywood Cemetery, Richmond, Virgina

Introduction

John Tyler was the first Vice-President to become President upon the death of the sitting incumbent. He established the right of the Vice-President to succeed completely to the Presidency. Before he became Vice-President he had served in the U.S. House of Representatives. During his term as President, the country continued to expand. The population passed twenty million for the first time and Florida joined the Union in 1845. Vast parts of the West were explored by Kit Carson and John C. Fremont and from 1841 thousands of settlers made their way towards the Pacific Northwest along the 2,000-mile (3,200km) Oregon Trail. In later life, Tyler was elected to the Confederate House of Representatives.

Background

John Tyler was born at Greenway estate in Charles City County, Virginia, on 29th March 1790, the son of a former state governor and former speaker of the Virginia House of Delegates. His aristocratic ancestors had emigrated from England and Tyler enjoyed a wealthy and privileged upbringing. He graduated from William and Mary College and then became a lawyer, being admitted to the Virginia bar in 1809. At the age of 21 he was elected to the Virginia House of Delegates. Shortly afterwards, on March 29th 1813, he married Letitia Christian, the daughter of a wealthy Virginia planter. They had five daughters and three sons. They lived on a plantation in Virginia and bought and owned slaves.

Entry into Politics

In 1816 he was elected to the U.S. House of Representatives where he opposed any measure that extended the powers of the government. He served as the governor of Virginia from 1825 to 1827 and was then elected to the U.S. Senate. His resistance to President Andrew Jackson's attempt to increase the powers of the federal government led him to leave the Democratic party and join the Whigs. The Whig party was a loose coalition of groups with no agreed policies or political beliefs. In 1840 they selected him as the Vice-Presidential running mate to William Henry Harrison based on his opposition to Jackson. In the election Harrison and Tyler defeated President Martin Van Buren with a large majority in the electoral college.

Tyler's Administration 1841 - 1845

Harrison died of pneumonia just one month after taking office and Tyler became President on 6th April 1841. He was at his plantation when he received the news of Harrison's death but quickly travelled to Washington and took the oath of office in his hotel room. He insisted on being called "President Tyler" rather than "Vice

President, Acting as President," and overcame opposition who felt his adoption of the Presidency was unconstitutional. An important precedent had been set concerning the orderly transfer of power upon the death of the President and was formally clarified in the Twenty-fifth Amendment to the Constitution in 1967.

The Whig leader in Congress, Henry Clay, submitted a legislative program that called for a new Bank of the United States and higher tariffs. This program conflicted with many of Tyler's long-held beliefs, many of which were more Democratic than Whiggish, and he vetoed every important bill that Congress passed. When Congress first attempted to pass a bill to create a Bank of the United States, Tyler responded with a sharply worded veto. That night an armed mob marched on the White House and threw bricks through the windows. Tyler issued guns to the White House staff and stood firm until the rioters had dispersed.

Congress then passed the bill a second time and once again Tyler vetoed it stating it included all the abuses of a private banking monopoly. Once again Whig mobs demonstrated against him, burning his effigy. All but one of his cabinet, Secretary of State Daniel Webster, resigned. Tyler then vetoed two further bills passed by Congress, one to give states money from the sales of public-land and one linking the distribution of this money with a higher tariff. Relations between Tyler and the Whigs became so bitter that they introduced impeachment resolutions into the House of Representatives, the first time this had happened. However, the impeachment attempt failed by 127 to 83.

Tyler did have some accomplishments in office. In 1841, he approved the *Pre-Emption Act* which speeded up the settlement of the Midwest by allowing a settler to claim 160 acres of land by building a cabin on the property. In 1842, he brought an end to the Seminole War in Florida and also settled a dispute with Britain concerning the border of Maine and Canada. In 1844, the United States signed a treaty with China that opened the way for trade between the two countries for the first time.

Election of 1844

Tyler sought the Whig nomination in 1844 but was unsuccessful. He briefly ran for election as an independent candidate but withdrew from the race so that the Democratic candidate, James Polk, could defeat the Whig candidate, Henry Clay. Although the result of the popular vote was close, Polk won 170 seats in the electoral college to 105 for Clay.

The second half of Tyler's term was dominated by the issue of the annexation of Texas. The Texans had declared their independence from Mexico in 1836 and sought to join the Union. Tyler favored annexation but was opposed by Northern Congressmen as Texas would be a slave state. However, when James Polk won the election of 1844 supporting annexation, Congress passed a joint resolution admitting Texas. Tyler signed the resolution on March 1st 1845. Two days later, on his last full day in office, he signed a bill admitting Florida to the Union. Texas formally joined the Union in December 1845, after Tyler had left office.

Letitia Tyler died from the effects of a paralytic stroke in September 1842. Her duties as First Lady were taken over firstly by her daughter-in-law, Priscilla Cooper Tyler, and then by one of her daughters, Letitia Tyler Semple. In 1844, the President was attending a naval review aboard USS Princeton when a gun accidently exploded killing eight people. Once of those that died was a former New York state senator, David Gardiner. After his death, Tyler grew close to Gardiner's daughter, Julia, and they married in New York City of 26th June 1844. Tyler was therefore the first President to be married while in office. Julia then fulfilled the role of First Lady during his last eight months in office. Their marriage produced seven children and his total of fifteen is a record for any President. One of Tyler's grandchildren is still alive more than 233 years after the President was born.

Later Years

After leaving office in 1845, Tyler retired to his estate and lived quietly. In 1861, however, he headed a Southern peace mission to Washington seeking a compromise on issues that threatened the Union but his proposals were rejected by Congress. Tyler then voted in favor of Virginia leaving the Union at a Virginia secession convention and later won election to the Confederate House of Representatives. However, he died before taking his seat on January 15th 1862 and was buried in Richmond, Virginia. He was the only President to die a citizen of the Confederacy and has sometimes been considered a traitor for being buried in its flag.

Summary

The tall, courteous and softly spoken Tyler has frequently been harshly criticized by historians and ranked very low among the Presidents. However, he often acted with great courage and since his time Vice-Presidents have always become President upon the death of the current incumbent.

CHAPTER 11 – JAMES POLK

11th President of the United States 1845 – 1849

Born: 2nd November 1795, Pineville, North Carolina

Married: Sarah Childress (1803-91), 1st January 1824

Number of Children: None

Died: 15th June 1849, Nashville, Tennessee

Final Resting Place: Tennessee State Capitol, Nashville, Tennessee

Introduction

James Polk was a slave-owning lawyer from the South that was elected as the 11th President of the United States. Before he entered the White House, he had served in the Tennessee House Representatives, the U.S House of Representatives, as Speaker of the House and as Governor of Tennessee. He took office as President after winning the election of 1844 and presided over the greatest territorial expansion in the history of the United States. During his four-year term of office, over one million square miles of territory was added to the country, later forming whole or part of no less than thirteen states. By 1849 the country had a population of nearly twenty-three million people and Americans enjoyed great prosperity. Polk is also remembered as being the only President that carried out every major promise made during his election campaign. However, despite his achievements, he failed to deal with America's growing social problems, in particular the divisive issue of slavery.

Background

Polk was born the eldest of ten children in Pineville, North Carolina on 2nd November 1795 and was brought up in Tennessee. His ancestors had emigrated from Ireland and his Presbyterian father made his fortune from farming, surveying, and land speculation. His plantation prospered, partly due to the hard work of fifty slaves. Polk studied mathematics and classics at the University of North Carolina and graduated in 1818. He then studied law in the office of Felix Grundy, one of the foremost lawyers and politicians in Tennessee, and was admitted to the bar in 1820.

Entry into Politics

It was then that he decided to enter a career in politics and in 1821 he became clerk of the Tennessee Senate. He entered the Tennessee House of Representatives in 1823 as a Democrat and worked to improve education and reduce taxes. On 1st January 1824 he married Sarah Childress, the daughter of a prosperous country merchant. They did not have any children. When she later became First Lady, she became the first wife of a President to serve as her husband's secretary.

In 1825 he entered the U.S. House of Representatives where he served seven consecutive terms. He became an enthusiastic supporter of President Andrew Jackson. In return, Jackson gave him his support and Polk became known as "Young Hickory," the protégé of "Old Hickory." Jackson's support was important in helping Polk become Speaker of the House in 1835. Further encouraged by Jackson, Polk then set his sights on becoming the Governor of Tennessee and he narrowly defeated Newton Cannon in the election of 1839. He hoped that this would be a springboard to even higher offices but he did not achieve any of his signature priorities and failed to get re-elected in 1841 and 1843.

Election of 1844

At this stage it looked like his career in senior politics was over as he could not even win his own state. However, in 1844 he was selected to represent the Democratic Party in the Presidential election. The early favorite for the nomination had been former President Martin van Buren but he lost support by openly opposing the annexation of Texas. Delegates at the Democratic presidential convention could not decide between Van Buren and his chief rival, Lewis Cass of Michigan, who had served as a former US minister to France. Polk, who was little known outside Tennessee, was proposed as a compromise candidate. He was known to favor the expansion of the United States to the south and west and this won him the critical support of Southern Democrats who believed it was America's *manifest destiny* to acquire new territory and clear the Native Americans from it. He won the nomination on the eighth ballot.

The delegates selected Senator Silas Wright of New York for Vice-President but, being a supporter of Van Buren, he rejected the nomination. This was the first time a man nominated for Vice-President had refused to run. The Democrats then nominated George M. Dallas, a lawyer from Pennsylvania.

Presidential Election of 1844		
Candidate	Popular Vote	Electoral College
James Polk (Democrat)	1,338,464	170
Henry Clay (Whig)	1,300,097	105

Polk's Whig opponent in the Presidential election was Senator Henry Clay of Kentucky, who was expected to win by a landslide. However, Clay tried to keep the issue of Texas out of the election fearing that if he supported annexation, it would lose him the antislavery vote in the North, whereas Polk took a forthright position for annexation. Polk then narrowly defeated him by little more than one percent of the total popular vote.

Polk's Administration 1845 - 1849

During his campaign, Polk had made four promises and each of these was carried out during his term. The first promise, to reduce tariffs, was achieved when Congress passed a new tariff law in 1846. Under this law, tariffs were to be based on the value of imports rather than the quantity for the first time. The second promise, to create an independent Treasury, was achieved a week later when Congress passed the Independent *Treasury Act* of 1846. Under the Act, an independent Treasury was set up to hold and disburse federal funds, and this remained in place until 1913, when the Federal Reserve System was established.

Polk's third objective was to reach agreement with Great Britain concerning the Oregon Territory. This territory covered not only the present-day state of Oregon but also parts of the states of Washington, Idaho, Wyoming, and Montana. Since 1843 thousands of pioneers had made their way along the Oregon Trail to settle in the territory, which enhanced America's claim. In the 1844 election campaign the Democrats used the slogan "Fifty-four Forty or Fight!" meaning that the U.S. should acquire the entire Oregon Territory as far north as the latitude of fifty-four degrees and forty minutes. However, once in office, Polk did not want a war with Britain and resolved the dispute peacefully. The two countries agreed the *Oregon Treaty* of 1846 which gave America all land south of the 49th parallel, except for Vancouver Island which remained in British hands. Oregon became a Territory in 1848.

Polk's fourth goal was to acquire California and this was achieved by a war with Mexico. The immediate cause of the war was America's annexation of Texas, which was also claimed by Mexico, in December 1845. Polk offered the Mexican government $30 million for their territory north of the Rio Grande and when this was refused war soon broke out. Polk expected a quick and victorious campaign against a disorganized and poorly resourced enemy but the war lasted more than two years and cost thirteen thousand American lives as well as twenty-five thousand Mexican.

The United States was ultimately victorious and in the *Treaty of Guadalupe Hidalgo* of February 1848, Mexico ceded territories that make up whole or part of the present-day states of California, Arizona, New Mexico, Utah, Colorado, and Wyoming. In return, the United States paid $15 million to the Mexican government. The territories were acquired without consulting the Native Americans who lived there and Polk seized their lands for settlement by white people. The settlement of California was given a boost when gold was discovered there in 1848 and thousands of people made their way west to seek their fortune.

American territory now stretched from the Atlantic to the Pacific. However, the acquisition of this territory only made worse the serious problems that America was already experiencing and which Polk did so little to resolve. During his term of office, three states joined the Union, namely Texas in 1845, Iowa in 1846 and Wisconsin in 1848. This brought the total number of states to thirty, equally split between those that permitted slavery and those that did not. Neither side had the power to control legislation through Congress and each feared that expansion westwards would give advantage to the other side.

Polk did little to resolve the tension that the issue of slavery was causing. Indeed, during his time in the White House, he bought no less than nineteen slaves of which thirteen were children. They were sent to work on a plantation in Mississippi from where it was harder for them to escape to the north. This was all kept secret from the American people to avoid an outcry. However, the fact that he was a slave-owner was one of the reasons that he did not ban slavery in the territories acquired from Mexico. During his term of office, Polk also did little to help the poverty of immigrants or tackle the hardships of children working in factories.

During his election, Polk had pledged to serve only one term. He was the first President not to seek re-election and he left the White House on the 4th March 1849. As he and his wife returned south, he fell ill, probably from cholera, and died in Nashville on 15th June, just three months after leaving office. His legacy was an enlarged America, but one that was on the brink of civil war.

Summary

James Polk is often portrayed by historians as mean and unfriendly man who was unsympathetic to the plight of slaves, poor immigrants and child laborers. However, he did keep all the promises that he made to get elected as well as expanding the country as far as the Pacific coast. For these reasons he is ranked in the middle of all the Presidents, being neither the best nor the worst.

CHAPTER 12 – ZACHARY TAYLOR

12th President of the United States 1849 – 1850

Born: 24th November 1874, Barboursville, Orange County, Virginia

Married: Margaret Mackall Smith (1788 – 1852), 21st June 1810

Number of Children: Six

Died: 9th July 1850, Washington D.C.

Final Resting Place: Zachary Taylor National Cemetery, Louisville, Kentucky

Introduction

Zachary Taylor was a hero of the Mexican-American War who was elected the 12th President of the United States. Before he entered the White House, he was a soldier that served in the War of 1812, the Black Hawk War, the Second Seminole War and the Mexican-American War. His victory over General Santa Anna's Mexican army of 20,000 men at the Battle of Buena Vista led directly to his nomination for President by the Whigs and he defeated the Democrat Lewis Cass in the election of 1848. He served as President when the country was dangerously divided between the free states of the North and the slave states of the South. The Union was then made up of thirty states with a population of just over twenty-three million. Half of the states permitted slavery but half did not and neither section could control legislation in Congress. However, he died in office before the slavery issue could be settled. His sixteen months as President was the third shortest spell of all the Presidents. He was also the last President to own slaves while in office.

Background

Zachary Taylor was born in Barboursville, Virginia on 24th November 1784, the third of nine children of one of the state's leading planters. He grew up on the frontier in Kentucky where his father had been rewarded for his service as an officer in the Revolutionary War with six thousand acres of land. This later grew to ten thousand acres and was worked by hundreds of slaves. Even though he came from a wealthy background, Taylor did not go to school and what education he had was provided by private tutors. Inspired by his father's tales of the Revolutionary War and living on frontier troubled by warfare, he joined the army as first lieutenant in 1808 and was promoted to captain two years later. In 1810 he met Margaret Mackall Smith, the orphaned daughter of a Maryland planter. They married on 21st June 1810 and had a son and five daughters, two of whom died as infants. Their son, Richard, later served as a General in the Confederate Army while one of their daughters, Sarah, married Jefferson Davis, the future President of the Confederacy.

During the War of 1812, Taylor defended Fort Harrison against Tecumseh in the Indiana Territory and won promotion to Major. He then spent many years defending the western frontier against Native American tribes. He served as a Colonel in the Black Hawk War in Wisconsin, receiving Black Hawk's surrender in 1832, and then in the Second Seminole War in Florida from 1837 to 1841. While there he earned the nickname "Old Rough and Ready" for his willingness to share the hardships of men. On December 25th 1837, he defeated the Seminole Indians at the battle of Lake Okeechobee and was rewarded with the honorary rank of Brigadier General.

However, his reputation was made in the war against Mexico which broke out in 1846 following the annexation of Texas. He led four thousand troops to the Rio Grande where they defeated the invading Mexicans at the battles of Palo Alto and Resaca de la Palma, driving them out of Texas. Taylor then invaded Mexico where he won the Battle of Monterrey in 1846. President Polk was concerned by his growth in popularity, particularly as Taylor was known to favor the rival Whig party. For this reason, he placed the invasion under the command of General Winfield Scott and transferred to him some of Taylor's soldiers and supplies.

Election of 1848

However, on 22nd February 1847, Taylor's army of five thousand men defeated General Santa Anna's Mexican army of 20,000 men at the *Battle of Buena Vista*. This victory made him a national hero and led to his nomination as a presidential candidate by the Whigs. They chose Millard Fillmore from New York as his running mate for the election in 1848. The Democrats nominated Senator Lewis Cass of Michigan while former President, Martin Van Buren, stood for the Free-Soil party. Of the candidates, only Van Buren campaigned on the issue of slavery. Although Van Buren did not carry a single state, he did succeed in taking votes from Cass. This was partly the reason that Taylor won the election by 36 electoral votes.

This was the first time that the Presidential election had been held in all the states at the same time. Margaret Smith Taylor had not been in favor of her husband running for President as she felt it would deprive her of her company. Because of her health, she would take little part in the social activities of the White House and her duties as hostess were performed by her daughter, Mary Elizabeth Bliss.

Presidential Election of 1848		
Candidate	Popular Vote	Electoral College
Zachary Taylor (Whig)	1,361,393	163
Lewis Cass (Democrat)	1,223,460	127
Martin Van Buren (Free Soil)	291,501	0

Taylor's Administration 1849 - 1850

President Taylor was due to be inaugurated on the 4th March 1849. However, as it was a Sunday, the religious Taylor postponed it until the following day. David R. Atchison, president pro tempore of the Senate, acted as acting President on March 4th as the presidency was vacant on that day.

There were some important achievements in his short term. In 1849, the Department of Interior was created and Taylor appointed Thomas Ewing as the first Secretary of the Interior. In 1850, the United States and Britain signed the *Clayton-Bulwer Treaty* which guaranteed the neutrality of any canal built across Nicaragua to link the Atlantic and Pacific oceans.

However, it was not long before the issue of slavery once again became important. At the time there were thirty states, equally split between those that permitted slavery and those that did not. In 1848, gold had been discovered in California leading to a gold rush the following year. Thousands of people, known as *forty-niners* headed west in search of their fortune. In 1849, California applied for admission to the Union as a free state. This created a dangerous situation as the slave states of the South refused to admit any new states fearing that it would upset the delicate balance between their slavery interests and the abolitionist North. Great debates were held in Congress where the Southerners threatened secession while the Northerners promised war to preserve the Union.

Taylor wanted to protect slavery in those states where it already existed, particularly as he was a slave owner himself, but opposed extending it to new states. Taylor was in favor of California joining the Union and opposed any compromise. However, before the issue could be settled, he became ill and died on the 9th July 1850. He may have contracted a bacterial infection after drinking iced water and milk at a ceremony for the new Washington Monument in Washington D.C. He was buried in the family cemetery in Louisville, Kentucky. His wife died two years later and was buried next to him. In 1991 his body was exhumed and examined for signs of poisoning but his corpse was badly decomposed and no conclusive evidence was found.

Summary

Zachary Taylor was a good military leader who served his country well as a soldier. As President he made little progress in resolving the issue of slavery during his short term and is often ranked low among the Presidents.

CHAPTER 13 – MILLARD FILLMORE

13th President of the United States 1850 – 1853

Born: 7th January 1800, Locke, Cayuga County, New York

Married: (1) February 5th 1826 – Abigail Powers (1798 – 1853) (2) 10th February 1858 – Caroline McIntosh (1813 – 1881)

Number of Children: Two with Abigail Powers, none with Caroline McIntosh

Died: 8th March 1874, Buffalo, New York

Final Resting Place: Forest Lawn, Cemetery, Buffalo, New York

Introduction

Millard Fillmore became the 13th President of the United States upon the death of Zachary Taylor. He was the second Vice-President to take office upon the death of the President. Before he was Vice-President, Fillmore had served in the New York House of Representatives, the U.S. House of Representatives and as Comptroller of New York. During his short spell as President, he approved and enforced the Compromise of 1850, which may have delayed the Civil War by more than ten years. During his administration, the population of the United States reached nearly twenty-six million people and continued expanding to the West. California became a state in 1850 and New Mexico and Utah became Territories. Faster settlement of the Midwest was aided by the completion of new railroads which provided faster cross-country travel. A direct rail service began between New York and Chicago in 1852.

Background

Millard Fillmore was born in Locke, New York, on 7th January 1800, the second of nine children of a poor farmer. He was raised in very humble circumstances. He attended school for only short periods and when he was fourteen, he became the unhappy apprentice of a clothmaker. He then studied law with a local judge and in 1823 opened his own legal practice in East Aurora. On February 5th 1826, he married his former school teacher Abigail Powers, who was two years his senior, and they later had two children.

Entry into Politics

In 1828 he commenced his political career when he was elected as a Whig to the New York House of Representatives. He was twice re-elected. In 1832 he was elected to the U.S. House of Representatives serving from 1833-35 and 1837-43. There he served as Chairman of the Ways and Means Committee and was the chief author of a new tariff in 1842, which raised duties on manufactured goods. In 1844 he unsuccessfully run for governor of New York. In 1846 he was the first chancellor of the University of Buffalo and the following year he was elected Comptroller of New York.

The Whigs nominated Fillmore as Zachary Taylor's running mate in the election of 1848. They were up against the Democratic nominees Senator Lewis Cass of Michigan for President and Congressman William Butler of Kentucky for Vice-President. However, the Democrats split over the issue of slavery and many voted for the Free Soil candidate Martin Van Buren. Taylor and Fillmore won the election by a margin of 36 votes. However, Taylor died on the 9th July 1850 and Fillmore took office the next day.

Fillmore's Administration

Fillmore took office at a time of great tension between the slave-owning states and slave-free states. At the time the country consisted of thirty states equally split between those that allowed slavery and those that did not. When slave-free California applied to join the Union in 1849, the Southern slave states opposed admittance as it would upset the delicate balance between slave-owning and the slave-free states. In addition, new territories had been recently been acquired following the successful war with Mexico and many Southerners wanted to expand slavery into them while many Northerners did not. Tension was increased when, supported by the other states of the South, Texas threatened to invade the territory of New Mexico in pursuit of a claim to land there. Had this happened then the Civil War may have started ten years earlier than it did.

Fillmore dealt resolutely with the issue. He sent federal troops to New Mexico to prevent an invasion and appointed men to his cabinet who were prepared to work towards a compromise. In September of that year, Congress passed a series of five Acts that became known as the *Compromise of 1850*. California was admitted to the Union as a slave-free state and slavery was also abolished in Washington DC. New Mexico and Utah were organized as territories from the land acquired from Mexico but the slavery question was left to each of them to decide. To satisfy the South, ten million dollars was paid to Texas to abandon its claims to New Mexico and a stricter law was passed for the return of runaway slaves. Known as the *Fugitive Slave Law* it was one of the harshest laws ever passed in the United States.

Many Northerners thought that the Fugitive Slave Law was too harsh and some states interfered with its enforcement. Many slaves escaped to Canada along what was known as *the underground railroad*. However, slavery did not become an issue again until the Kansas-Nebraska act of 1854 made slavery legal in territories where it had been prohibited. It is sometimes said that the Compromise of 1850 helped to delay the Civil War for more than ten years.

The compromise of 1850 was not Fillmore's only accomplishment in office. In 1852 he sent Matthew Perry on an expedition to the Far East. This voyage resulted in America's first trade treaty with Japan two years later.

When the Whigs met to nominate their presidential candidate for the election of 1852, the Southerners supported Fillmore. However, he had faithfully and zealously enforced the Compromise of 1850, including its provision for the return of runaway slaves. This lost him the support of most Northerners and he was rejected in favor of an antislavery candidate, General Winfield Scott.

Abigail Filmore, who found her duties as First Lady a heavy burden, died one month after Fillmore left office and was buried in Washington DC. During her time in the White House, she had set up the first library there and carefully chose the books for it. She was also the first ever First Lady to work both before and after her marriage. On 10th February 1858 Fillmore married a wealthy widow, Mrs. Caroline Carmichael McIntosh.

Later Years

After leaving the White House, Fillmore returned to Buffalo and resumed his law practice. The Whigs nominated him for the presidential election in 1856 but he came third behind Democrat James Buchanan and Republican General John C. Fremont. During the Civil War he opposed many of Abraham Lincoln's policies. After the war, he favored the reconstruction program of President Andrew Johnson. He died in March 1874 and was buried in Buffalo.

Summary

Largely forgotten and unknown by today's Americans, Millard Fillmore was a modest self-made man who rose from humble origins to take over the nation's highest office. Although he failed to win the nomination in 1852, his approval of the Compromise of 1850 may have delayed the Civil War by ten years. His vigorous support of the Fugitive Slave Law, one of the harshest laws in American history, means that he is usually ranked low among the Presidents.

CHAPTER 14 – FRANKLIN PIERCE

14th President of the United States 1853 – 1857

Born: 23rd November 1804, Hillsborough, New Hampshire

Married: Jane Appleton (1806 – 63), November 10th 1834

Number of Children: Three

Died: 8th October 1869, Concord, New Hampshire

Final Resting Place: Concord, New Hampshire

Introduction

Franklin Pierce was elected as the 14th President of the United States at the age of 48 and was the youngest President up to that time. Before he entered the White House, he served in the New Hampshire House of Representatives, the U.S. House of Representatives, the U.S. Senate and as a Brigadier General in the Mexican-American War. As President he approved the Kansas-Nebraska Act which created great and violent tensions over the issue of slavery and led to the formation of the Republican Party. During his presidency, the United States added to the territory of Arizona and New Mexico with the Gadsden Purchase and concluded America's first ever trade agreement with Japan. Pierce served at a time of great prosperity. The population of the United States had reached twenty-nine million people and settlers were attracted to the West by the California gold rush and assisted by railway lines that extended across the country.

Background

Franklin Pierce was born in Hillsboro, New Hampshire, on 23rd November 1804, the seventh of nine children of a former state governor. He was educated at academies in Hancock and Francestown before entering Bowdoin College. After graduating in 1824, he studied law and in 1827 set up his own legal practice in Concord. On November 10th 1834 he married Jane Means Appleton, the daughter of a former president of Bowdoin College. They had three children but two sons died in early childhood.

Entry into Politics

He began his political career in 1829 when he was elected to the New Hampshire House of Representatives. Two years later won re-election and served as speaker of the house. In 1833, he was elected to the US House of Representatives, where he served two terms. In 1837, he was elected to the US Senate where, aged 37, he was the youngest Senator. However, his wife disliked Washington and suffered from tuberculosis and depression following the death of her two young children. In accordance with his wife's wishes, Pierce resigned from the Senate in 1842, shortly before his term ended.

When the Mexican-American war began in 1846, President James Polk commissioned Pierce as colonel in the US Army. Shortly afterwards he was promoted to brigadier general. He served under General Winfield Scott in the advance to Mexico City and commanded a brigade in the attack on Churubusco, where he was injured in the leg. After the war, he resumed his legal practice in Concord and became one of the leading Democrats in New Hampshire.

Election of 1852

At the national convention in 1852, the delegates had difficulty in selecting a candidate for the presidential election that was acceptable to all the factions in the party. The four strongest candidates were Senator Stephen A. Douglas from Illinois and three former cabinet members – James Buchanan, William L. Marcy and Lewis Cass. After 34 ballots it appeared that none of the four strongest candidates could win the nomination. Delegates from Virginia then nominated Pierce who won on the 49th ballot after several delegates swung to him from James Buchanan. Pierce received support from the North because he was from New England but also from the South because he had supported the Compromise of 1850 including the strict enforcement of the Fugitive Slave Law.

In the presidential election of 1852, his running mate was Senator William R.D. King of Alabama. The Whigs nominated General Winfield Scott for President and Secretary of the Navy, William Graham, for Vice-President. At first it appeared that no real issues separated the two parties but during the campaign it became clear that Scott was opposed to slavery. This lost him support in the South and Pierce won both the popular vote and carried more states in the electoral college.

Presidential Election of 1852		
Candidate	Popular Vote	Electoral College
Franklin Pierce (Democrat)	1,601,117	254
Winfield Scott (Whig)	1,385,453	42

Pierce's Administration 1853 – 1857

Sadly, Pierce's administration began in the aftermath of a tragedy in which their eleven-year-old son, Benjamin, was killed in a railroad accident. Mrs. Jane Pierce collapsed from grief and did not attend her husband's inauguration. She led a secluded life in the White House until 1855 while many of her duties as First Lady were carried out by her aunt, Mrs. Abby Kent Means. Another tragedy was that Vice-President King died in April 1853 after a severe illness before he had the chance to perform any of the duties of his office.

Pierce tried to unite his party by selecting men from all factions for his cabinet. At first, he was successful. However, in January 1854 Senator Stephen Douglas introduced a bill that he hoped would hasten frontier settlement. It proposed to carve two new territories, Kansas and Nebraska, out of the Indian lands to the west and provided that the settlers in the new territories could decide for themselves whether to permit slavery. The bill permitted slavery in Kansas for the first time since it had been prohibited there by the Missouri Compromise of 1820 and threatened the uneasy balance achieved by the Compromise of 1850. However, Pierce supported it and it became law on May 30th 1854. Both slavery and anti-slavery settlers poured into Kansas each seeking to control the territory. In 1855, thousands of settlers from Missouri, known as *Border Ruffians*, crossed into Kansas and elected a pro-slavery legislature that then established slavery in the territory. Meanwhile, anti-slavery settlers, known as *Free Staters*, organized a rival government. Their rivalry soon developed into armed clashes known as *Bleeding Kansas*.

Both Northerners and Congress were outraged by Pierce's approval of the *Kansas-Nebraska Act* and there was a violent realignment of the political parties. The Democrats defended the existing law on slavery and remained strong in the South. The Whigs, already weakened by sectionalism, disintegrated and two new parties were born. Firstly, the *Republican Party* was formed from the anti-slavery Democrats, Free-Soilers and northern Whigs. Secondly, the *Know-Nothing* or American Party was created which opposed to granting rights to immigrants.

Pierce pursued an aggressive foreign policy aimed at territorial expansion. In 1853, he achieved an early success when the *Gadsden Purchase* acquired further territory from Mexico. In return for a payment of ten million dollars, the United States gained the land which now makes up the southern parts of Arizona and New Mexico. This gave America a more direct railroad route from the Southern states to the Pacific Coast as well as a settled boundary with her southern neighbor.

Many Southerners also wanted to acquire Cuba, which would enable the expansion of slavery and enhance their security and commerce. In 1854, Spanish authorities in Cuba seized an American ship, the *Black Warrior*. American diplomats then drafted what became known as the *Ostend Manifesto* which claimed that the United States had the right to seize Cuba if the Spanish would not sell it to them. Although the document had been drafted in secret, it became known to the public and led to great protests, especially in the North.

Pierce successfully concluded America's first trade agreement with Japan in 1854. However, when he recognized the Nicaraguan regime of William Walker, an American adventurer who had set himself up as dictator, he annoyed the government of Great Britain who had commercial interests in that country.

By the time his term ended, his handling of the slavery issue and as well as opposition to the Ostend Manifesto meant that few Democrats supported his re-election and James Buchanan was nominated as the party's candidate for the 1852 presidential election.

Later Years

After Buchanan was inaugurated, Pierce and his wife travelled to Madeira in an unsuccessful attempt to improve her health. In 1863, shortly after they returned to America, Mrs. Pierce died. In later life, Pierce became a fierce critic of President Abraham Lincoln and blamed his leadership for the Civil War. He died in October 1869 and was buried next to his wife in Concord.

Summary

Franklin Pierce was President during one of the most prosperous periods of American history. Settlers continued to move westwards and the Gadsden Purchase acquired new territory in Arizona and New Mexico. However, Pierce failed to effectively deal with the increasingly bitter division between the North and South over the issue of slavery. The Kansas-Nebraska Act, which he supported, led to fighting and bloodshed. This is a key reason why he is often ranked as one of the worst Presidents.

CHAPTER 15 – JAMES BUCHANAN

15th President of the United States 1857 – 1861

Born: 23rd April 1791, Cove Gap, Pennsylvania

Married: Unmarried

Number of Children: None

Died: 1st June 1868, Lancaster, Pennsylvania

Final Resting Place: Woodward Hill Cemetery, Lancaster, Pennsylvania

Introduction

James Buchanan was elected 15th President of the United States and led the country in the critical years leading up to the Civil War. During his presidency, seven of the fifteen Southern states seceded from the Union and formed the Confederate States of America. He did not attempt to force them to rejoin fearing that this would cause the remaining Southern states to also secede. Before he entered the White House, he rose from a humble upbringing in a log cabin to serve in the Pennsylvania legislature, the U.S House of Representatives, the U.S. Senate, as the U.S. Minister to Russia and Great Britain, and as Secretary of State. He became President after winning most of the electoral votes in the election of 1856 even though he failed to win a majority of the popular vote. During his administration the U.S. population exceeded more than 32 million people and three new states joined the Union, namely Minnesota in 1858, Oregon in 1859 and Kansas in 1861. Congress also created three new territories in Colorado, Nevada and Dakota. He was noteworthy as the only bachelor to become President.

Background

James Buchanan was born in a log cabin near Mercersburg, Pennsylvania, in April 1791. His father had moved to America from Ireland and opened a country store. James was initially schooled at home, taking lessons from a local pastor. He later graduated from Dickinson College in Carlisle, Pennsylvania, and then studied and practiced law in Lancaster. In the War of 1812, he volunteered as a private and took part in the defense of Baltimore.

After the war had ended, Buchanan began his political career serving two terms in the Pennsylvania legislature. However, in 1816 he returned to his law practice in Lancaster. He met and fell in love with Anne Coleman, the daughter of an iron manufacturer and they became engaged in 1819. However, shortly afterwards, Anne died while visiting her married sister in Philadelphia. Buchanan never got over her death and is still the only President to remain a bachelor.

He decided once again to return to politics and successfully ran for the U.S. House of Representatives in 1820. He supported the Presidential candidacy of Andrew Jackson, the leader of the Democratic Party, in 1824. However, Jackson was defeated by John Quincy Adams. Jackson was later elected President in 1828 and rewarded Buchanan by appointing him Minister to Russia in 1831. In 1832, he negotiated the first trade treaty between the United States and Russia.

Buchanan returned to America in 1833 and the following year was elected to the U.S. Senate by the Pennsylvania legislature. He served there until 1845 and became one of Jackson's leading supporters. During his spell as a Senator, he served for a time as the chairman of the committee on foreign affairs. In 1844 President James Polk appointed him Secretary of State and negotiated the entry into the Union of the state of Texas. This led to the Mexican-American War and the acquisition of much new territory in the southwest. He also negotiated a compromise settlement with Britain concerning Oregon's border with Canada, which still forms the present boundary.

In 1849 the Whig party regained the presidency. Buchanan retired to Wheatland, his estate near Lancaster, Pennsylvania. In 1852 he ran for the Democratic presidential nomination but lost to Franklin Pierce who then went on to win the presidential election. Pierce the appointed Buchanan as Minister to Great Britain and he spent two years attempting to modify the Clayton-Bulwer Treaty of 1850. The treaty provided that neither nation should occupy territory in Central America. After the treaty had been signed, the British said that it did not apply to territory that they already had while Americans said that if they had known this then they would not have ratified the treaty. However, Buchanan could not persuade the British to give up their territory. Buchanan was also an author of the controversial Ostend Manifesto of 1854 which said that the United States should seize Cuba if the Spanish refused to sell the island to them.

Election of 1856

Many of the leading Democrats had supported the Kansas-Nebraska Act of 1854 and therefore found it hard to get enough support to win the nomination for presidency in 1856. Buchanan had been serving as the U.S. Minister in London when this act was passed and had therefore not taken a stand on it. He returned to the United States in April 1956 and was nominated the Democratic candidate for President the following month. John C. Breckinridge, a former Kentucky congressman, was nominated for Vice-President. The Republicans nominated two former Senators, John C. Fremont of California and William L. Dayton of New Jersey. The Whigs nominated the former President, Millard Fillmore, and the No-Nothings nominated Andrew J. Donelson, the former Minister to Prussia. The Democrats appealed to those that wanted to preserve the Union while the Republicans openly fought slavery using the slogan "Freedom, Freemen, Fremont." In the election, Buchanan won a large majority of the electoral votes even though he failed to win a majority of the popular votes.

Presidential Election of 1856		
Candidate	Popular Votes	Electoral Votes
James Buchanan (Dem.)	1,836,072	174
John C. Fremont (Rep.)	1,342,345	114
Millard Fillmore (American)	873,053	8

Buchanan was inaugurated in 1857. During his time in the White House his niece, Harriet Lane, served as his hostess. She organized a brilliant social life with one reception and ball following another. The most spectacular parties centered around the visit of the Prince of Wales, later King Edward VII, of Great Britain. He brought such a large party that Buchanan had to sleep in the hallway to provide enough accommodation for his guests.

Buchanan's Administration (1857 - 1861)

Buchanan entered the White House at a time when the nation was bitterly divided by the issue of slavery. He said that he opposed slavery but that the Constitution protected it in the states of the South. However, when he appointed his Cabinet, he failed to include representatives from all the major factions within his party. There were no Northern Democrats and he seemed to rely heavily on pro-slavery Southern Democrats. Of the seven members of his Cabinet, four were Southern slave-owners and at least one of the others was a *doughface*, the derogatory term given to those Northerners who held pro-Southern views. Consequently, he was accused of listening to only a narrow range of opinion and, as a result, of taking pro-slavery positions and actions.

Shortly after his inauguration in 1857 he announced his support for the Supreme Court's decision in the *Dred Scott Case*. The decision has been described by some constitutional historians as the worst ever made by the Supreme Court and said that a slave called Dred Scott could not be free even though he lived in a state where slavery was prohibited; that African-Americans were not and could never be citizens of the United States; and that Missouri Compromise, which prevented the extension of slavery to a large part of the West, was unconstitutional.

Later in 1857 Buchanan endorsed the *Lecompton Constitution*, which had been produced by pro-slavery settlers in Kansas to allow slavery in the new state. He said that he favored "popular sovereignty," which meant letting the people who lived in Kansas vote on whether to allow slavery. However, the U.S. Congress refused to approve the constitution and sent it back to the people of Kansas in 1858. Anti-slavery voters there then defeated it.

Buchanan's stand on the Kansas question greatly angered people living in the North. In the congressional elections of 1858, Northern candidates opposed to the President won both a majority in both Houses. With Congress now hostile to him, his proposals to build a railroad to the Pacific, enlarge the army and navy, and develop canals across Central America were rejected. He vetoed several bills including one to give free land to settlers in the west.

He was more successful in his foreign policy, partly due to his experience in foreign affairs. He established better relations with Great Britain and approved of the treaties that the British signed with Nicaragua and Honduras that solved the problem of complying with the Clayton-Bulwer Treaty. However, Congress refused to allow Buchanan to send troops to Central America to prevent European powers intervening in the disorder there.

The Election of 1860

Buchanan made it clear that he did not wish to stand for re-election in 1860 but even if he had there was little support for his renomination. Different candidates were nominated by the Northern and Southern Democrats, which split the party's vote and ensured that the election would be won by the Republican ticket of Abraham Lincoln of Illinois and Senator Hannibal Hamlin of Maine.

It was during the period between Lincoln's election and his inauguration that Buchanan faced his greatest crisis. Shortly after Lincoln's victory, South Carolina seceded from the Union and was followed by six other states. They then established the Confederate States of America. Buchanan said that the states had no right to secede but that the Constitution provided no legal way to prevent it. He took very little action other than to call for an amendment to the Constitution. He believed that if he attempted to force the seven states to return to the Union then it would cause the eight remaining slave states to also secede. He also felt that, if left alone, the seven Confederate states would soon disagree among themselves and seek a return to the Union.

On December 26th 1860, a small garrison of Union troops were moved to Fort Sumter in Charleston Harbor in South Carolina. South Carolina then sent commissioners to Buchanan to demand their withdrawal but the President refused. Two of his Southern Cabinet members then resigned because they thought he was being too hard. However, the Secretary of State, Lewis Cass, also resigned because he thought Buchanan was not being hard enough. Buchanan now filled the vacant posts with members that were loyal to the Union and sent the steamer *Star of the West* to relieve the garrison at Fort Sumter. On 9th January 1861, South Carolina batteries opened fire on the vessel and forced it to turn back. Buchanan still hoped that a peaceful settlement could be reached and said that he did not regard this as an act of war as no blood had been shed. In March 1861, he left the White House and Abraham Lincoln became President. Lincoln initially attempted to continue Buchanan's policy but in April 1861 Confederate troops fired on Fort Sumter and the Civil War began.

Later Years

After Lincoln's inauguration Buchanan retired to his home at Wheatland where he spent much of his time writing a book in defense of his policies. He urged his fellow Democrats to support Lincoln's prosecution of the war. Buchanan died on 1st June 1868 and was buried in Woodland Hill Cemetery in Lancaster, Pennsylvania.

Summary

James Buchanan is usually ranked among the worst Presidents in the history of the United States. His time in office was affected by the gathering storm over the issue of slavery as well as by economic problems and unemployment. He opposed slavery but said that the Constitution protected it in the states of the South. When seven states seceded from the Union, he did not attempt to force them back. To many historians, he did too little to either end slavery or save the Union.

CHAPTER 16 –
ABRAHAM LINCOLN

16ᵗʰ President of the United States 1861 - 1865

Born: 12ᵗʰ February 1809, Sinking Spring Farm, Hodgenville, Kentucky

Married: Mary Todd (1818 – 82), November 4ᵗʰ 1832

Number of Children: Four

Died: 15ᵗʰ April 1865, Washington D.C.

Final Resting Place: Oak Ridge Cemetery, Springfield, Illinois

Introduction

Abraham Lincoln rose from a humble background to be elected as the 16ᵗʰ President of the United States in 1860. Before entering the White House, Lincoln had served in the Illinois State Legislature and the U.S. House of Representatives. As President, he led the country through the entire four years of the Civil War. In 1862 he issued the Emancipation Proclamation which freed the slaves in the states of the Confederacy. In 1863 he delivered the Gettysburg Address, one of the most famous speeches in history, in which he defined democracy as "government of the people, by the people, for the people," and promised that it would not "perish from the earth." In 1864 he was re-elected with a substantial majority of both the popular vote and the electoral vote. In 1865 he offered generous and reconciliatory terms to the defeated Confederate states and asked that they be welcomed back into the Union. Less than a week after the end of the war he was shot in the back of the head by a Confederate plotter while watching a performance of *Our American*

Cousin at Ford's Theatre in Washington D.C. He died early the following day and was the first President to be assassinated. Thousands of mourners lined the tracks as a train carried his body from Washington D.C. to his burial in Springfield, Illinois. Today he is remembered as the man that saved the Union and as one of the two greatest Presidents along with George Washington.

Background

Abraham Lincoln was born on February 12th 1809 in a log cabin in Hardin (near Hodgenville), Kentucky. His ancestors migrated from England to Massachusetts in the 17th century. Over the years the Lincoln family spread over different states and Abraham's father, Thomas, worked as a carpenter in the frontier state of Kentucky. Abraham was the middle of three children. His younger brother died in infancy. The family moved to Indiana where they lived in a log cabin built by Abraham and his father. Abraham's mother died when he was nine years old and his father then remarried. Abraham's step-mother moved into their log cabin with her three children from a previous marriage.

There were no good schools on the wild frontier of Indiana but Abraham learned reading, writing and arithmetic. He had less than one year of formal education and was rarely able to read a book. However, his parents did own a bible and he came to know it thoroughly. He left his father's home at 22 and moved to New Salem where he lived for six years. In 1831 he volunteered to fight in the Black Hawk War but saw no action. He then ran a store in New Salem but the business failed after a few months. He then briefly earned a living as a surveyor. In 1834, while campaigning for a seat in the legislature, he began to study law and received his license to practice law in 1836. The following year he became a junior partner in a legal practice in Springfield, the state capital. He later served as a partner in other law practices.

On November 4th 1832 he married Mary Todd, a woman from Kentucky that he met in Springfield. They had four children, three of whom died young.

Entry into Politics

Lincoln made his first attempt to win election to the Illinois state legislature in 1832 but was unsuccessful. However, in 1834 he ran again and this time won. He then served four successive two-year terms as a Whig in the legislature's lower house. In the legislature, his wit and skill in political debates made him a prominent figure. It was also at this time that he made his first speeches criticizing slavery. In 1846 he was elected to the U.S. House of Representatives but his opposition to the popular war against Mexico ruled out an attempt at a second term. He briefly returned to his law practice in Springfield, Illinois, and became known as one of the leading lawyers in the state.

Lincoln re-entered politics due to a sudden change in the national policy towards slavery. The Missouri Compromise of 1820 had prohibited slavery in new territories north of the east-west line that was an extension of Missouri's southern boundary. In 1854, Congress passed the Kansas-Nebraska Act which repealed the Missouri Compromise and provided that the settlers of new territories should decide for themselves whether they wanted slavery. Lincoln was outraged. Although he believed that the Constitution protected slavery in the states where it already existed, he also believed that slavery was evil and should not be spread. He resolved to return to politics and reverse the Kansas-Nebraska Act. He made powerful speeches throughout Illinois condemning the Act and was once again elected to the state legislature. Shortly afterwards he attempted to be elected to the U.S. Senate but was unsuccessful.

In 1856 he joined the antislavery Republican party, which was then only two years old. In 1858 he was nominated to run against Senator Stephen A. Douglas for a seat in the U.S. Senate. It was Douglas that had introduced the bill into Congress that led to the Kansas-Nebraska Act. Lincoln accepted the nomination with a famous speech in which he said: "A house divided against itself cannot stand." He predicted that America would become either wholly slave-owning or wholly slave-free. Lincoln and Douglas then took part in a series of debates which focused on the extension of slavery into free territory. Both candidates fought an exhausting campaign, but in the election, Douglas won by 54 votes to 46. Lincoln's campaign speeches and performance in the debates had, however, made him a national figure and he now set his eyes on the White House.

Election of 1860

When Lincoln ran for President in 1860 his main opponents were Senator William H. Seward of New York and Senator Salmon P. Chase of Ohio. Seward was the frontrunner but he also had many political enemies. Lincoln had never held a prominent national office and did not have any bitter enemies. His humble background and moderate views on the slavery question also attracted him support. At the Republican national convention in Chicago, Seward clearly won the first ballot with 173 and a half votes to Lincoln's 102. However, Lincoln began to gain strength and on the second ballot he almost tied with Seward with 181 votes to 184 and a half. On the third ballot Lincoln won the votes of Ohio from Chase and these helped him to pass the 233 votes needed to win the nomination.

Presidential Election of 1860		
Candidate	Popular Votes	Electoral Votes
Abraham Lincoln (Rep.)	1,865,908	180
John C. Breckinridge (Dem.)	848,019	72
John Bell (Con. Union)	590,901	39
Stephen A. Douglas (Dem.)	1,380,202	12

In the election he faced two candidates from the Democratic party, which had split into two factions. The Northern Democrats nominated Senator Douglas while the Southern faction nominated Vice-President John C. Breckinridge. A fourth party, calling itself

114

the Constitutional Union party, nominated former Senator John Bell of Tennessee. The split in the Democratic party assisted Lincoln enormously, and in the election, he received 180 electoral votes to 72 for Breckinridge, 39 for Bell and 12 for Douglas. Lincoln received 1,865,593 votes compared to a combined total of 2,923,975 for his three opponents. All his electoral votes and nearly all his popular votes came from the North.

Lincoln's First Administration 1861 - 1865

The Southern states threatened to withdraw from the Union if Lincoln won the election. On 20th December 1860, South Carolina became the first state to secede from the Union followed by six more before Lincoln was inaugurated. Four more seceded later. Together the eleven seceded states formed the Confederate States of America with its capital in Richmond, Virginia. In his inauguration address on March 4th 1861, Lincoln said that he did not wish to end slavery in states where the Constitution protected it and urged the preservation of the Union. He felt that the break-up of America would be a tragedy not only for the country but for the world. The survival of freedom and democracy in the world depended on it.

As the eleven states seceded, they occupied most of the forts belonging to the Federal government. In his inauguration address, Lincoln had vowed to "hold, occupy and possess" the Federal government's forts and other property in the South. Fort Sumter in the harbor of Charleston, South Carolina, was still in Federal hands. Lincoln knew that to reinforce the garrison there would be seen as an act of war by the Confederacy. He therefore ordered that it should only be supplied with provisions. However, the leaders of South Carolina still regarded this as a hostile act and on 12th April 1861 General Pierre G. T. Beauregard ordered Confederate artillery to fire on the fort, which surrendered the next day. The American Civil War had begun.

Lincoln dealt with the crisis with great energy. He called on the militia to suppress the "insurrection," greatly expanded the army, blockaded the Southern ports, and suspended Habeas Corpus in those parts of the North where many of the people were actively sympathetic to the South. He justified his actions when Congress met for the first time in his administration in July 1861. The North received far more volunteers for its army than it could equip but by July a large force had been assembled near Washington. An equally large Confederate army was stationed just across the Potomac River in Virginia. At this point many people in the North thought that the South could be defeated in a single battle and newspapers urged Lincoln to order an advance on Richmond. However, when the two armies clashed in the first *Battle of Bull Run* on 21st July the Union forces were decisively defeated. The public then realized that the war would be a long one.

In 1862, Northern forces under General George B. McClennan once again tried to capture Richmond but their campaign ended in failure and Lincoln relaced McClennan with General John Pope. However, Pope's troops were then defeated in the *Second Battle of Bull Run* and Lincoln reappointed General George B. McClennan to lead the defense of Washington D.C. McClennan achieved an important victory at the *Battle of Antietam* but Lincoln replaced him in November with General Ambrose E. Burnside. However, he led his troops to defeat at the *Battle of Fredericksburg* on December 13th. His successor, General Joseph Hooker, was then defeated at the *Battle of Chancellorsville* in May 1863.

One of Lincoln's concerns as President was to ensure that the remaining states of the Union remained united. The four border states of Kentucky, Missouri, Delaware and Maryland would have seceded if the North's war aim was to end slavery. Had they done so then the task of winning the war would have become much more difficult. Lincoln therefore repeated stressed that the aim of the war was to preserve the Union. His moderate position played an important part in keeping all the border states in the union. Another of Lincoln's concerns was to ensure that there was no foreign intervention in the Civil War. In November 1861, the U.S. Navy stopped a British ship and removed two Confederate commissioners. The outraged British threatened war if the two men were not released. Lincoln released the two men and formally apologized to Britain.

The demands of war and running the country meant that Lincoln spent most of administration staying in the White House. During his four-year term he was away from Washington for only one month. The war also made demands on his family. Mrs. Lincoln's brother and other members of her family were serving in the Confederate forces. On February 20th 1862, their young son William Wallace died in the White House.

As the war progressed more and more people in the North wanted to see slavery stamped out. By the late summer of 1862, Lincoln decided that it was time to change his policy towards slavery. He decided to issue a proclamation freeing the slaves. The Union victory at *Antietam* on 17th September 1862 created favorable circumstances for the *Emancipation Proclamation* to be issued and five days later Lincoln declared that from 1st January 1863 all slaves in Confederate states would be free. A final proclamation was then issued on 1st January. However, the Proclamation could not be enforced in those areas still held by the Confederacy. In addition, the Proclamation did not end slavery in those border states that had remained loyal to the Union's side. Lincoln urged those states to free their slaves in return for financial help from the federal government but they did not do so. However, the Proclamation did lead to the 13th Amendment to the United States Constitution in December 1865, which ended slavery in all parts of the United States.

In July 1863 the war at last turned in the North's favor. General George G. Meade led Union forces to victory at the *Battle of Gettysburg* in Pennsylvania, and General Ulysees S. Grant's troops captured Vicksburg, the last Confederate stronghold on the Mississippi River. In November, Lincoln attended a ceremony dedicating a cemetery on the Gettysburg battlefield and was asked to make a short speech. In what became known as the *Gettysburg Address*, Lincoln spoke for three minutes and famously declared that "government of the people, by the people, for the people, shall not perish from the earth." In 1864, Lincoln put Grant in command of all the Union armies and they advanced on the South on every front.

Election of 1864

In June 1864, the Republican national convention renominated Lincoln for the presidency. Former Senator Andrew Johnson of Tennessee was nominated for Vice-President. The Democrats nominated General George B. McClellan for President and Representative George H. Pendleton of Ohio for Vice-President. At this time the war's slow progress and high casualties had badly affected Lincoln's popularity and it appeared that his administration would not be re-elected. However, a series of Union victories helped him to win re-election and he defeated McClennan by 212 electoral votes to 21 and a popular majority of over 400,000.

Presidential Election of 1864		
Candidate	Popular Vote	Electoral College
Abraham Lincoln (Rep.)	2,218,388	212
George B. McClellan (Dem.)	1,812,807	21

Lincoln's Second Term 1865

When Lincoln attended his second inauguration on 4th March 1865, the end of the war was in sight. The forces of the South were melting away as Union armies advanced. Lincoln saw the opportunity to re-unite the nation and made an inaugural address calling for peace, unity and reconciliation. On 9th April 1865, General Robert E. Lee surrendered to Grant at Appomattox Court House in Virginia. Under authority from Lincoln, Grant extended generous terms to Lee and his defeated troops. A great wave of joy swept the North when the fighting ended. In his last public address on April 11th, Lincoln asked that the returning states be welcomed back into the Union.

Assassination

On the evening of April 14th 1865, Lincoln attended a performance of *Our American Cousin* at Ford's Theatre in Washington D.C. Just after 10pm, one of the best-known actors of the day, John Wilkes Booth, entered the President's box and shot him in the head from behind with a pistol. Lincoln was carried unconscious into a neighboring house where, surrounded by family and senior government officials, he died at 7.22am on 15th April. Thousands of mourners lined the tracks as a train carried his body from Washington to Springfield, Illinois, where he was laid to rest in Oak Ridge Cemetery. On April 26th, Booth was killed by Federal troops in Virginia as he tried to escape. Booth had been plotting with other conspirators to kill senior figures in the government and Union army. The other conspirators were arrested and put on trial. Eight people were convicted and four of them were hanged on 7th July. The remaining four were imprisoned where one died. The other three were pardoned by President Andrew Johnson in 1869.

Lincoln is remembered with a large memorial situated at the west end of the Mall in Washington D.C. Designed by the architect, Henry Bacon, it is a large monument of white marble 30 meters tall (99 feet), 58 meters long (190 feet) and 36 meters wide (119 feet), and surrounded by a colonnade of 36 fluted Doric columns. It was completed between 1915 -1922 and its main chamber contains a marble statue of Lincoln by Daniel Chester French, which is more than six meters high (20 feet) and took four years to cut. In two smaller rooms of the memorial are bronze plaques that give the text of two of his most famous speeches. Lincoln's is also one of the enormous (18 meters or sixty feet tall) four faces cut into the side of Mount Rushmore under the direction of Gutzon Borglum between 1927 and 1941.

Summary

Abraham Lincoln was one of the greatest men of all time. He showed that a man could rise from humble origins to win the highest office in America. His courageous and resolute leadership in the Civil War helped to preserve the Union and save democracy. He was a talented public-speaker able to express what he believed clearly and with great force. His Gettysburg Address is one of the greatest speeches in history a provides a clear definition of democracy. Most importantly, he was man of noble ideas, values and character at a time when America and the cause of human freedom needed them most. Lincoln shares with Washington the distinction of being "the greatest   President."

CHAPTER 17 – ANDREW JOHNSON

17th President of the United States 1865 – 1869

Born: 29th December 1808, Raleigh, North Carolina

Married: Eliza McCardle (1810 – 76), 17th May 1827

Number of Children: Five

Died: 31st July 1875, Elizabethton, Tennessee

Final Resting Place: Andrew Johnson National Cemetery, Greeneville, Tennessee

Introduction

Andrew Johnson rose from poor and humble circumstances to become the 17th President of the United States following the death of Abraham Lincoln. He was the third Vice-President to become the President following the death of the Chief Executive and the first to do so following an assassination. Before he became Vice-President, Johnson served in the U.S. House of Representatives, as Governor of Tennessee and in the U.S. Senate. As President he took over a divided country in the aftermath of a bitter Civil War. His attempts to quickly restore the South to the Union brought him into conflict with the Radical Republicans in Congress and led to his impeachment trial in 1868. Against the President's will, Congress passed a harsh series of Reconstruction laws that established a military administration in the South. Two important Amendments to the Constitution came into effect during his Presidency: the 13th Amendment freed all the remaining slaves and the 14th made them citizens. During his time in office, Alaska was purchased from

Russia in 1867, Wyoming was organized as a territory in 1868, and Nebraska was admitted to the Union as the 37th state in 1869. The total population of the United States then exceeded 39 million people. After he left the White House, he became the first and only former President to be elected to the U.S. Senate.

Background

Andrew Johnson was born in December 1808 in Raleigh, North Carolina, the son of a handyman in a tavern. His father died when he was three years old and his mother supported her son's upbringing by sewing and undertaking laundry. He was one of the few Presidents never to go to school. When he was thirteen, he was apprenticed to a tailor, where he learned to read. He later set up his own business as a tailor in Greenville, Tennessee. On 17th May 1827, he married Elizabeth McCardle, the daughter of a Scottish shoemaker, and they had five children together.

Entry into Politics

He entered politics in 1828, when he was elected as an alderman and then as mayor of Greenville. In 1835, he was elected to the Tennessee House of Representatives. Later he was elected to the state senate. In 1843 he was elected to the U.S. House of Representatives, where the issue of slavery was becoming increasingly important. Although he owned slaves, he did not always support the interests of slavers in Congress, attempting to steer a middle course. For instance, he voted to admit Texas as a slave state but favored admitting California and Oregon as free. For many years he fought for a homesteading bill that would open federal lands to poor white settlers. However, he was opposed by those slaveholders who feared that this would lead to more free states joining the Union.

In 1853 he successfully campaigned to become the Governor of Tennessee where he supported laws that would provide the public with free education. He was re-elected in 1855. In 1857 the

Tennessee state legislature elected him to the U.S. Senate where he once again pushed for a Homestead Act. It was passed in 1862, after the Civil War had begun and the Southern slave-owners had resigned from Congress. As the slavery question became more critical, he continued to steer a middle course. He opposed the anti-slavery Republican party as he felt the Constitution guaranteed the right to own slaves. He supported Buchanan's proslavery administration and approved of the Lecompton constitution in Kansas. At the same time, he made it clear that his devotion to the Union was greater than his devotion to slavery.

In 1860 Abraham Lincoln defeated Democrat John C. Breckinridge in the presidential election and the Southern states began to leave the Union. In March 1861 Johnson denounced the secessionists as traitors. In Tennessee they held a special vote to decide whether the state should secede. When they voted to do so he was the only Southern Senator who refused to secede with his state. The Tennessee militia had orders to arrest him as a traitor but he escaped.

In 1862 Union armies won control of western Tennessee and Lincoln appointed Johnson as the military governor of the state. He planned to restore Tennessee to the Union by holding free elections for voters who would take an oath against the rebellion and accept the Emancipation Proclamation. In March 1864, Tennessee sent representatives to Congress.

Johnson's devotion to the Union and his record as a military governor made him a national figure. He had become the most prominent of the loyal, or War, Democrats. This group joined with the Republicans in 1864 to form the National Union Party. This party then nominated Lincoln for a second term and selected Johnson for Vice-President. Lincoln and Johnson then comfortably won the 1864 election. He was inaugurated as Vice-President on 4th March 1865 but appeared to be drunk when he made his acceptance speech. On 14th April 1865, just six weeks after the inauguration, Lincoln was shot and died early the following day. That morning Johnson took the presidential oath of office in his hotel room

Johnson's Administration (1865 - 1869)

When Johnson became President, he had to decide how best to restore the defeated South to the Union. Like Lincoln he favored restoring the Southern states to the Union as quickly as possible and without punishing them. Congress was not in session until December and so for eight months Johnson was able to unilaterally proceed with his own restoration and reconstruction plan for the South. On 29th May 1865 he issued a proclamation of amnesty which pardoned all those that were prepared to take an oath of allegiance but said that the Confederate leaders would require Presidential pardons. He took steps to abolish slavery but did nothing to stop the Southern states from adopting discriminatory new "black codes" which prevented the newly freed slaves from enjoying full equal rights. As a result, many African-Americans endured a condition little better than slavery. He appointed provisional governors for the Southern states who then set up state governments and arranged for the election of representatives to Congress. Johnson was prepared to allow each state to determine whether to grant African-American the right to vote.

When Congress met in December 1865 it immediately ratified the 13th Amendment to the U.S. Constitution which abolished slavery. However, many members were angered by Johnson's lenient policies which had allowed the South to keep their prewar leaders and to impose many new restrictions upon African-Americans. The most critical opponents were the so-called Radical Republicans under the leadership of Representative Thaddeus Stevens of Pennsylvania and Senator Charles Sumner of Massachusetts. Motivated by a desire for revenge as well as to end slavery, they called for harsh measures against the South including the punishment of the Confederate Leaders and the imposition of military rule. They also called for all African-Americans to be given the vote.

The Radical Republicans refused to allow the southern Congressmen to take their seats and began to pass a less-forgiving series of *Reconstruction* bills. Johnson vetoed these bills claiming that they could not be passed legally unless the Southern states were represented in Congress. Many of the bills were then passed over his veto. In June 1866, Congress passed the 14th Amendment to the U.S. Constitution which was designed to protect the rights of African-Americans and bar from rebels from holding office. Johnson opposed the Amendment and toured to country to gain support before the mid-term Congressional elections. However, the tour did not go well and the Radicals then won a majority in Congress.

Congress then attempted to put a limit the President's power and passed the *Tenure of Office Act*. It said that the President could not remove any official without the Senate's approval if his appointment had been confirmed by the Senate. Johnson attempted to resist the Act by suspending the Secretary of War, Edwin M. Stanton, and appointing General Ulysees S. Grant to the office of temporary secretary. However, in January 1868, Grant gave his office back to Stanton. Johnson then attempted to dismiss Stanton and appoint General Lorenzo Thomas. However, Stanton locked himself in his office and refused to let Stanton take over. He then stayed in office until after Johnson's impeachment trial.

Congress now decided to introduce impeachment proceedings against Johnson. On 24th February 1868, the House of Representatives voted to impeach Johnson by 126 votes to 47. On the 2nd and 3rd of March, eleven articles of impeachment were adopted by the House. The two most important articles were the first, which charged that the President had violated the Tenure of Office Act by dismissing Stanton, and the eleventh, which charged that he had conspired against Congress and the Constitution and cited his claim that Congress did not properly represent all the states. On 5th March 1868, Congress organized itself as a court to hear the impeachment trial with Salmon P. Chase, Chief Justice of the United States, presiding.

The impeachment trial began on 13th March and it soon became apparent that the Radicals did not have a strong case. Many Americans came to believe that the Senators were more interested in punishing Johnson than they were in obtained justice. Johnson did not appear at the trial but was defended by a team of lawyers. At that time there were fifty-four members in the Senate and a conviction required the vote of two-thirds of them. This meant that Johnson would be convicted if 36 Senators voted for it or acquitted if there were less. Tremendous pressure was brought upon the Senators to convict Johnson and one member even received a letter from a Radical voter that said: "Any Republican Senator who votes against impeachment need never expect to get home alive."

Johnson's opponents felt that the eleventh charge was the one that had the best chance of securing a conviction and the vote took place on 16th May. Thirty-five Senators voted to convict Johnson and so he was acquitted by one vote. Ten days later, the Senate voted on the second and third articles with the same result. No further votes were then taken and the trial ended.

After the impeachment trial, the final months of his administration were largely uneventful. The most important event was the adoption of the 14th Amendment in July 1868, which allowed all African-Americans born in the United States to become citizens. Johnson sought the Democratic nomination for the presidential election of 1868 but was unsuccessful. The Democrats nominated former Governor Horatio Seymour of New York, who then lost the election to Ulysses S. Grant. Johnson's last important official act was on Christmas Day 1868 when he proclaimed a complete pardon for all Southerners that had taken part in the Civil War.

During his term of office, there were two important foreign policy achievements. A French army had overthrown the Mexican government and Napoleon III named Maximilian of Austria as Emperor of Mexico in 1864. This violated the Monroe Doctrine but the U.S. was too involved in the Civil War to do more than protest. In 1865, the US government sent troops to the border and the Secretary of State, William Seward, told the French ambassador that the army would remove the French by force if necessary. In 1867 Napoleon withdrew his troops and Maximilian was overthrown.

Seward's second accomplishment was the purchase of Alaska from Russia in 1867. The Russians feared that they might lose the colony to Great Britain and offered it to America for $7,200,000. Seward finally persuaded Congressmen to vote for the purchase and for many years Alaska was known as "Seward's folly." However, it joined the Union as the 49th state in 1959.

Later Years

After leaving the White House Johnson ran unsuccessfully for Congress in 1869 and 1872. He was elected to the U.S. Senate in 1874 and thus became the only President to later serve as a Senator. He attended a special short session in March 1875 where he was greeted with applause and flowers. However, when he returned Tennessee, he suffered a paralytic stroke and died a few days later, on 31st July 1875. He was buried in Greeneville. Mrs. Johnson died five and half months later and was buried next to her husband.

Summary

Andrew Johnson is usually ranked low all the Presidents. This is because he did not deliver long-promised freedoms to African-Americans, began a harsh occupation and reconstruction of the South, and was the first President (and for many years the only President) to be impeached. He is usually portrayed by historians as tactless, humorless and unpopular. However, some of these judgements may be unfair. He was an honest and self-made frontier man who rose to the White House without ever having been to school. The acquisition of Alaska during his presidency was an important   and   lasting   achievement.

CHAPTER 18 – ULYSEES S. GRANT

18th President of the United States 1869 – 1877

Born: 27th April 1822, Point Pleasant, Ohio

Married: Julia Dent (1826 – 1902), 22nd August 1848

Number of Children: Four

Died: 23rd July 1885, Wilton, New York

Final Resting Place: Grant's Tomb, Morningside Heights, New York City

Introduction

Ulysees S. Grant was a Union hero of the Civil War that was elected as the 18th President of the United States. As a young man, Grant had served bravely in the Mexican-American War and been promoted to the rank of Lieutenant. He then left the army to be with his family and worked in a number of civilian roles. However, he rejoined the army as a Colonel when the Civil War broke out and showed himself to be a brilliant commander. He was promoted to Brigadier General, to Major General, to Lieutenant General and then put in charge of all the Union armies. He accepted the final surrender of the Confederate leader, Robert E. Lee, at Appomattox Court House on 9th April 1865 and the war ended. He comfortably won the presidential election of 1868 and served two terms in the White House. Unfortunately, his term in office was clouded with disgrace and dishonesty as Congressional investigations revealed widespread corruption in all levels of government. During his presidency, America continued to recover from the war and expand westwards. In 1869 the first transcontinental railroad was completed. In 1872, Congress established Yellowstone National Park, the first national park in the United States. Colorado became a state in 1876 and the country had a population exceeding 47 million people.

Background

Hiram Ulysees Grant was born on April 27th 1822 in Point Pleasant, Ohio, the eldest of six children of a prosperous tanner and farmer. In his childhood he as always known as Ulysees or "Lyss." He attended schools in Georgetown, Ohio, and academies in Maysville, Kentucky, and Ripley, Ohio. In 1839, he gained admittance to the U.S. Military Academy at West Point where his name was erroneously recorded as Ulysees Simpson Grant, Simpson being his mother's maiden name. Grant preferred this arrangement of names and so never corrected it.

Grant graduated from West Point in 1843 and was commissioned as a Second Lieutenant to the Fourth Infantry Regiment near St. Louis. When war broke out with Mexico in 1846, he became the regimental quartermaster, in charge of supplies. In 1847, he took part in the capture of Mexico City where he was praised for his skill and bravery. He was then further promoted and reached the rank of Lieutenant by the end of the war. He then returned to St. Louis where he married Julia Dent on August 22nd 1848. They had four children.

Grant was then posted to Oregon Territory but could not take his wife and children as his pay would not be enough to support them in the West. He was promoted to Captain in 1853 and transferred to Fort Humboldt in California. However, he did not like being separated from his family and resigned from the Army in 1854. He then settled with his family in St Louis. Over the next six years he had a succession of jobs as a farmer, a rent collector, a custom official and a storekeeper but did not make a success of any of them.

Grant opposed both slavery and secession. When the Civil War began in 1861, he saw it as his duty to fight for the Union. He applied for a commission as a Colonel and several months later was appointed Colonel of a regiment that became the 21st Illinois Volunteers. Grant led his troops on a successful campaign against the Confederates in Missouri and was promoted to Brigadier General by President Abraham Lincoln in August 1861. As the war progressed, Grant showed all the qualities of a great military commander. In 1862 he attacked Fort Henry and then nearby Fort Donelson, insisting on the *unconditional surrender* of all the enemy troops. Northerners claimed that his initials, U.S., stood for "Unconditional Surrender." He was then promoted to Major General.

After victories at Shiloh and Vicksburg he was promoted put in charge of all the Union armies in west. His consistent successes there led to his promotion to Lieutenant General in 1864 and he was put in charge of all the Union armies. He began a campaign against the forces of Robert E. Lee and forced them to retreat towards the confederate capital in Richmond, Virginia. After a bitter campaign, his troops captured Richmond in the following spring and Lee surrendered at Appomattox Court House, Virginia, on 9th April 1865.

Election of 1868

Presidential Election of 1868		
Candidate	Popular Vote	Electoral College
Ulysees S. Grant (Rep.)	3,013,421	214
Horatio Seymour (Dem.)	2,706,829	80

After the end of the war, Grant became a hero to the people of the North. Many Southerners also appreciated the generous terms that he had offered to Lee. In 1868, the Republicans unanimously nominated Grant as their presidential candidate. They nominated Speaker of the House Schuyler Colfax of Indiana for Vice-President.

The Democrats nominated Governor Horatio Seymour of New York for President and former Representative Francis P. Blair Jr., of Missouri as his running mate. In the election, Grant defeated Seymour by a decisive majority of the electoral votes.

Grant's First Administration 1869 – 1873

Grant was inaugurated on 4th March 1869. In his inaugural address he promised to rule independently from professional party politicians. When selecting his cabinet, he did not consult party leaders about appointments. He also appointed friends, relatives and army officers to other government offices.

During his first term, Grant worked hard to bring the North and South closer together. Many former Confederate leaders were pardoned and the use of federal troops stationed in the South was limited. Grant did use troops to protect African-Americans from the Ku Klux Klan and other white groups that had been organized in the South to prevent black people from voting. In 1870, the 15th Amendment to the U.S. Constitution came into effect which gave all African-Americans the right to vote. In the following two years, Congress passed three *Enforcement Acts* which enforced their voting rights.

During Grant's term of office, political corruption spread to all levels of government. Some state governments in the South were controlled by corrupt *carpetbaggers*. In Northern cities, organized political machines made huge profits from graft on city contracts. Some of the men appointed by Grant were also dishonest. One of the reasons for the low state of public morality was the spoils system, by which successful political candidates rewarded their supporters by giving them government jobs. As a result, many high government positions were taken by incapable or dishonest people. Grant urged Congress to reform the civil service so that people were appointed on merit. However, they refused to appropriate money for this purpose.

During his first term, Grant had mixed success in matters of foreign policy. In 1869, he agreed a treaty with the Dominican Republic to annex that country to the U.S.A. However, the treaty was rejected by the Senate. On the other hand, in 1872 a tribunal in Geneva ruled that Great Britain should pay the United States $15.5 million dollars in compensation for the destruction to Northern shipping caused by the *Alabama* and other British-built warships in the Civil War. The two countries had signed the *Treaty of Washington* on 8th May 1871 agreeing to submit America's claims for compensation to an independent arbitration committee in Switzerland.

Election of 1872

Grant's first term achieved several successes including the reduction of the national debt and the settling of the war claims dispute with Britain. However, many politicians were disappointed that he had not reformed the civil service or reduced the high tariffs then in effect. Discontented Republicans formed the *Liberal Republicans* and held a convention which nominated Horace Greeley, Editor of the New York Tribune, for President. The Democrats supported this nomination hoping to topple the corrupt Republican administration. However, the Democrats ran corrupt political machines in several big cities and found it hard to cooperate with the Liberal Republicans.

The Republicans renominated Grant for President and chose Senator Henry Wilson of Massachusetts as his running mate. They knew that they could count on the black vote in the South. Their campaign was also expertly run by experienced politicians. In the election, Grant won by even greater majority than he had won before.

Presidential Election of 1872		
Candidate	Popular Votes	Electoral Votes
Ulysees S. Grant (Rep.)	3,596,745	286
Horace Greeley (Dem.)	2,843,446	3

Grants Second Administration 1873 – 1877

Grant's second term got off to a bad start when an investigation revealed that many congressmen had taken bribes to perform favors for the Union Pacific Railroad. Congress reprimanded several members for their part in the scandal. Then in September 1873 the country was swept by a financial panic after the failure of several important banks which hit farmers and manufacturers hard. Voters reacted strongly to the panic and the continued evidence of corruption in the government and the Democrats won a sweeping victory in the congressional election of 1874.

The new Congress investigated the *Whiskey Ring* and found that whiskey distillers in St Louis and other cities had conspired with tax officials to rob the government of excise taxes. Grant had to defend his secretary, General Babcock, who was accused of protecting the ring from exposure. In 1876, another investigation revealed that the Secretary of War, William W. Belknap, had accepted bribes from a trader at an Indian post. He resigned but the House of Representatives attempted to impeach him anyway. However, he was acquitted on a technicality.

In 1874, Grant's daughter Nellie married a wealthy Englishman, Algernon Sartoris. Their wedding was held in the White House and attracted international attention. On 4th July 1876, The United States celebrated its one hundredth birthday. President Grant was preparing to lead the celebrations when a message arrived at the White House saying that on 25th June 1876 General George Armstrong Custer and 225 soldiers of the Seventh Cavalry had been wiped out to the last man by the Sioux and Cheyenne Indians in the Battle of the Little Big Horn. The news had taken nine days to travel to Washington from the battlefield in Montana 1,500 miles away. The day then became one of mourning.

In 1876, many Republicans wanted to nominate Grant for a third term despite the growing list of scandals. However, he refused to run again and in June 1876 the Republicans nominated Rutherford B. Hayes of Ohio for President. Hayes won the presidency by a margin of only one vote.

Later Years

After he left office, Grant travelled to Europe and the Far East with his family and received an enthusiastic welcome wherever he went. When he returned home in 1879, he settled in a house in Galena, Illinois. In 1881 he moved to New York City. He invested his life savings in the banking firm of Grant & Ward but the company failed in 1884 leaving him penniless. In 1885 he moved to Mount McGregor, New York, and died there from cancer on July 23rd, shortly after completing his memoirs. His body was entombed in New York City. His wife died in 1902 and was buried beside him. When the memoirs were published, they earned $500,000 for his family.

Summary

Ulysees Grant was a heroic soldier whose skill as a general helped to bring the Civil War to a successful conclusion and led to his election as President. However, his time in the White House was less successful and his administration became known for its dishonesty, corruption, and scandals. America's one hundredth birthday was spent in mourning for the Seventh Cavalry defeated and killed at the Battle of the Little Big Horn. Grant deserves a high ranking among America's soldiers but a much lower one among America's Presidents.

CHAPTER 19 –
RUTHERFORD HAYES

19th President of the United States 1877 – 1881

Born: 4th October 1822, Delaware County, Ohio

Married: Lucy Ware Webb (1831 – 1889), 30th December 1852

Number of Children: Eight

Died: 17th January 1893, Fremont, Ohio

Final Resting Place: Oakwood Cemetery, Fremont, Ohio

Introduction

Rutherford Hayes was elected the nineteenth President of the United States in 1876 in what was then the closest and most disputed election in American history. Congress had to create a special Electoral commission to decide the winner and he was awarded victory by a margin of one vote. Before he entered the White House, Hayes had served in the U.S. House of Representatives and as Governor of Ohio. He became President at the time when the country was still developing rapidly after the Civil War. The population had reached fifty-one and a half million people and New York had become the first American city with more than a million inhabitants. In 1877 Thomas Edison invented the phonograph and sound could be recorded for the first time. He later demonstrated his invention to Hayes in the White House. Hayes also brought the problem of Reconstruction in the South to an end and tried to find solutions to a business depression and political scandals.

Background

Rutherford Birchard Hayes was born 4th October 1822 in Delaware, Ohio. He was the youngest of five children of a successful store owner. However, his father died two months before he was born and the children were raised by an uncle. Rutherford attended schools in Norwalk, Ohio, and Middletown, Connecticut. In 1838 he entered Kenyon College in Gambier, Ohio, and graduated as head of his class in 1842. The following year he entered Harvard Law School from where he graduated in 1845 and was admitted to the bar. He began practicing law in Lower Sandusky, Ohio, and in 1850 opened a law office in Cincinnati.

On December 30th 1852 he married Lucy Ware Webb, the daughter of an Ohio physician. She was the first President's wife to have a college degree having graduated from Wesleyan Female College in Cincinnati in 1850. They had eight children but three died in infancy. She championed leading moral causes of the day including the abolition of slavery and the prohibition of alcohol. In 1858 he was elected city solicitor of Cincinnati.

In the Civil War, he served as a major of a regiment of Ohio volunteers and distinguished himself in several battles. He was wounded four times and had four horses shot from under him. He spent four years in the army and earned rapid promotion. On June 8th 1865, two months after the war ended, he resigned from the army with the rank of brevet major general.

Entry into Politics

In 1864 he was nominated for the U.S. House of Representatives. He received the news while fighting in the Shenandoah Valley under General Philip H. Sheridan. He refused to campaign for the office because the outcome of the war was still in doubt. He won the election but did not take his seat in Congress until December 1865. He then won re-election in 1866. However, he resigned from the House in 1867 when he was nominated for Governor of Ohio.

In 1867 he won election to the first of three terms as Governor of Ohio. He planned to retire at the end of his second term in 1872. However, Republican leaders persuaded him to run for Congress. He was defeated and spent the next three years at home in Fremont, Ohio, where he lived quietly and dealt in real estate. In 1875 he won a third term as Governor.

The Election of 1876

As President Grant's second term drew to a close, the Republican party was torn by corruption. The party split into two factions. The *Stalwarts* under Roscoe Conkling of New York favored a third term for Grant. The *Half-Breeds* led by Representative James G. Blaine of Maine opposed the Stalwarts. However, Grant refused to run for a third term. Neither side had enough votes to nominate a Presidential candidate. Hayes was then supported as a compromise candidate and at the Republican National Convention in June 1876 he won the presidential nomination on the seventh ballot with William A. Wheeler of New York nominated for Vice-President. Their Democratic opponent was Samuel J. Tilden of New York with Governor Thomas A. Hendricks of Indiana nominated for Vice-President. The new Greenback Party nominated Peter Cooper for President.

As election day approached, President Grant sent federal troops to South Carolina and Louisiana to protect the rights of African-American voters and gain support for the Republicans.

When the election was held, Tilden won the popular vote. However, the states of Louisiana, South Carolina, Florida and Oregon all submitted two sets of electoral returns, one for the Democrats and one for the Republicans. As a result, both parties claimed victory. On December 6th the Electoral College awarded the disputed votes to Hayes. This gave Hayes 185 electoral votes to Tilden's 184. Democrats in Congress accused the Republicans of fraud and challenged the decision. In January 1877 Congress appointed a fifteen-man Electoral Commission to decide which electoral votes should count for Hayes and which for Tilden. Its decision was to be final unless both houses of Congress voted otherwise. As Inauguration Day approached Southern Democrats agreed not to oppose the decision of the Commission, thus making Hayes president. In return, the Republicans promised to end Reconstruction and withdraw federal troops from the South. Southerners thus regained complete control over their state and local governments for the first time since the Civil War. On March 2nd 1877, just 56 hours before Inauguration Day, Hayes was formally announced as winner of the election.

Presidential Election of 1876		
Candidate	Popular Votes	Electoral Votes
Rutherford B. Hayes (Rep.)	4,284,020	185
Samuel J. Tilden (Dem.)	4,,026,572	184
Peter Cooper (Greenback)	83,726	0

Hayes' Administration 1877 – 1881

Hayes was inaugurated as President on 4th March 1877. Rutherford and Lucy Hayes gained respect for trying to set a high moral standard to all Americans. The First Lady refused to serve alcoholic drinks, even at formal dinners and receptions, and became known as "Lemonade Lucy." In 1878 she introduced custom of Easter egg rolling by children on the White House lawn

One of Hayes first acts as President was to withdraw federal occupation forces from the south as promised. On April 10th 1877 the soldiers left South Carolina and on April 24th the last federal troops left Louisiana. Hayes hoped this would benefit the Republicans but the Democrats soon restored their solid hold on the South.

He announced he would serve only one term as President. This made it easier for him to reform the Civil Service as he did not have to give political jobs to win support. Hayes based his appointments on merit rather than the spoils system. He even appointed a Southern Democrat, David M. Key, to his cabinet. He forced the removal of three fellow Republicans from their jobs at the New York Custom House, one of which was Chester Arthur, later the 21st President of the United States. This angered members of his own party and Congress refused to act on the Civil Service legislation that he proposed. However, he was the first President to fight Congress on the Civil Service issue and his struggle gained wide public support. This opened the way for later presidents to make civil service reforms.

Because of the depression of the 1870's, many people demanded "cheap money". They wanted the government to issue more paper and silver money even though it could not be backed by large amounts of gold in the treasury. Hayes favored a conservative money policy and resisted their demands. In 1878 he vetoed the Bland-Allison Act which required the Treasury to buy and coin between $2 million and $4 million worth of silver a month. But the Treasury coined only the minimum amount required in an effort to limit inflation. In 1879 he restored financial confidence by resuming payment of specie (metal coin) for "greenbacks," paper money issued to finance the Civil War.

Later Years

When Hayes' term ended in 1881, he said "Nobody ever left the Presidency with less regret than I do." No one seemed sorry that he did not run for a second term. However, his friend and political supporter, James A. Garfield was elected President. Hayes believed that this showed public approval of his administration. He completely withdrew from politics and returned home to Spiegel Grove near Fremont, Ohio. He devoted himself to philanthropic work in education, prison reform, and veterans' affairs. Mrs. Hayes died in June 1889. He died on 17th January 1893 after a short illness and was buried in Fremont.

Summary

Rutherford Hayes is a largely forgotten President and as a result is usually accorded a low ranking. However, he was a hard-working and good-natured man that was widely respected for his honesty and sincerity. He presided over rapid industrial and economic expansion, and his achievements in office include ending the Reconstruction and initiating reform of the Civil Service.

CHAPTER 20 – JAMES A. GARFIELD

20ᵗʰ President of United States 1881

Born: 19ᵗʰ November 1831, Orange Township, Ohio

Married: Lucretia Rudolph (1832 – 1918), 11ᵗʰ November 1858

Number of Children: Seven

Died: 19ᵗʰ September 1981, Elberon, New Jersey

Final Resting Place: Lake View Cemetery, Cleveland, Ohio

Introduction

James Garfield was born in a log cabin in 1831 and rose from poverty and obscurity to become the 20ᵗʰ President of the United States. Before he entered the White House, he served a Major General in the Union Army and in the U.S. House of Representatives. As President, he led the country at a time when the population had reached more than fifty-one million people and a network of railways was expanding across the country. However, politics was then known for the spoils system by which the best government jobs were filled with the President's supporters. Large numbers of government employees lost their jobs every time there was a new President. Garfield did not have time to make the necessary reforms before he was assassinated by a deranged office-seeker. He was the second President to be assassinated and the fourth to die in office.

Background

James Abram Garfield was born in Orange, Cuyahoga County, Ohio on November 19th 1831. He was the youngest of five children of pioneers from the East. He was the last President to be born in a log cabin. His father died before he was two years old and his mother made a living from their thirty-acre farm. She later became the first woman to attend a son's inauguration as President. He was educated at the Geauga Academy in Chester and the Western Reserve Eclectic Institute in Hiram, Ohio. He then attended Williams College in Williamstown, Massachusetts, for two years and graduated in 1856. He then returned to Hiram College as professor of ancient languages and literature. The following year, at the age of twenty-six, he was chosen president of the college. He could write Latin with one hand while writing Greek with the other. On November 11th 1858 Garfield married Lucretia Rudolph, the daughter of an Ohio farmer. They had seven children, two of whom died as infants.

Shortly after the outbreak of the Civil War he was commissioned as a Lieutenant Colonel of the Ohio volunteers by Governor William Dennison. In January 1862 he won a minor battle at Middle Creek and was promoted to Brigadier General, the youngest in the Union Army. He then took part in the Battle of Shiloh and the operations around Corinth. In 1863 he distinguished himself at the Battle of Chickamauga by riding under heavy fire to deliver an important message to General George H. Thomas. After the battle he was promoted to Major General.

Entry into Politics

He first showed an interest in politics in 1856 when he campaigned for John C. Fremont, the Republican candidate for President. He was elected to Ohio State Senate in 1859 and the U.S. House of Representatives in 1862. At the time he was serving in the Union army and did not resign his commission until December 1863. He won re-election to the House eight times. He served as chairman of the Appropriations Committee and as a member of the committees on Military Affairs, Ways and Means, and Banking and Currency. He supported the harsh Reconstruction measures of the Radical Republicans and voted for the impeachment of President Andrew Johnson. In 1872 he was one of several congressmen accused of accepting gifts of stock from the Credit Mobilier, a corporation seeking favors from the government, but he denied the charge and it was never proved. However, he did admit to taking a £5,000 fee from a company trying to get a paving contract for the City of Washington contending that his services were not improper. He served on the commission that settled the disputed Hayes-Tilden election of 1876 and drew up the bargain that gave Hayes the presidency.

During Hayes presidency, Garfield became floor leader of the Republicans in the House. At that time the party was divided into two factions. The first faction was called the *Stalwarts* and were led by Senator Roscoe Conkling on New York. The second fraction were called the *Half-Breeds* and were led by Senator James G. Blaine of Maine. These groups quarreled over personal differences and government jobs rather than political principles. Garfield was closer to the Half-Breeds but stood between the two factions and had the respect of both.

Election of 1880

The Ohio legislature elected Garfield to the U.S. Senate in 1880. However, before he took his seat there, he led his state's delegation to the Republican national convention in Chicago. The Half-Breeds tried to nominate Blaine for President while the stalwarts wanted former President Ulysses S. Grant. Neither could get enough votes to become President. The Half-Breeds then swung towards Garfield, a "dark horse" or little-known candidate and the convention finally chose him on the 36th ballot. Chester A. Arthur, a Stalwart, was nominated for Vice-President.

In the election, Garfield defeated his Democratic opponent, Winfield Scott Hancock, by nearly 40,000 popular votes. In the electoral college, Garfield gained 214 votes to 155 for Hancock.

Presidential Election of 1880		
Candidate	Popular Votes	Electoral Votes
James A. Garfield (Rep)	4,453,295	214
Winfield S. Hancock (Dem)	4,414,082	155
James B. Weaver (Greenback)	305,997	0

Garfield's Administration – 1881

Garfield was inaugurated in 1881. He owed his nomination to the Half-Breeds and he now favored this faction by handing out jobs. Blaine was made Secretary of State and others were appointed to important offices. The Stalwarts received only minor positions. When Conkling failed to stop these appointments in Congress he resigned. These party quarrels distracted Garfield from the business of government. However, he did support an investigation by Postmaster General Thomas L. James, who found fraud in the awarding of contracts to transport the mail

2nd July 1881 Garfield was about to leave Washington to attend the 25th reunion of his class at Williams College. As he stood at the railroad station, a stranger stepped out of the crowd and fired two pistol shots at him and he fell to the ground. The assassin cried: "I am a Stalwart and Arthur is President now!" The assassin, Charles J. Guiteau, was immediately arrested. He held a grudge because Garfield had refused to appoint him U.S. Consul in Paris. At his trial he behaved like a madman and his lawyer argued he was innocent on the grounds of insanity. However, he was convicted and hung in 1882.

Garfield lay near death for eighty days. One of the bullets had grazed his arm but another had lodged in his back and could not be found.

During this period his only official act was to sign an extradition paper. The Vice-President did not step in for fear of disturbing Garfield and the Cabinet supported this decision. At that time there were no x-rays or antiseptics available and an infection set in. He was moved to a seaside cottage near Elberon, New Jersey, and died on there on 19th September 1881. He was buried in Cleveland.

Summary

Garfield was murdered before he could achieve anything and therefore is neither ranked a good nor bad President. Two years after his death, Congress began to reform the civil service and end the *spoils system* by passing the Pendleton Civil Service Act.

CHAPTER 21 – CHESTER A. ARTHUR

21ˢᵗ *President of the United States 1881 – 1885*

Born: 5ᵗʰ October 1829, Fremont, New York

Married: Ellen Herndon (1837 - 1880), 25ᵗʰ October 1859

Number of Children: Three

Died: 18ᵗʰ November 1886, New York City

Final Resting Place: Albany Rural Cemetery, Menands, New York

Introduction

Chester Arthur was sworn in as the 21ˢᵗ President of the United States following the assassination of James Garfield in 1881. It was the fourth time that a Vice-President had succeeded to the presidency following the death of the Chief Executive. Before he became Vice-President, Arthur had served as Collector of the New York Customs House but had been removed from this position after an investigation had revealed that he had used his office to reward Republicans and strengthen his party. At the time he became President, Americans were very concerned by the widespread dishonesty in government and protests forced Congress to pass the Civil Service Act in 1883. Arthur signed the Act and further tackled fraud and waste in the government even though he had previously been corrupt. While in the White House, Arthur learned that the was suffering from a serious kidney disease called Bright's Disease. For this reason, he did not stand in the election of 1884 and died soon afterwards. Despite the dishonesty of its politicians, America continued to develop rapidly and by 1885 had the largest economy of any country in the world. By this time there were thirty-eight states in the Union with a population of fifty-one million. In 1883, the Brooklyn Bridge was completed, its 1,595 feet (486m) span then the longest in the world. That same year, Standard Time was adopted by the railroads and its system of time zones gradually became accepted by the public. In 1884, the World's First Skyscraper, the Home Insurance Building, was built in Chicago.

Background

Chester Alan Arthur was born on October 5th 1829 in Fairfield, Vermont. He was one of ten children of a teacher and Baptist minister that had emigrated to America from Northern Ireland. The family frequently moved to various villages in Vermont and Upstate New York. At the age of eighteen he graduated from Union College in Schenectady in New York and began studying law while working as a teacher in a school. In 1854 became a partner in a law firm in New York City and soon became known as a defender of civil rights for African-Americans. In 1855 he won a case that established the right of black people to travel on any streetcar in the city. On October 25th 1859 he married Ellen Lewis Herndon, the daughter of a naval officer and they had two sons and a daughter. However, the older son died aged two and a half and Ellen died in 1880, the year before he became President.

Entry into Politics

In 1854 Arthur attended a meeting that led to the creation of the Republican Party in New York. When Republican Edwin D. Morgan became governor of New York in 1859 he obtained a position on Morgan's staff. Soon afterwards Morgan named Arthur state engineer-in-chief with the rank of brigadier-general. When the Civil War began in 1861, Morgan put Arthur in charge of outfitting the New York militia for federal service. In 1862 Morgan appointed Arthur inspector general of the militia. Later that year he appointed him state quarter-master general.

In the 1860s Arthur became an associate of Senator Roscoe Conkling, leader of the New York Republican organization. In 1871 President Grant appointed him collector of the New York Customs House. With more than one thousand employees it was then the nation's largest federal office. Officially, he supervised the collection of import duties. Politically, however, he strengthened the Republican Party largely by giving jobs to party workers. He soon became the leader of the party organization in New York City. He became Chairman of the Republican state committee and all customs employees paid part of their salaries into Republican campaign funds. Some money collected from customs violations also ended up in the party treasury. Politicians in all parts of the country also took similar advantage of the *spoils system*. Protesters said that this resulted in dishonest and incompetent officials.

When Rutherford Hayes becomes President in 1877, he issued an order forbidding government employees from taking part in the management of a political party. Hayes set up a commission to investigate the New York customs house which uncovered evidence of corruption, inefficiency and waste. It also found continued involvement by top customs house officials in Republican Party affairs. In 1877, Hayes asked Arthur and two chief aides to resign. However, they refused to do so until the Senate had confirmed new appointees, as then required by the law. In 1878 Hayes suspended Arthur and one of the aides. Senator Conkling then temporarily blocked the confirmation of new appointees but in 1879 the Senate approved new officials.

The Election of 1880

At the Republican National Convention in 1880, Senator-elect James Garfield of Ohio was nominated for President with Arthur for Vice-President. They defeated their Democratic opponents, General Winfield Scott Hancock, and former Congressman William H. English of Indiana.

Assassination of Garfield

After Garfield entered the White House in 1881, Conkling demanded that the President consult him on all federal appointments in New York. However, Garfield named Conkling's chief political enemy, James G. Blaine, as Secretary of State and another of his opponents as Collector of the New York Customs House. Conkling was furious and, along with Senator Thomas C. Platt, resigned and asked the New York Legislature to show their disapproval of Garfield by re-electing them. However, they were defeated.

Garfield never had a chance to enjoy the benefits of his victory over Conkling. 2nd July 1881 he was shot by Charles J. Guiteau and died on September 19th. Arthur took the Presidential oath in his home in New York City at 2.15am the next day.

Arthur's Administration 1881 - 1885

One of his first acts as the new President was the renovation of the White House, which he said looked like "a badly kept barracks." On December 7th 1881 he moved into the newly decorated White House. About a year after he became President, he learned that he was dying of a kidney disease called *glomerulonephritis* or Bright's Disease. He often suffered great pain but kept his illness a secret.

After Garfield's death there was a great popular demand for a better system of filling public offices. In response to this demand, Congress passed the *Pendleton Civil Service Act* in which offices were to be filled based on the results of competitive exams. Most Americans regarded Arthur as a machine politician who would oppose Civil Service reform. However, he signed the bill on January 16th 1883 and named attorney Dorman B. Eaton, the author of the bill, as Chairman of the first Civil Service Commission.

During Garfield's term, two of Arthur's close political allies were charged with fraud. They had been accused of obtaining money by giving false estimates on the cost of operating postal star routes. Arthur renewed the prosecutions and his administration worked vigorously for convictions. A jury acquitted the accused men after two trials but the postal frauds were halted.

In 1882 Congress authorized money to be spent on improvements to waterways. Arthur knew many of the improvements were extravagant and so vetoed the bill. However, Congress passed the bill over Arthur's veto. Congress also passed the Edmunds Anti-Polygamy Act 1882. This was aimed at the Mormons of Utah and made it illegal for a man to have more than one wife. That same year Congress passed a bill to limit Chinese migration for twenty years. Arthur vetoed the bill saying it violated a treaty with China but Congress then amended it to ten years and it became law.

American consumers pressured him into lowering import tariffs. In 1882 he appointed a commission to study tariff rates and they urged sharp tariff cuts. However, Congress ignored the commission and passed a law in 1883 that only lowered tariffs slightly.

The Election of 1884

Arthur tried hard to avoid major involvement in Republican party affairs during his presidency. In 1882 he was blamed for the defeat of his secretary of the treasury, Charles A. Folger, in the race for governor of New York. Folger lost to Democrat Grover Cleveland. High-ranking Republicans in his administration also achieved little when they tried to build Republican strength in the South.

Because of his illness, Arthur did not actively pursue the nomination in 1884 and discouraged friends from working to help him. However, at the Republican National Convention in Chicago, he still received a third of the votes. Former Secretary of State, James G. Blaine, won the nomination but lost the election to the Democratic candidate, Grover Cleveland.

Later Years

After he left the White House, Arthur returned to New York City. His health steadily declined and he died of a cerebral hemorrhage on

November 18th 1886. He was buried beside his wife in Albany, New York.

Summary

Chester Arthur was soon forgotten after he left office. Historians of today generally rank him in the bottom half of all the Presidents. Americans in the early 1880's were surprised by the honesty and efficiency of his Administration and he began to reform and modernize the Civil Service. However, there were few other real achievements   in   his   term.

CHAPTER 22 – GROVER CLEVELAND

22ⁿᵈ President of the United States (1885-89)

Born: 18ᵗʰ March 1837, Caldwell, New Jersey

Married: Frances Folsom (1864 – 1947), 2ⁿᵈ June 1886

Number of Children: Five

Died: 24ᵗʰ June 1908, Princeton, New Jersey

Final Resting Place: Princeton Cemetery, New Jersey

Introduction

Grover Cleveland is the only President to serve two non-consecutive terms in office. He was first elected in 1884 and served four years as the 22ⁿᵈ President of the United States. In 1888 he lost the presidential election to Benjamin Harrison, who then served as the 23ʳᵈ President. However, in 1892 Cleveland once again ran for President and won the election against Harrison. He then served a further four years as the 24ᵗʰ President. His second spell in office is covered in Chapter 24.

Before he entered the White House, Cleveland had served as the Governor of New York where he earned a reputation for honesty and good government. In the presidential election of 1884 this reputation helped him to defeat a candidate who had been implicated in a financial scandal. His victory meant that he was the first Democratic President since before the Civil War. He took office at a time of great economic and social change. At that time there were thirty-eight states in the Union with a population of nearly 62 million. The divisions of the war had begun to heal and voters were more concerned by corruption and waste in the government. Workers demanded higher wages and better working conditions while farmers were heavily in debt and demanded lower tariffs to reduce prices. Many of the most important decisions taken by Cleveland in his first term concerned the economy and labor reforms.

Background

Stephen Grover Cleveland was born the fifth of ten children on March 18th 1837 in Caldwell, New Jersey. He dropped his first name while still a boy. His father was a Presbyterian minister and a relative of Moses Cleaveland, the founder of Cleveland, Ohio. His mother was the daughter of a publisher. The family lived a hard life with very little money and moved several times. He attended schools in Fayetteville and Clinton, New York, and then at the age of fourteen went to work as a clerk in a general store in Fayetteville. At the age of sixteen his father died and he moved to New York City to teach at the New York Institution for the Blind.

At the age of seventeen he decided to look for better opportunities. He moved to Buffalo where he spent six months working for his uncle. He then decided to become a lawyer and worked as a clerk at the office of Rogers, Bowen and Rogers while studying for his exams. He continued to work for the same firm after he was admitted to the bar in 1859. When the Civil War broke out, Cleveland paid for a substitute to take his place in the Union army while he looked after his mother and sisters. This was a common and lawful practicebut was later used against him by his political enemies.

Entry into Politics

He entered politics as a ward worker for the Democratic Party in Buffalo. He served as a ward supervisor in 1862 and later as assistant district attorney in Erie County. In 1870 he was elected sheriff and served three years. During this time, he sprang the traps to hang two convicted murderers saying that he would not ask anyone to do anything that he would be unwilling to do. He then returned to his law office.

Buffalo suffered from corrupt administration and there was growing demand for reform. In 1881, Cleveland was selected by the Democrats to run for mayor. He won the election and then vetoed many padded city contracts. In 1882, the Democrats nominated him for Governor of New York. He won comfortably and became a conscientious administrator working hard to reform the government of New York.

The Election of 1884

Cleveland's reputation for good government made him a national figure. In 1884, the Republicans nominated James G. Blaine for President even though he had been implicated in a financial scandal. Many influential Republicans were outraged. Known as *Mugwumps*, they withdrew from the convention and said that they would rather vote for the Democratic candidate if he was an honest man. The Democrats responded by nominating Cleveland. Governor Thomas A. Hendricks of Indiana was nominated as the candidate for Vice-President. Each side conducted their campaign by attacking the other with scandalous personal stories rather than facing the issues. The tide turned when one of Blaine's supporters said a vote for Cleveland would be a vote for "rum, Romanism and rebellion." This was deeply resented by Catholics and Blaine repudiated it. However, the damage was done and Cleveland won by a slim majority of 23,005 votes. He was the first Democratic President to be elected since James Buchanan in 1856.

Presidential Election of 1884		
Candidate	Popular Votes	Electoral Votes
Grover Cleveland (Dem)	4,874,986	219
James G. Blaine (Rep)	4,851,981	182

Cleveland's First Administration 1885 - 1889

Cleveland was inaugurated in 1885. However, with the Senate in Republican hands, Cleveland had to restore government efficiency by making effective use of the presidential powers of veto, appointment and administrative control. He was a hard-working President and often stayed up to the early hours of the morning going over official business.

Cleveland's most important task was to eliminate corruption and waste in the government. Cleveland ordered the members of his cabinet to eliminate "abuses and extravagances" in their departments. As a result, the Department of the Navy tightened its supervision of shipbuilding and added several new vessels to the fleet, including the battleship *Maine*. The Department of the Interior forced western railroad companies to return vast amounts of unused excess right-of-way land to the public domain. The spoils system still flourished but he did award more jobs based on merit.

Cleveland also had to deal with severe labor problems. Farmers had heavy debts, workers suffered from low wages and harsh working conditions, and employers felt little sense of responsibility for their employees. Reforms were demanded by the public and by 1886, 700,000 people had joined a labor group, The Knights of Labor. Its strike at the McCormick-Harvester plant in Chicago led indirectly to the bloody Haymarket Riot in which ten people died, including eight policemen. Cleveland distrusted workers movements and worked for the best interests of the country. He was the first President to devote an entire congressional message to the subject of labor. However, nothing came of his proposal for a permanent government arbitration board.

He opposed many measures concerning Veteran's pensions, defying powerful pressure groups such as the Grand Army of the Republic. The pension rolls were full of fraud. Many healthy veterans claimed to be unfit for work and many widows still collected government money after they had remarried. Cleveland vetoed hundreds of dishonest claims. He vetoed the Dependent Pension Bill, which would have extended pension coverage to all disabled veterans even if their disabilities were not connected with military service. The bill was later passed in 1890.

Two of the most important issues facing Cleveland in his first term were the currency and the tariff. The bankers and industrialists of the East wanted a high tariff to protect high prices and a "sound" money system based on gold. Farmers in the South and West wanted low tariffs so that they did not have to pay high prices for imported manufactured goods. As they had heavy debts, they wanted money to be cheap. At this time the currency was based on gold. Limited amounts of silver could be sold at the Treasury for gold in the fixed proportion of 16 to 1, or 16 ounces of silver for 1 ounce of gold. The Bland-Allison Act of 1878 required the Treasury to purchase and coin a minimum of $2 million worth of silver a month. Meanwhile, new silver mines had been discovered and the world price of silver fell. People could buy silver on the open market and make a profit by selling it to the government for gold. As a result, gold was rapidly drained from the Treasury. Cleveland asked Congress to repeal the Bland-Allison Act, but it refused. The government then issued bonds and sold them to banks for gold. This helped matters for a short time but the drain on the Treasury's gold continued. Cleveland felt that tariffs should be reduced and in 1887 he asked Congress to lower tariffs. Congress refused but national opinion was now focused on this problem.

At forty-nine years of age, Cleveland became the first and only President to get married in the White House when he took the vows with Frances Folsom (1864 – 1947) in the Blue Room on 2nd June 1886. At only twenty-one years old, she was the youngest First Lady in the nation's history. She was the daughter of one of Cleveland's law partners and had been his ward since her father died in 1875. Together they had five children, the first of which, Esther Cleveland (1893-1980), was the first and only child of a President to be born in the White House.

Other notable events in Cleveland's first term of office included the *Presidential Succession Act* of 1886, which settled questions regarding succession to the presidency. On October 28th 1886, Cleveland dedicated the *Statue of Liberty* in New York. *The*

Interstate Commerce Act of 1887, was the first federal act to regulate railroads and other forms of transportation. In 1889, the *Department of Agriculture* was made into an executive agency by Congress and its head was given Cabinet rank.

The Election of 1888

The tariff became the main issue in the 1888 election. The Republican candidate, Benjamin Harrison, opposed tariff reduction. Neither Cleveland nor the Democratic Party waged a strong campaign. His attitude towards the spoils system had antagonized party politicians. His policies on pensions, the currency and tariff reform hadmade enemies among veterans, farmers,and industrialists. Although Cleveland still won the popular vote, Harrison won the electoral college vote and the election.

Please see Chapter 24 for Grover Cleveland's Second Term

CHAPTER 23 –
BENJAMIN HARRISON

23ʳᵈ President of the United States 1889 – 1893

Born: 20ᵗʰ August 1833, North Bend, Ohio

Married: (1) Caroline Lavinia Scott (1832 – 1892), 20ᵗʰ October 1853 (2) Mary Lord Dimmick (1858 – 1948), 6ᵗʰ April 1896

Number of Children: Three – two with Caroline Scott, one with Mary Dimmick

Died: 13ᵗʰ March 1901, Indianapolis, Indiana

Final Resting Place: Crown Hill Cemetery, Indianapolis, Indiana

Introduction

Benjamin Harrison, the 23ʳᵈ President of the United States, was the only grandson of a President to also become President. His grandfather, William Henry Harrison, served as the ninth President of the United States in 1841. There was a great deal in common between the two men. Both were successful army commanders, both served in the U.S. Senate and both ran for the Presidency twice, winning once and losing once. Before he entered the White House, Harrison had been a successful army commander in the Civil War and served in the U.S. Senate. His family background and military record helped him to defeat Grover Cleveland in the presidential election of 1888 even though he won fewer popular votes. He became President when the country was rapidly growing. During his term of office, six new states joined the Union – North Dakota, South Dakota, Montana, Washington, Idaho and Wyoming – and a new Territory was established in Oklahoma. The forty-four states had a population of 67 million people. However, he found it difficult to solve the nation's growing economic and social problems and was defeated by Cleveland in the election of 1892.

Background

Benjamin Harrison was born the second of ten children on August 20th 1833 on his grandfather's farm in North Bend, Ohio. His father, John Scott Harrison, was the son of President William Henry Harrison and the only man whose father and son both became President. John Harrison was a farmer who had served two terms in Congress and Benjamin grew up on a farm. Benjamin was named after his great-grandfather who had signed the Declaration of Independence. He was educated at the Farmers' College in Cincinnati for three years and graduated from Miami University, Ohio, in 1852. He then trained as a lawyer with a firm in Cincinnati and was admitted to the bar in 1854. Harrison met his wife, Caroline ("Carrie") Lavinia Scott while at college and they married on October 20th 1853. They later had two children. Her father was the president of a women's college. Harrison was deeply religious man that taught at a Sunday school. In 1857 he became a deacon of the Presbyterian Church, and was elected an elder of the church in 1861.

Entry into Politics

Harrison's name was already familiar to voters because of the political careers of his father and grandfather. He was also a gifted public-speaker. In 1857 he successfully ran for City Attorney of Indianapolis. In 1858 he became secretary of the Republican state central committee and in 1860 was elected reporter of the State Supreme Court, being re-elected twice.

In 1862, Governor Oliver P. Morton asked Harrison to recruit and command the 70th Regiment of Indiana Volunteers in the Civil War. Serving as a Colonel, Harrison molded his regiment into a well-disciplined unit that fought in many battles. A fearless commander, he rose to the rank of Brigadier General. Like his grandfather,

159

"Tippecanoe," he was given a nickname. His men called him "Little Ben" because he was only 5 feet 6 inches tall (168cm)

After the war, he continued to work as a lawyer. In 1876 he ran unsuccessfully for the governorship of Indiana. In 1879, President Hayes appointed him to the Mississippi River Commission, a post he held until 1881. In January 1881 he was elected to the U.S. Senate where he supported Civil Service reform, a protective tariff, a strong navy and regulation of the railroads, and criticized President Cleveland's vetoes of veteran's pension bills. When he sought re-election for a second term, his bid was defeated by Indiana's Democratic legislature by one vote.

Election of 1888

James G. Blaine, who lost the election to Cleveland in 1884, refused to run again in 1888. Harrison was nominated because of his war record, the familiarity of voters with his name and his popularity with veterans. A banker from New York City, Levi P. Morton, was nominated for Vice-President. The Democrats nominated Cleveland with Allan G. Thurman, a former Ohio Senator, as his running mate. Harrison ran a "front porch" campaign from his home. He supported high tariffs, which were the chief issue of the election. Cleveland favored lower tariffs. As a hero of the Civil War, Harrison was able to make much of Cleveland never having served in the Union army. Cleveland did not actively campaign as he felt it was below the dignity of the President. In the election, Harrison trailed Cleveland by 90,000 votes. However, he won more votes in the electoral college.

Presidential Election of 1888		
Candidate	Popular Votes	Electoral Votes
Benjamin Harrison (Rep.)	5,447,129	233
Grover Cleveland (Dem.)	5,537,857	168
Clinton B. Fisk (Prohibition)	249,819	0

Harrison's Administration 1889 – 1893

Harrison was inaugurated in 1889. During his term, the White House was thoroughly photographed for the first time and electric lights and bells were installed in 1891. The Harrisons lived there with their daughter and her husband and two children. During his campaign he promised to extend the Civil Service Law to cover more jobs. He did this by increasing the number of classified positions from 27,000 to 38,000.

The four most important laws of his administration were all passed in 1890. During a period of rapid industrialization in the 1880's, many corporations formed trusts that controlled market prices and destroyed competition. Farmers and small businesses demanded protection from the government. *The Sherman Antitrust Act* fulfilled a campaign pledge and outlawed trusts or other monopolies that hindered trade. *The Sherman Silver Purchase Act* met another demand of farm voters. This act increased the amount of silver that could be coined. The government purchased this silver and paid for it with treasury notes that could be redeemed in either silver or gold. Farmers hoped this would stop farm prices falling. However, as most people redeemed their notes in gold, it later led to a financial panic in 1893 as people feared a resulting drain on the Treasury's gold reserves. *The McKinley Tariff Act* was designed to mainly protect American manufacturers. Tariffs were increased on imported farm products. As passed by Congress, the law set tariffs at record highs and domestic prices shot upward leading to an increase in the cost of living. *The Dependent Pension Bill* broadened pension qualification to include all Civil War veterans who could not perform manual labor. The cost of pensions soared from $88 million in 1889 to $159 million in 1893.

Harrison and Secretary of State James G. Blaine pursued a vigorous foreign policy. Harrison launched a program to build a two-ocean navy and expand the merchant marine. Cooperation was promoted among the nations of *Latin America* by the creation of the Pan American Union at first Pan American Conference that met in Washington in 1889. As US tariffs grew higher, *foreigntrade* with other nations was being threatened. Therefore, Harrison began to

161

negotiate reciprocal trade agreements. This was a compromise between manufacturers who wanted competitive markets and those who favored competitive tariffs. In *Hawaii*, Queen Liliuokalani lost her throne in a revolution led by American planters in 1893. The new Hawaiian government asked the U.S. to make Hawaii a territory. Harrison presented a treaty of annexation before Congress but there was not time to enact it before he left office. Cleveland then withdrew it saying the whole affair had been dishonorable to the U.S.

The Harrison government also settled many old quarrels. A long-standing dispute with Britain over fur seals in the Bering Sea was settled by arbitration. In 1889 the U.S. joined Germany and Britain in establishing a protectorate over Samoa, when a quarrel seemed likely over ownership of the islands. In 1892 Congress passed the *Oriental Exclusion Act*, prohibiting Asians from entering the United States, which long remained a sore spot in America's relations with China and Japan.

Election of 1892

In 1892 the Republicans nominated Harrison with Whitelaw Reid, editor of the New York Tribune, as his running mate. The Democrats nominated Cleveland for President with Adlai E. Stevenson, a former Illinois Congressman, for Vice-President. Discontented farmers turned from the Republicans to the new Populist party, which had been formed in protest against falling farm prices. There was also opposition to the McKinley Tariff Act which was blamed for a large increase in consumer prices. Tragedy struck Harrison two weeks before the election when his wife died on October 25th. Harrison received 5,182,690 popular votes to Cleveland's 5,555,426 while the Populist candidate, James B. Weaver, received more than a million votes. Cleveland won 277 electoral votes to Harrison's 145 while Weaver received 22.

Later Years

After he left the White House, Harrison returned to Indianapolis and the practice of law. In 1896 he married Mrs. Mary Dimmick, who had nursed his wife during her last illness. They had one child, Elizabeth. In 1897 he wrote a book *This Country of Ours* and in 1899 he represented Venezuela in the arbitration of a dispute with Britain over the boundary with British Guiana. In 1901 he published his memoirs, *Views of an Ex-President*. He died in his home on March 13th 1901 and was buried in Indianapolis.

Summary

Benjamin Harrison is surprisingly ranked quite highly among all the Presidents. A hero of the Civil War and a talented public speaker, he receives credit from historians for his attempts to deal with the economic problems of the time. Among his achievements in office were the curbing of monopolies and better cooperation with the other countries in the Americas.

CHAPTER 24 – GROVER CLEVELAND

24ᵗʰ President of the United States 1893 – 1897

For details of Cleveland's first term please see Chapter 22

Introduction

The election of 1888 returned Grover Cleveland to the White House for his second spell as President. In some ways the country had changed enormously even in the short spell since his first term. The number of states had grown from thirty-eight to forty-four and the population had expanded from sixty-two million to more than seventy-two million people. However, some of the economic and social problems remained the same. There was a great deal of labor unrest and important issues concerning tariffs and the currency. The country continued to expand and change. Utah joined the Union as the forty-fifth state in 1896 and the first gasoline-powered motor cars appeared on America's roads.

Background

After he left the White House in 1889, Cleveland moved to New York City and resumed the practice of law. The Harrison administration reversed many of his stringent policies. It boosted the tariff, increased the purchase of silver and extended pension coverage. As a result, both prices and government expenditure reached new heights. Cleveland criticized Harrison's program from the sidelines.

The Election of 1892

By the end of Harrison's term, he had grown unpopular with discontented factory workers and farmers. Many Americans were ready to once again ready to consider voting for Cleveland as President. At the Democratic national convention held in Chicago in 1892, Cleveland was nominated for President on the first ballot with Adlai E. Stevenson, a former Illinois congressman, as his running mate. The Republicans nominated Harrison with Whitelaw Reid for Vice-President. Cleveland also faced the challenge of a new Populist Party that was formed from the Knights of Labor and other disaffected groups. All sides focused on economic issues in their campaigns. In the election Cleveland won a comfortable victory winning 277 votes in the electoral college to 145 for Harrison. The populist party won over a million popular votes and 22 votes in the electoral college.

Presidential Election of 1892		
Candidate	Popular Votes	Electoral Votes
Grover Cleveland (Dem.)	5,551,883	277
Benjamin Harrison (Rep.)	5,179,244	145
James B. Weaver (Populist)	1,024,280	22
John Bidwell (Prohibition)	270,770	0

Cleveland's Second Administration 1893 - 1897

When they left the White House in 1889, Mrs. Cleveland told the servants to take good care of all the furniture and ornaments until they returned four years later. In March 1893, Cleveland and his wife returned to the White House. He enjoyed greater popularity at the start of his second term than at any other time in his presidency. Unlike his first term, he had Democratic majorities in both houses and he was free to deal with the country's problems as he saw fit. However, two months after he took office a serious financial panic swept the country. It led to 15,000 business failures and put four million people out of work. It was caused by a farm depression, a business slump abroad and the drain on the country's gold reserve. Cleveland felt that the economic problems were caused by the Sherman Silver Purchase Act of Harrison's administration. In June 1893 he called a special session of Congress to repeal the Act. They did so but the nation's gold reserves had depleted alarmingly. They were replenished by four bond issues in the next three years.

At this crucial time, doctors found he had cancer of the mouth. It was kept secret and he had a successful operation on his friend's yacht as it steamed up the East River in New York. The public only gradually became aware of it.

The business slump caused labor unrest to grow more serious. Due to his belief in order and limited understanding of changing conditions, he used force rather than constructive solutions to deal with it. In May 1894 workers of the Pullman Company went on strike after their pay had been reduced by thirty percent. The American railway Union supported them by refusing to handle Pullman cars. A general railroad strike resulted. Disorders broke out near Chicago and Cleveland sent in federal troops. The government broke the strike and most people approved of his action. However, critics said he had exceeded his constitutional powers and violated states' rights. The state militia were standing ready.

In his first term, Cleveland had been unsuccessful in persuading Congress to lower tariffs. In his second term he once again resumed his campaign for tariff reform and again asked Congress to lower import duties. He outraged members of his party by accusing uncooperative democrats of "party perfidy and party dishonour." As a result, the *Wilson-Gorman Bill* was passed in 1894 but fell short of his goal.

With America's growing strength in the world, foreign affairs were a more important concern in Cleveland's second term than in his first. Many Americans wanted a colonial empire. Cleveland wanted the U.S. to respect the rights of smaller, weaker nations. However, his principles were tested by events in Hawaii and Venezuela. In

Hawaii, American settlers had brought about a revolution at the end of Harrison's administration and asked the U.S. to annex the islands. Cleveland's second term began before the Senate could ratify the treaty of annexation. He withdrew it as he felt the Americans in Hawaii had involved the U.S. in a dishonorable action and the islands remained independent until 1898.

In Venezuela there was a boundary dispute between Great Britain. The British government had refused several times to allow its claim to be settled by a board of arbitration. In 1895, Secretary of State Richard Olney declared that the US was sovereign on its continent and would decide the matter. Cleveland hinted armed force may be necessary to settle the matter. Britain then agreed to submit the Venezuela boundary to international arbitration and settlement was reached in 1899. Historians have criticized Cleveland's intervention as extreme and provocative.

Later Years

By 1896, the economic and labor problems had made Cleveland unpopular and he did not seek re-election. The Democrats then nominated William Jennings Bryan for President. After he left the White House for a second time, Cleveland spent his last years in Princeton, New Jersey where he became a lecturer and trustee of Princeton University. He shared a friendship with Woodrow Wilson, president of the university, who later became President of the United States. He also reorganized the Equitable Life Assurance Society after its reputation had been damaged by financial scandals. As a result, he regained the respect of the public. He died after a three-month illness on June 24th 1908 and was buried at Princeton. Five years after Cleveland's death, his widow married Thomas J. Preston Jr., a Princeton professor.

Summary

Grover Cleveland is often regarded as the most important and capable President to occupy the White House between Abraham

Lincoln and Theodore Roosevelt. He is highly regarded for his courage, firmness, integrity and sense of duty. However, there were few positive achievements in either of his two terms and he ranks in the bottom half of all the Presidents.

CHAPTER 25 – WILLIAM MCKINLEY

25th President of the United States 1897 – 1901

Born: 29th January 1843, Niles Ohio

Married: Ida Saxton (1847 – 1907), 25th January 1871

Number of Children: Two

Died:14th September 1901, Buffalo, New York

Final Resting Place: Canton, Ohio

Introduction

William McKinley was a distinguished veteran of the Civil War who was elected as the 25th President of the United States. He was the last President of the 19th Century and the first of the 20th Century. Before entering the White House, McKinley had served in the U.S. House of Representatives and as the Governor of Ohio. He won the election of 1896 by promising Americans greater prosperity. At that time the country had 45 states and a total population of over 77 million. During his term of office, America won the Spanish-American War and began to play an important part in world affairs. The first cars appeared on American roads and the use of electric lights and telephones became more widespread. He was re-elected in 1900 by a large majority but six months into his second term, McKinley was shot by an anarchist in Buffalo, New York. He was the third President to be assassinated and the fifth to die in office.

Background

Wiiliam McKinley was born on 29th January 1843 in Niles, Ohio, a small rural town with a population of about 300. His ancestors migrated to America from Ireland in 1743 and his father owned a country store. He was the seventh of nine children and first attended school in Niles. He was later educated at a private school called the Poland Seminary and then Allegheny College in Meadville, Pennsylvania. When the Civil War broke out in 1861, he was the first man from his hometown to volunteer. He served as a Commissary Sergeant but his bravery under fire at the Battle of Antietam led to his promotion to Second Lieutenant. By the end of the war, he had been promoted to Brevet Major.

After the war, McKinely decided to become a lawyer and he studied in the office of County Judge Charles E. Glidden in Youngstown and at the law school in Albany, New York. He was admitted to the bar in 1867 and began practicing law in Canton, Ohio. On 25th January 1871, he married Ida Saxton, who worked as a cashier in her father's bank. They had two daughters but both died very young. The shock and grief caused Mrs. McKinley to become an invalid and William cared for her for the rest of his life.

Entry into Politics

In 1869 he won his first public office as prosecuting attorney of Stark County. In 1876 he was elected to the U.S. House of Representatives where he served until 1891, except for one short break of ten months. He gained a reputation for supporting high tariffs and in 1890 sponsored a tariff bill that raised duties to new highs. However, the measure proved unpopular due to a large increase in consumer prices, and he lost his bid for an eighth term in Congress. In 1891 he was elected Governor of Ohio where he improved the state's roads and canals, and established a state board of arbitration to deal with labor disputes. His widening political fame attracted the support of Cleveland millionaire, Marcus A. Hanna, who later sponsored his bid for the presidency.

Election of 1896

With Hanna's support, McKinley ran for the Republican nomination for President in 1896. At the national convention in St. Louis, McKinley won the nomination on the first ballot. Senator Garrett A. Hobart of New Jersey was nominated for Vice-President. The Democrats nominated William Jennings Bryan for President and Arthur Sewall, a wealthy Maine shipbuilder, for Vice-President. They campaigned against McKinley and Hobart as symbols of the plutocracy, or "rule of the rich." The chief issue of the campaign concerned the nation's prosperity. McKinley promised the protection of tariffs and the gold standard. As he had to care for his epileptic wife, McKinley conducted his campaign from his front porch in Canton. Thousands of people travelled to his home to hear his well-prepared speeches. In the election, McKinley won by over 600,000 votes. He gained 271 votes in the electoral college to 176 for Bryan. In the largest Republican victory since 1872, he won all the states north of the Mason-Dixon Line and east of the Mississippi.

Presidential Election of 1896		
Candidate	Popular Votes	Electoral Votes
William McKinley (Rep.)	7,102,246	271
William Jennings Bryan (Dem.)	6,492,559	176

McKinley's Administration 1897 – 1901

McKinley was inaugurated in 1897. During his term of office, the First Lady would sit next to the President at official dinners so that he could aid her if necessary. This differed from the usual protocol that directed that the President's wife be seated across the table from him. During his first term, Congress passed two important acts. They raised the tariff in 1897 and passed the Gold Standard Act of 1900.

It was during McKinley's first term that America first became an important player in world affairs. When he took office the people of Cuba were in revolt against their Spanish rulers. McKinley sought to maintain neutrality but on February 15th 1898, the battleship U.S.S. Maine blew up in Havana harbor. Although the exact cause of the explosion was never determined, many Americans thought that the ship had been sunk by the Spaniards and demanded war. McKinley relented and declared war in April. The war only lasted 113 days but it greatly increased America's influence in both Europe and the Far East. In the peace treaty with Spain, America acquired Guam, the Philippines and Puerto Rico. As American influence in the Pacific increased, Hawaii was annexed in 1898. The following year, America began the "Open Door" policy which asked for equality of trade in the potentially vast market of China.

The Election of 1900

The Republicans renominated McKinley for President in 1900. Governor Theodore Roosevelt of New York, a hero of the Spanish-American War, was nominated for Vice-President. The Democrats once again nominated Bryan and named Adlai E. Stevenson, Vice-President from 1893 to 1897, as his running mate. Prosperity became the central issue of the campaign. Republicans claimed that McKinley's re-election would give people "four more years of the full dinner pail." In the election, McKinley won 292 electoral votes to 155 for Bryan.

Presidential Election of 1900		
Candidate	Popular Votes	Electoral Votes
William McKinley (Rep.)	7,218,491	292
William Jennings Bryan (Dem.)	6,356,734	155

Mckinley's Second Term 1901

Although McKinley's second term was only a short one, there were several events of international significance. The Supreme Court affirmed that the residents of the newly acquired territories did not have the same rights as U.S. citizens and that Congress could impose tariffs on their trade. A civil government had been established by the U.S. in Puerto Rico and free trade was set up with it. In 1901, Cuba added an amendment to its constitution which allowed the United States to intervene in its affairs under certain circumstances. William Howard Taft was appointed the civil governor of the Philippines and began to improve the lives of the Filipino people living there.

Assassination

In September 1901 McKinley attended the Pan-American Exposition in Buffalo, New York. On the 6th September he held a public reception in the exposition's Temple of Midas where hundreds of people waited to shake his hand. Standing in the crowd as an anarchist called Leon F. Czolgosz. As McKinley reached out to shake his hand, Czolgosz fired two shots from a revolver concealed beneath his handkerchief. McKinley fell to the floor saying "Am I shot?" The crowd seized Czolgosz and began to beat him but the President implored them to stop. Czolgosz was arrested as the President was rushed to hospital for emergency surgery. He appeared to be making a recovery but died on 14th September. Czolgosz was later found guilty of his murder and electrocuted.

Mrs. McKinley did not learn of the shooting for several hours. She was so shocked that she never returned to the White House nor attended the burial rites. She lived in Canton until her death in 1907 when she was buried next to her husband at the McKinley Memorial. Vice-President Theodore Roosevelt was sworn in as President.

Summary

William McKinley was one of six Republican Presidents elected between 1876 and 1920 that were born in the state of Ohio. He is usually ranked high among all the Presidents because he both delivered prosperity and led the country to victory in the Spanish-American War. His murder meant that he did not have the chance to deal with some of the important problems that faced America including the growing power of business trusts.

CHAPTER 26 – THEODORE ROOSEVELT

26th President of the United States 1901 – 1909

Born: 27th October 1858, Manhattan, New York

Married: (1) Alice Lee (1861 – 1884), 14th February 1884 (2) Edith Carrow (1861 – 1948), 2nd December 1886

Number of Children: Six (1) One with Alice (2) Five with Edith

Died: 6th January 1919, Sagamore Hill, Oyster Bay, New York

Final Resting Place: Youngs Memorial Cemetery, Oyster Bay, Long Island, New York

Introduction

Theodore Roosevelt, the twenty-sixth President of the United States, was the youngest man ever to become President when he succeeded William McKinley in 1901. He was the third Vice-President in less than forty years to become President because of an assassination. However, Roosevelt was one of the most talented and accomplished men ever to become President. He had already been successful as a scholar, a rancher, a writer, a naturalist, a state legislator, a civil service commissioner, a police commissioner in New York City, an assistant secretary of the navy, a colonel in the army, a hero of the Spanish-American War and a Governor of New York. As President he approved laws to limit the power of trusts and promote the interests of workers and consumers. He pursued an active foreign policy that gave America control of the Panama Canal Zone and won the Nobel Prize for Peace by negotiating an end to the Russo-Japanese War. When he left office, America was a prosperous country of 90 million people and a respected world power. It was during his Presidency that the Wright Brothers made their first flight and cars, telephones and electric lights came into common use.

Background

Theodore Roosevelt was born in New York City on 27th October 1858, the second of four children of an importer of plate glass. His ancestors, the Van Roosevelts, emigrated from the Netherlands in the 1640s and settled in New Amsterdam, which was later renamed New York. The Roosevelt family were mostly wealthy landowners and businessmen. His mother came from Georgia and sympathized with the South in the Civil War. As a child, Roosevelt was tutored privately and travelled widely with his parents, visiting Europe and the Middle East. In 1876 he entered Harvard University and graduated in 1880. On 14th February 1884 he married his first wife Alice Hathaway Lee, the daughter of a wealthy investor. Unfortunately, she died two days after the birth of her first daughter. Sadly, Roosevelt's mother died of typhoid fever the same day.

Entry into Politics

After he graduated from Harvard, he enrolled into the University of Columbia Law School but showed little interest in the courses. He wrote a book called "The Naval War of 1812." He then decided to enter politics and joined a Republican club in New York City. In 1881, at the age of 23, he won election to the New York assembly where he showed an interest in Civil Service reform. He was re-elected in 1882 and 1883. In 1882 he briefly served as minority leader but was removed by Republican bosses because he did not follow the party line.

In 1884 he left politics after the death of his wife and mother and bought two cattle ranches in Dakota territory. Hard work as a rancher helped him to overcome the sorrow of their passing. He then wrote further books including the four-volume "The Winning of the West." In 1886 he returned to New York City and ran for mayor, but was heavily defeated. On December 2nd 1886 he married Edith Kermit Carow, a former childhood friend. They had five children, one of whom fought as an aviator in World War One and was killed in an air battle with a German pilot. Edith also looked after Alice, the child from Roosevelt's first marriage.

In 1888 Roosevelt made speeches in support of Benjamin Harrison, who had won the Republican nomination. When Harrison was elected President in November, he rewarded Roosevelt by appointing him to the Civil Service Commission. This body had previously attracted little attention but Roosevelt brought it publicity. While there, he established exams for some Civil Service jobs to improve the merit system. In 1893 he was reappointed by Cleveland. In 1895, Roosevelt became President of the Board of Police Commissioners in New York City. During his two years in the office, he attempted to stamp out dishonesty in the police force.

In 1896 Roosevelt campaigned vigorously for William McKinley. When McKinley won the election, he made Roosevelt the Assistant Secretary of the Navy. At that time rebels in Cuba were fighting the Spanish government. In 1898 the *USS Maine* was blown up in Havana harbor and on the 25th April the United States declared war on Spain. He resigned as Assistant Secretary so he could go to Cuba and fight the Spanish. He recruited men for a cavalry regiment known as the First Volunteer Cavalry Regiment. Most of its men were former college athletes or western cowboys and under his command it won fame as the *Rough Riders*. On 1st July 1898 he won national fame when he led his men in a cavalry charge up Kettle Hill.

His war record helped him become the Governor of New York in 1898, where he supported mild reform legislation. When McKinley was renominated for President in 1900, Roosevelt agreed to become his running mate. The Republicans nominated both men by acclamation. In the election McKinley and Roosevelt defeated their Democratic opponents, William Jennings Bryan and former Vice-President Adlai E. Stevenson. However, on 6th September 1901, six months after his second inauguration, McKinley was shot and later died on 14th September. That day Roosevelt took the oath of office as President.

Roosevelt's First Administration 1901 – 1905

Roosevelt became President six weeks before his 43rd birthday. He kept all the members of McKinley's Cabinet and said he would continue to pursue his predecessor's policies. The Republicans controlled Congress throughout his Presidency but conservative opposition made it difficult for his more progressive legislation to be passed. During his time as President the White House was remodelled and enlarged. The east and west wings were built and plumbing, heating and electrical systems were installed. In 1906, his daughter Alice married Nicholas Longworth in the executive mansion in what was a big Washington social event.

Many Americans were concerned by the rapidly growing number and power of large business monopolies known as *trusts*. Many people thought that they were responsible for increasing prices. Roosevelt wanted the government to supervise and control them so that they would continue to increase productivity and the standard of living but not attempt to raise prices nor reduce competition. In 1902 the government sued the *Northern Securities Company* on charges of trying to reduce competition. The company had been formed by financiers such as JP Morgan to control key railroads in the West. The government's view was upheld by the Supreme Court in 1904 and it dissolved the National Securities Company. During Roosevelt's presidency, the government filed suits against 43 other corporations and ended John D. Rockefeller's oil trust. Roosevelt earned a reputation as a *trust buster* but he said he wanted government to regulate not bust trusts.

Roosevelt wanted the government to act justly towards the labor unions as well towards business and he intervened in several labor disputes on behalf of the workers. In May 1902, 140,000 members of the United Mine Workers went on strike in the hard coal fields of Pennsylvania to achieve higher pay and better working conditions.

They enjoyed the support of the public but as winter approached supplies of coal began to run low. Roosevelt called a conference involving the leaders of both sides and suggested that the strike be settled by Arbitration. At first, the miners agreed but the mine-owners refused. The President then threatened to have the army seize and operate the mines. At Roosevelt's request, J.P. Morgan helped to negotiate a compromise for the mine owners and the miners received a pay increase the following March. Roosevelt said he tried to give the miners a "square deal" and later used this phrase to describe his social reforms. In 1903 Congress established the Department of Commerce and Labor.

Roosevelt also made notable achievements in conservation. During his term of office, 125 million acres were added to the National Forests. In 1902 the Reclamation Act provided for the reclamation and irrigation of dry western lands. Twenty-five irrigation and reclamation projects were started by Roosevelt.

In matters of foreign policy, Roosevelt liked to use the Native American proverb, "Speak softly and carry a big stick." The "big stick" referred to was the threat to use force. In 1902, British and German warships blockaded Venezuelan ports to force repayment of their loans that they had raised in Europe. Roosevelt was concerned that Germany planned to seize Venezuelan territory and warned them that he would use force if they took any part of Venezuela. As a result, the Germans withdrew their warships and Roosevelt was able to help resolve the dispute peacefully. In 1904 Santo Domingo (now the Dominican Republic) found it could not pay its debts to some European countries. Roosevelt again feared European intervention and announced that in cases of wrongdoing or incompetence the US would act as an "international police power." This became known as the "Roosevelt Corollary" of the Monroe Doctrine. The U.S. took control of Santo Domingo's customs system and brought order to that country's finances.

The foreign policy achievement of which Roosevelt was most proud was the treaty agreed with Panama which granted the United States the right to control and use the strip of land on which the Panama Canal was built. Between 1902 and 1905 the U.S. built ten battleships and four armored cruisers. These needed to move rapidly between Atlantic and Pacific oceans and therefore a canal across Central America was necessary. In 1902 the U.S. began negotiating a treaty with Colombia to build a canal across what was then the Colombian province of Panama. When the Colombian senate rejected the treaty, Roosevelt supported a revolutionary government that took control of Panama. The U.S. then recognized the state of Panama. Two weeks later the U.S. and Panama signed a treaty granting the U.S. the right to control and use the strip of land on which to dig the canal. In 1906 Roosevelt visited Panama and became the first President to travel to a foreign country while in office.

Another foreign policy achievement was the successful resolution of a boundary dispute in Alaska. Until 1896, no-one cared about the exact boundary between Canada and Alaska. However, that year gold was discovered in the Klondike and both Canada and America then disputed where the exact boundary lay. Canada claimed a line which gave it control of important routes to the goldfields. Britain asked for the matter to be settled by Arbitration and Roosevelt agreed providing the members of the tribunal were impartial. In 1903 the tribunal ruled in favor of the United States.

Election of 1904

Roosevelt was unanimously nominated by Republicans in 1904 and Senator Charles W. Fairbanks was chosen for Vice-President. The Democrats nominated Judge Alton B. Parker of the New York Supreme Court for President and Henry G. Davis of West Virginia for Vice-President. In the campaign, Roosevelt asked voters to vote for his "square deal policies" while Parker appealed for an end to what he called the "usurpation of authority" by the President. In the election, Roosevelt won election by more than 2.5 million votes, the largest majority achieved by any President up to that time.

Presidential Election of 1904		
Candidate	Popular Votes	Electoral Votes
Theodore Roosevelt (Rep.)	7,626,593	336
Alton B. Parker (Dem.)	5,082,898	140
Eugene V. Debs (Socialist)	402,489	0

Roosevelt's Second Administration 1905 – 1909

During his second administration, Roosevelt had to deal with America's pressing domestic problems. He believed that laws were needed to better control the nation's railroads. In 1903 the *Elkin's Act* was passed which aimed to prevent railroads from making rebates to favored shippers. However, the Act did not stop this practice, which put rival shippers out of business, and so Congress therefore passed the *Hepburn Railway Act* in 1906. That same year the *Meat Inspection Act* and the *Federal Food and Drug Act* were also passed to reform the food and drug industries. In 1907 the stock market slumped and financial panic spread throughout the country. However, prosperity returned in 1909.

During Roosevelt's second term there was increasing friction between the United States and the increasingly important country of Japan. In 1905 Roosevelt helped to end the Russo-Japanese war when he mediated the *Treaty of Portsmouth*, New Hampshire. This led to him becoming the first American to win a Nobel Prize in 1906 when he won the *Nobel Prize for Peace*. However, relations with the Japanese became strained when Roosevelt opposed their demands for compensation from Russia. The Japanese were also offended when the San Francisco School Board decided to segregate children of Japanese descent. Roosevelt persuaded them to end this policy and negotiated a "Gentlemen's Agreement" with Japan to keep Japanese laborers out of the U.S. In 1908 the United States and Japan signed the *Root-Takahira Agreement* by which both nations promised not to seek territorial gains in the Pacific and to honor the Open-Door policy in China. In 1907, as part of his "big stick" diplomacy, Roosevelt sent *The Great White Fleet* of sixteen new battleships on a worldwide tour where they were welcomed in Japan and other countries.

At that time Europe was divided into two alliances of nations, one headed by Germany and the other by Britain and France. In 1905 war threatened to break out when Germany demanded a share of control in Morocco, which was then dominated by France. Roosevelt persuaded Germany to attend an international conference in Spain in 1906. There the U.S. sided with France and Great Britain, because of which Germany then back down in its demand.

A split in the Republican party developed near the end of his presidency as Conservative Republicans opposed his progressive policies and resisted his proposals in Congress. In 1909, Roosevelt kept a pledge made five years earlier that he would not run again. He wanted William Howard Taft, his Secretary of War, to succeed him. Taft won the Republican nomination and comfortably defeated Democrat William Jennings Bryan in the presidential election of 1908.

Later Years

In March 1909 Roosevelt left the Presidency to hunt big game. When he returned home the following year, Progressive Republicans wanted him to be their next presidential candidate as they felt the Taft had betrayed them. At first, Roosevelt tried to bring conservatives and progressives together but when failed he decided to run for a third term in 1912. When Taft won the party's nomination, Roosevelt formed a separate party that offered a progressive policy which he called *New Nationalism*. When he told reporters that he felt "as strong as a bull moose," the party became known as the *Bull Moose* Party. On October 14th 1912 he was shot by saloonkeeper John N. Schrank but survived because the glasses case in his pocket saved his life. He recovered in two weeks and Schrank was sent to a mental hospital. However, Roosevelt's candidacy split the Republican vote and the Democratic candidate, Woodrow Wilson, won the election.

In 1914 Roosevelt explored the River of Doubt in the Brazilian jungle. However, he contracted jungle fever which adversely affected his health. In 1918 he had operations to remove abscesses on his leg and ears. It was also about this time that he revealed that he had lost an eye in 1903 while boxing with an aide in the White House. On January 6th 1919 he unexpectedly died of a blood clot in the heart. He was buried at Sycamore Hill in Oyster Bay, New York.

Summary

Theodore Roosevelt was the youngest man yet to become President when he took over from the assassinated William McKinley. He was one of the most talented men ever to occupy the White House. Always very popular, he was known as *Teddy* or *TR*, the first President to become known by his initials. It was he that gave his name to "Teddy" bears. He is regarded as one of America's best Presidents. At home he was a *trustbuster* that also passed important conservation measures. Overseas he made America a respected world power and won the Nobel Peace Prize for bringing the Russo-Japanese War to an end. He is remembered today with one of the four faces on Mount Rushmore.

CHAPTER 27 – WILLIAM HOWARD TAFT

27ᵗʰ President of the United States 1909 - 1913

Born: 15ᵗʰ September 1857, Cincinnati, Ohio

Married: Helen "Nellie" Herron (1861 – 1943), 19ᵗʰ June 1886

Number of Children: Three

Died: 8ᵗʰ March 1930, Washington D.C.

Final Resting Place: Arlington National Cemetery, Washington D.C.

Introduction

William Howard Taft was a lawyer and judge that was elected as the 27ᵗʰ President of the United States. Before entering the White House, Taft served as Solicitor-General of the United States, as Governor of the Philippines and as Secretary of War. He was elected President at a time when the country had a population of nearly 97 million people and was continuing to expand with New Mexico and Arizona joining the Union in 1912. During his presidency, America became an increasingly urbanized society and women had the right to vote in twelve states. The world was also rapidly changing. Europe was on the brink of the First World War while a revolution overthrew the Emperor of China in 1912. Explorers reached both the North Pole and the South Pole for the first time. After leaving the White House, Taft claimed that he had not wanted to be President and said that his time in office was a lonely and unhappy one. He then spent a more personally fulfilling period as Chief Justice of the United States. He is usually remembered as the largest man ever to become President.

Background

William Howard Taft was born in Cincinnati, Ohio, on 15th September 1857. His ancestors had emigrated from England in the 1600's and he was the third of six children of a Vermont judge. He was educated at Woodward High School in Cincinnati and then at Yale College, where he graduated second in his class. He then studied law at Cincinnati Law School and after receiving his degree in 1880 was admitted to the Ohio bar. On 19th June 1886 he married Helen "Nellie" Herron, the daughter of a lawyer, and they had three children. Their eldest child, Robert Aphonso Taft, later became a famous U.S. Senator and leader of the Republican Party while their youngest, Charles Phelps Taft, served as mayor of Cincinnati from 1955 to 1957.

Entry into Politics

Taft served as an assistant prosecuting attorney of Hamilton County, Ohio, in 1881 and 1882 and was then appointed collector of internal revenue for the first district, by President Chester Arthur, with headquarters in Cincinnati. A year later he resigned and formed his own law partnership. He was encouraged to enter politics by his father and in 1885 he was appointed assistant county solicitor for Hamilton County. In 1887, the Governor of Ohio, J. B. Foraker appointed him to a vacancy in the Cincinnati Superior Court. The following year he was elected to the court for a five-year term.

In 1890, President Benjamin Harrison appointed him as the Solicitor General of the United States. During his first year in the office, he won fifteen of the eighteen government cases that he argued before the Supreme Court. In March 1892 President Harrison appointed Taft a judge of the newly established federal Circuit Court of Appeals and he spent the next eight years as a circuit judge. From

1896 to 1900 he also served as Dean of the University of Cincinnati Law School.

In 1900 President William McKinley appointed Taft chairman of the civil commission to govern the Philippines, which the United States had just acquired from Spain. The following year Taft was named as the first civil governor of the islands where he established new schools and courts, and had built new roads and harbors. His commitment to the Philippines led him to turn down an appointment to the Supreme Court in 1902 even though that had always been his main ambition. In 1904, President Theodore Roosevelt appointed him as the Secretary of War and he returned to Washington. There he helped to supervise the construction of the Panama Canal and set up a government in the canal zone. He also assisted the President in negotiating the Treaty of Portsmouth, which ended the Russo-Japanese War.

Election of 1908

Presidential Election of 1908		
Candidate	Popular Votes	Electoral Votes
William Howard Taft (Rep.)	7,678,908	321
William Jennings Bryan (Dem.)	6,409,104	162
Eugene V. Debs (Socialist)	420,380	0

When Roosevelt fulfilled his pledge not to run for a further term, Taft sought the party's nomination for President and won it on the first ballot at the Republican National Convention in Chicago. Representative James S. Sherman of New York was nominated for Vice-President. The Democrats nominated Williams Jennings Bryan for President and John W. Kern, a party leader from Indiana, as Vice-President. Jennings had already made two unsuccessful attempts to win the Presidency and Taft's campaign used the slogan

"Vote for Taft now, you can vote for Bryan anytime." Taft won the election by more than a million popular votes, gaining 321 votes in the electoral college against 162 for Bryan. It was the Republicans fourth consecutive victory in presidential elections.

Taft's Administration 1909 – 1913

Taft was inaugurated on a wintry day in March 1909. As President, he continued with Roosevelt's policy of supervising and controlling large business monopolies. During his four years in office, nearly twice as many "trust-busting" prosecutions took place for violations of the Sherman Antitrust Act as had occurred during Roosevelt's administration of almost eight years. There were also other achievements during his term. In 1910 he signed the Postal Savings Bank Act which created the postal savings system. In 1912 he signed a bill which created the Federal Children's Bureau. That same year, New Mexico and Arizona joined the Union as the 47th and 48th states and Alaska was established as a territory. In 1913, the Sixteenth Amendment to the Constitution was ratified authorizing Congress to collect income taxes. Taft also took steps to create a balanced federal budget and to make public details of campaign expenses.

However, his time in office was marked by increasing tensions with Congress. The Republicans controlled both houses of Congress but were bitterly divided. Liberal Republicans under the leadership of Representative George W. Norris of Nebraska, wanted to restrict the powers of the Speaker of the House, Joseph Cannon. When Taft refused to support them, it alienated them against him. They were further antagonized by his stand in the *Pinchot Case*. In late 1909, Chief Forrester Gifford Pinchot accused the Secretary of the Interior, Richard A. Ballinger, and his department of making illegal transactions in the sale of Alaskan coalfields as well as selling land concessions to water and power companies too cheaply. Taft supported Ballinger, who was later cleared by a congressional investigating committee. Taft then dismissed Pinchot. Liberal Republicans, however, were convinced that some of Pinchot's charges were true and their support began to drain away from Taft.

It was Congress that forced higher tariffs than Taft wanted. He believed in tariff protection but felt that lower tariffs would help to control trusts. Soon after entering office, he called a special session of Congress to pass a tariff-reduction law. However, Senator Nelson W. Aldrich of Rhode Island led a campaign to keep tariffs high and the resulting law, the *Payne-Aldrich Act*, left the general rate as high it had been previously, although some rates were lowered slightly. Taft refused to veto the bill and suffered from the unpopularity that the new tariffs received. The Act also established the Tariff Board which undertook the first scientific investigation of tariff rates.

In foreign affairs, Taft's administration is associated with *dollar diplomacy*. This meant providing financial support and assistance to foreign countries in return for influence over the policies of their governments. The U.S. sought to obtain influence in China, Nicaragua and Honduras by making loans to those countries. Taft did have some achievements in his foreign policy. In 1909, he ended the American occupation of Cuba. In 1910, the International Court of Arbitration in the Hague resolved a dispute with Britain concerning the fishing grounds of Newfoundland.

Election of 1912

In 1910, Theodore Roosevelt had returned from an African hunting trip. He had supported Taft's bid to become President but their relationship chilled once Taft was in the White House. Roosevelt denied an interest in running for the presidency again but began making speeches advocating a *New Nationalism*. Under this slogan, Roosevelt called for a more honest government, stronger controls on big business, further conservation measures, and old age and unemployment insurance. Roosevelt found support from the Liberal Republicans that had been alienated by Taft. Conservative Republicans meanwhile with lined up the Taft against Roosevelt.

Although Roosevelt won most of the primary elections, most of the delegates to the nominating convention were pledged to Taft. The president was renominated on the first ballot and James S. Sherman was renominated for Vice-President. Roosevelt and progressive republicans accused Taft of "stealing" the convention by only recognizing the votes of pro-Taft delegations. They organized a Progressive party with Roosevelt as their nominee and chose Senator Hiram W. Johnson of California as his running mate. The Democrats nominated Governor Woodrow Wilson of New Jersey for President and Governor Thomas R. Marshall of Indiana for Vice-President.

With the Republican vote divided, Taft faced inevitable defeat. In the election he received only eight electoral votes against 88 for Roosevelt and 435 for Wilson.

Later Years

After Taft left the White House in March 1913, he became professor of constitutional law at Yale University. That same year he was elected president of the American Bar Association. During World War One, President Wilson appointed Taft joint chairman of the National War Labor Board.

In 1921, President Warren G. Harding appointed Taft as the Chief Justice of the United States. Taft regarded this appointment as the achievement of his greatest ambition. During his time in office, he achieved the passage of the Judiciary Act in 1925 which enabled the court to function more effectively. Taft was also instrumental in obtaining congressional approval for a new court building. He became an important adviser to President Calvin Coolidge. Taft later remarked that his time as Chief Justice was more enjoyable than his time as President of the United States and he found the work personally more fulfilling.

Taft was the largest and heaviest man to ever be President. In later life he attempted to control his weight and managed to maintain it at around 300 pounds (136kg). In an attempt to maintain his health and fitness, he used to walk the three miles between his home and the court almost every morning and evening. However, in February 1930 he was forced to retire from the strain of overwork and health problems, including heart trouble. On 8th March 1930, he died and was buried in Arlington National Cemetery. Taft and President John F. Kennedy are the only presidents to be buried there.

Summary

William Howard Taft is often remembered as the largest man ever to occupy the White House. During his time in office, America grew to forty-eight states when Arizona and New Mexico joined the Union. He was an honest, straightforward, and pleasant man who did not really want to become President and he was happy to leave the office after an unhappy stay. He later became Chief Justice of the United States, which gave him far greater fulfilment. He is often ranked in the middle of all the Presidents.

CHAPTER 28 –
WOODROW WILSON

28th President of the United States 1913 – 1921

Born: 28th December 1856, Staunton, Virginia

Married: (1) Ellen Louise Axson (1860 – 1914), 24th June 1885 (2) Edith Bolling Galt (1872 – 1961), 18th December 1915

Number of Children: Three (all with Ellen)

Died: 3rd February 1924, Washington D.C.

Final Resting Place: Washington National Cathedral, Washington D.C.

Introduction

Woodrow Wilson is known for being the President that led America into the First World War. Before he entered the White House, he had been a successful scholar, teacher and president of Princeton University as well as the Governor of New Jersey. As President of the United States, he passed important political reforms which stopped unfair trading practices and limited child labor. In 1917 he felt that he had no option but to declare War on Germany after German submarines began to attack American ships without warning. In 1918 he proposed Fourteen Points to be used as a guide for a peace settlement. These included a proposal for an association of nations that would help to keep world peace. In 1919 the Treaty of Versailles created the League of Nations but many Americans did not want their country to join it and the Senate refused to ratify the treaty. Wilson began to suffer from poor health and had to run the country from his sickbed after he collapsed. In 1920 he won the

Nobel Prize for Peace for his work in founding the League of Nations. When he was in office, America had 48 states and a population of over 108 million people. In 1920, the 19th Amendment to the Constitution gave women the right to vote.

Background

Thomas Woodrow Wilson was born on 29th December 1856. He dropped his first name shortly after graduating college. He was the third of four children of a Presbyterian minister. His father's ancestors had emigrated to America from Northern Ireland and his mother was born in Carlisle, England. He was the only President to have been a citizen of the Confederacy and his first memories were of the Civil War. His father's church in Georgia was used as a hospital for wounded Confederate soldiers. It was because of the war that he did not start school until he was nine years old. Until then he was taught at home by his father. At the age of 17 he entered Davidson College in Davidson, North Carolina. In September 1875 he enrolled at Princeton University in New Jersey where he graduated 38th from a class of 106 in 1879. He then entered the University of Virginia Law School in Charlottesville but withdrew in 1880 because of ill-health.

In 1882 he established a legal practice in Atlanta, Georgia but was unsuccessful in attracting new clients. In 1883 he entered John Hopkins University to study history and political science. Two years later he published his first book, "Congressional Government, A Study of American Politics." When he presented this as his doctoral thesis in 1886, he was awarded a doctorate by the university. On 24th June 1885 he married Ellen Louise Axson and they later had three daughters. He then became a teacher a Bryn Mawr College before being appointed the professor of history at Wesleyan University in Middletown. In 1890 he was invited to become the professor of jurisprudence and political economy at Princeton University and there he gained a reputation as a scholar, a distinguished lecturer and a teacher.

192

Entry into Politics

In October 1910 Wilson resigned from Princeton to campaign to become the Governor of New Jersey. The Democrats had nominated him for Governor as they felt his honesty and public-speaking skills would appeal to the public. His campaign speeches stirred votes throughout the state and he was elected with the largest majority ever received by a Democrat in New Jersey up to that time.

As state governor, Wilson gained a reputation as a reformer. Schools were improved and business corruption was tackled. These reforms brought him national attention and he became a candidate for the Democratic presidential nomination in 1912. At the party's national convention in Baltimore, Wilson was nominated on the 46th ballot. The convention nominated Governor Thomas R. Marshall of Indiana for Vice-President.

The Election of 1912

The Republican party was badly split. The conservative Republicans re-nominated President William Howard Taft whereas the progressive Republicans nominated former President Theodore Roosevelt. The public were once again stirred by Wilson's campaign speeches which promised to tackle the country's problems with liberal reforms. In the election he won an overwhelming majority in both the popular votes and in the electoral college.

Presidential Election of 1912		
Candidate	Popular Votes	Electoral Votes
Woodrow Wilson (Dem.)	6,293,454	435
Theodore Roosevelt (Pro.)	4,119,538	88
Willam Howard Taft (Rep.)	3,484,980	8
Eugene V. Debs (Socialist)	900,369	0

Wilson's First Administration 1913 – 1917

Wilson was inaugurated on 4th March 1913. He was the last President to ride to his inauguration in a horse-drawn carriage. On 15th March he became the first President to hold a press conference. He felt that people were entitled to receive reports on the progress of his administration. With the Democrats controlling Congress, Wilson was able to lead a great reforming government. In October, Congress passed Wilson's first important measure of reform, the *Underwood Tariff Act*, which lowered or removed tariffs on imports. In December, Congress passed the *Federal Reserve Act*, the most effective banking and currency bill in the nation's history. The following year, Congress established the Federal Trade Commission to investigate and stop unfair trade practices, and passed the *Clayton Antitrust Act* which gave the federal government more powers to police unfair practices of big businesses. In 1916, the *Adamson Act* established an eight-hour working day for Railroad employees and the *Child Labor Act* limited children's working hours. Other measures were taken to improve education and roads in rural areas.

Three important amendments were made to the U.S. Constitution during Wilson's term of office. In his first administration, the 17th Amendment provided for the election of Senators by popular vote rather than by state legislatures (1913). In his second administration, the 18th Amendment banned the manufacture, sale and transportation of alcoholic beverages (1919) and the 19th Amendment gave women the right to vote (1920).

Wilson had to deal with several foreign policy problems during his first term of office. In April 1914, American troops occupied the Mexican port of Veracruz after the military dictator of Mexico, Victoriana Huerta, arrested 14 American sailors that had gone ashore in Tampico. Wilson accepted an offer by Argentina, Brazil and Mexico to arbitrate in the dispute and as a result Huerta left Mexico and was replaced by Venustiano Carranza. But relations remained poor and in 1916 American troops under General John J. Pershing penetrated deep into Mexico in pursuit of Pancho Villa, a renegade general that had led raids across the Rio Grande. Open war with Mexico was only narrowly averted. During his first term of office,

American troops were also sent to occupy Haiti, Nicaragua and the Dominican Republic to restore political stability to those countries.

In August 1914, World War One broke out in Europe and the United States initially remained neutral. However, on 7th May 1915, the British liner Lusitania was sunk by a torpedo fired from a German submarine and 123 Americans were killed. Wilson then negotiated an agreement with the Germans whereby their submarines would not attack neutral or passenger ships.

During Wilson's first term of office his wife became ill and died on 6th August 1914. He was so saddened by her death he almost lost the will to live. However, in March 1915 he met Mrs. Edith Bolling Galt, the widow of a Washington jeweler. They soon fell in love and were married in Washington D.C. on 18th December 1915. Two of the President's daughters also married during his first term of office.

The Election of 1916

In June 1916 the Democrats once again nominated Wilson for President and Marshall for Vice-President. The Republicans nominated Supreme Court Justice Charles Evans Hughes for President and former Vice-President Charles W. Fairbanks as his running mate. The war in Europe overshadowed all other issues in the campaign. Under the slogan "He kept us out of the war," Wilson appealed to those that favored peace but he also emphasized the reforms achieved by his first administration. The election was a close one with Wilson's victory only assured when he won the state of California by 4,000 votes.

Presidential Election of 1916		
Candidate	Popular Vote	Electoral College
Woodrow Wilson (Dem.)	9,129,606	277
Charles Evans Hughes (Rep.)	8,538,221	254

Wilson's Second Administration 1917 – 1921

After his re-election Wilson continued with his attempts to halt the fighting in Europe. However, in February 1917 the Germans began unlimited submarine warfare against all merchant shipping, including American ships. Wilson immediately broke off diplomatic relations. Later that month, British agents uncovered a German plot to start a war between the United States and Mexico. In March, the Germans began to attack American ships without warning. With an enraged public calling for war, Wilson realized that the United States could no longer remain neutral and on 2nd April he addressed a joint session of Congress where he asked for a declaration of war to be made against Germany to make the world "safe for democracy." On 6th April 1917, Congress passed a joint resolution declaring war on Germany. Wilson soon proved himself a great war leader. He clearly defined the aims for which America fought, plainly explained the great issues of the war, and rallied the people with stirring speeches.

The Fourteen Points

As he led America through the war, Wilson gave great thought as to how peace could be achieved and maintained. In a speech to Congress on January 8th 1918, Wilson presented fourteen points he said should be used as a guide for a peace settlement. The first five points set out his general ideals. He said that he wanted to avoid secret treaties, establish the freedom of the seas, remove all economic and trade barriers, reduce armaments, and impartially adjust all colonial claims. The next eight points all concerned immediate political and territorial problems. He wanted German troops to be withdrawn from all the Russian, Belgian and French territory that they occupied and Italy's borders to be adjusted along lines of nationality. He called for the countries of the Balkans and Poland to be made independent and for the peoples of the Austro-Hungarians and Turkish empires to be granted self-government. The final of the fourteen points was the most important. He called for the creation of an association of nations to help keep world peace.

The speech undermined German morale in the last months of the war but it also gave them a basis upon which to appeal for peace. In the summer and fall of 1918, allied armies broke through the German lines and advanced along with Western Front, forcing the Germans to retreat. On November 9th 1918, with his armed forces on the verge of mutiny and collapse, Kaiser Wilhelm II gave up control of the German government. On 11th November 1918, an armistice negotiated by Wilson was proclaimed.

The Paris Peace Conference

After the armistice had been signed, Wilson led the United States delegation to the peace conference in Paris. He wanted to make certain that the peace would be based on his fourteen points. He was particularly determined that his plan for a League of Nations was included in the peace settlement. He was the first serving President to cross the Atlantic Ocean and arrived in Brest, France, on 13th December 1918. The following day he rode through the streets of Paris and was given a joyous reception by the people there. He received similar welcomes in London, where he stayed at Buckingham Palace, and in Rome, where he became the first serving President to meet the Pope.

The Paris Peace Conference took place from January to June 1919. The conference was dominated by Wilson, Prime Minister Lloyd George of Great Britain, and Prime Minister Georges Clemenceau of France. Wilson was successful in having the League of Nations included in the peace settlement but this was achieved only by compromising on several major issues. In February he briefly returned to the United States to discuss the peace treaty and the League of Nations with the Senate. There he realized that he would not win the Senate's approval for the League without some amendments. When he returned to France, he successfully negotiated some of these and the Treaty of Versailles was signed on 28th June 1919.

In July 1919, Wilson returned to America with the treaty. His peace delegation had included neither a Senator nor a senior Republican.

He therefore faced a hard fight to have his treaty accepted by the Senate. Some Senators were isolationists who felt the U.S. should not be involved in European affairs. Others wanted to reduce or eliminate America's obligations to the League. Wilson decided to tour the country making speeches that would try and win public support for the treaty. However, his health was in decline and on 25th September he collapsed from fatigue and nervous tension while he travelling to Wichita in Kansas. He cancelled his tour and returned to Washington but suffered a paralytic stroke on 2nd October. He spent the rest of his life as an invalid.

However, he continued as President, leading the country from his sick bed. In November 1919, the Senate were asked to vote upon the treaty. The Republicans had proposed several amendments including one that declared that the United States assumed no obligation to support the League of Nations unless Congress specifically approved it by joint resolution. Wilson claimed that this would destroy the League and instructed Democrats in the Senate to vote against approving the amended treaty. As a result, the treaty failed to win the two-thirds majority that it required for approval. A second attempt was made to approve the treaty in March 1920 but once again it failed.

With Wilson unfit to run in the election of 1920, the Democrats nominated James M. Cox for President but he was overwhelmingly defeated by his Republican opponent Warren G. Harding. The Democratic platform had endorsed the League while the Republican platform opposed it. Harding's victory meant that the United States never joined the League of Nations. In December 1919, Wilson won the Nobel Peace Prize for his work is founding the League of Nations and seeking a fair peace agreement.

Later Years

After he left office, Wilson lived in quiet retirement in Washington D.C. He died in his sleep on February 3rd 1924 and was buried in Washington Cathedral. He is the only President interred in Washington D.C.

Summary

Woodrow Wilson was a man of great honesty and integrity who provided America and the world with strong and purposeful leadership at the time of a great crisis. Although he was an effective war leader, he was also a peace-loving man with high moral standards. It was largely due to his intervention that the First World War was brought to a successful close and peace returned to the world. For this reason, he ranks highly among all the Presidents.

CHAPTER 29 – WARREN G. HARDING

29th President of the United States 1921 – 1923

Born: 2nd November 1865, Blooming Grove, Ohio

Married: Florence Kling DeWolfe (1860 – 1924), 8th July 1891

Number of Children: One (with Nan Britton)

Died: 2nd August 1923, San Francisco, California

Final Resting Place: Harding Tomb, Marion, Ohio

Introduction

Warren Harding was a former schoolteacher and newspaper magnate who was elected as the 30th President of the United States. Before he entered the White House, he had served in the Ohio State Senate and the U.S. Senate. He became President of the United States in the aftermath of World War One. At the that time, there were 48 states in the Union with a total population of 111,000,000 people, and the country was one of the most powerful in the world. However, the American people were weary of world problems and warfare. They longed to reduce their international responsibilities and return to normal life as soon as possible. Harding was elected President promising a "return to normalcy." However, the popularity of his government was affected by economic depression and corruption. In 1923 he became the sixth President to die in office.

Background

Warren Gamaliel Harding was born the eldest of eight children on 2nd November 1865, on a farm near Corsica (now called Blooming Grove), Ohio. His ancestors had emigrated to America from England in 1624. His father was a farmer who supplemented his income by working as a homeopathic doctor. After attending grammar schools in Corsica and Caledonia, he studied at Ohio Central College in Iberia.

In 1882 he qualified as a teacher but only taught one term in a schoolhouse near Marion, Ohio. He was more interested in a becoming a journalist and joined the Marion Democratic Mirror. However, he was fired in 1884 for supporting the Republican candidate, James G. Blaine, for President. He then joined two friends in purchasing the Marion Star, a bankrupt weekly newspaper, for three hundred dollars. He built the Star into a prosperous daily newspaper with the help of his wife, Florence Kling DeWolfe, whom he married in 1891. The ambitious daughter of a prominent Marion banker, she was a divorcee five years his senior. They had no children.

Entry into Politics

Harding first entered politics in 1898 when he was elected a state senator for the Republican party in 1898. He was then elected lieutenant governor in 1903 but lost the election for state governor in 1910. His career in politics was helped by his friendship with a political strategist from Ohio, Harry M. Daugherty, who worked hard to make him President. In 1912, Harding was chosen to nominate William Howard Taft for a second term at the Republican national convention. He later served as permanent chairman at the national convention in 1916 where he made a keynote speech.

In 1914, he ran successfully ran for the Senate where he served six years. There he voted for women's suffrage even though he admitted being indifferent to it. In early 1919 he was first mentioned by the U.S. press as a potential candidate for President. Daughety and his wife persuaded him to stand and Daugherty became his campaign manager. When the Republican national convention opened in June 1920 most of the delegates supported either Governor Frank O. Lowden of Illinois; Major General Leonard Wood, former army chief of staff; or Senator Hiram W. Johnson of California. However, Daugherty persuaded delegates to vote for Harding as their second- or third-choice candidate.

On the first day of voting there was deadlock after four ballots. That night powerful Senators and political bosses met in the Blackstone Hotel in what Daugherty described as "smoke-filled rooms." At two o'clock in the morning they agreed on Harding as the compromise candidate even though he was the first choice of none of them. They were tired and wanted to go home and there was no other compelling alternative. The next day the delegates nominated Harding as President with governor Calvin Coolidge of Massachusetts as his running mate.

The Election of 1920

The election of 1920 took place in the aftermath of World War One. The Democratic candidate, James M. Cox, wanted to create a League of Nations to safeguard world peace. However, Americans were tired of the world and its problems and longed for their lives to return to normal. Harding promised a "return to normalcy" and denounced the League of Nations.

Presidential Election of 1920		
Candidate	Popular Votes	Electoral Votes
Warren G. Harding (Rep)	16,152,200	404
James M. Cox (Dem)	9,147,353	127
Eugene V. Debs	915,490	0

Harding conducted a "front porch" campaign from his home in Marion. There he made speeches and received visiting delegations. In the election, Harding won an overwhelming victory and became the first man to be elected President while serving in the Senate. It was also the first presidential election in which women could vote, and in which returns were broadcast on the radio.

Harding's Administration 1920 – 1923

Harding was inaugurated in 1921. Once he took office, he quickly signed peace treaties with Germany and Austria which excluded any terms that committed America to join the League of Nations. In 1921, a disarmament conference was held in Washington D.C. under the leadership of the Secretary of State, Charles Evans Hughes, whereby the world's leading powers agreed to limit the size of the navies. Congress took the lead in terms of domestic legislation. In1921, it reduced taxes and placed quotas on immigration for the first time. In 1922, it raised tariffs to their highest ever level.

A depression that badly affected America's farmers caused the Republicans to slip badly in the 1922 Congressional elections. Confidence in Harding's administration was also affected by several government scandals. The most shocking of these was the *Teapot Dome scandal* in which the Secretary of the Interior, Albert Fall, had leased the government's oil reserves at Teapot Dome, Wyoming, and Elk Hills, California, to private oil producers in return for bribes worth $300,000 and $100,000 respectively. Fall resigned in 1923 and was later sent to prison in 1931.

Harding 's friends were linked to some of these scandals. When he arrived in Washington, he gave important jobs to friends from his home state. They soon became known as "the Ohio gang," and many of them were untrustworthy and corrupt. Daugherty, who had been appointed as Attorney General, was tried in 1926 on charges concerning his administration of the Alien Property Custodian's office. He was freed after two juries failed to agree on a verdict. Daugherty's friend, Jesse W. Smith, committed suicide in 1923 after it was revealed that he was arranging settlements between the Department of Justice and violators of the law. There was also graft in other government agencies. Misuse of funds in the Veteran's Bureau resulted in the suicide of a legal adviser to the agency, Charles F. Cramer, and the imprisonment of a director, Charles R. Forbes.

In 1923, Harding embarked on a speaking tour in to revive confidence in his administration. He crossed the country accompanied by his wife and a large official party and made the first presidential visits to Canada and Alaska. En route he received a long, coded message which informed him that the Senate was investigating oil leases. Shortly afterwards he fell ill as his train was passing through Seattle. When he reached San Francisco, doctors reported that he had pneumonia and on the 2nd August 1923 he died. No autopsy was performed and so the exact cause of death was not known at the time. Sorrowful crowds gathered along the route as Harding's body was returned to Washington. Harding's wife attempted to protect his memory by burning as much of his correspondence as she could. She died the following year and was buried beside him in Marion.

After his death two books were published which severely affected his reputation and may also explain how and why he suddenly died. In 1927, Nan Britton published *The President's Daughter,* which gave lurid details of their extra-marital affair and claimed that Harding had secretly fathered her daughter. In 1930, *The Strange Death of President Harding* by Gaston Means was published which said that the President had been poisoned by his wife and doctor.

Summary

Warren G. Harding is remembered as one of America's worst Presidents. He was a poor judge of character and this is one of the reasons that his administration is associated with corruption and graft. He probably became aware of widespread corruption in the summer of 1923 and anxiety about it may have affected his health and caused his early death. There is also the possibility that he was poisoned. He was only 57 when he became the sixth President to die in office. The Great Depression began only six years later and reinforces the impression that he made serious policy errors in his unimpressive   term.

CHAPTER 30 – CALVIN COOLIDGE

30th President of the United States 1923-1929

Born: 4th July 1872, Plymouth Notch, Vermont

Married: Grace Anna Goodhue (1879 – 1957), 4th October 1905

Number of Children: Two

Died: 5th January 1933, Northampton, Massachusetts

Final Resting Place: Plymouth Notch Cemetery, Massachusetts

Introduction

Calvin Coolidge, the 30th President of the United States, was the sixth Vice-President to become President upon the death of the incumbent. Prior to becoming Vice-President, he had served as the Governor of Massachusetts. As President, he led the country when there were 48 states in the Union and the population had reached 122 million people. The nation had achieved a new level of prosperity and people enjoyed jazz music and the first "talking" motion pictures. The era of the "Roaring Twenties" is associated in American minds with the baseball player Babe Ruth, the heavyweight boxer Gene Tunney, and the aviator Charles Lindbergh, who made the first non-stop solo flight across the Atlantic in 1927. Some Americans defied Prohibition and gangsters such as Al Capone grew rich supplying them with bootleg liquor. Coolidge was a popular President and may well have been re-elected in 1929. However, he surprised everybody when he chose not to run.

Background

Calvin Coolidge was born on Independence Day, 4th July 1872 in Plymouth Notch, Vermont. His ancestors had arrived in America from England in 1630. He was the eldest of two children and his father was a farmer and a local politician who had served three terms in the Vermont house of representatives and one term in the state senate. His mother died when he was twelve. He sister died while he was still at school. He graduated from the Black River Academy in Ludlow in 1890 and then entered Amherst College in 1891. It was there that he first showed an interest in politics and made his first speech in 1892, when he gave an Independence Day address in his home town. He graduated cum laude in 1895. He then studied to become a lawyer with the firm of Hammond and Field in Northampton, Massachusetts and passed the bar examination in 1897. Seven months later he opened his own law office in Northampton.

Entry into Politics

Coolidge joined the Republican party and was elected to Northampton city council in 1898. In 1900 he became city solicitor. On 4th October 1905 he married Grace Anna Goodhue (1879 – 1957), a teacher for the Clarke School of the Deaf in Northampton. They had two sons. In 1906 he was elected to the Massachusetts house of representatives in 1906 and was re-elected the following year. In 1909 he won election as the Mayor of Northampton and was returned in 1910. From 1912 to 1915 he served in the state senate with two terms as president of that body. In 1915 he was elected lieutenant governor and twice won re-election. Then in 1918 he was elected as Governor of Massachusetts. In September 1919, the police force in Boston went on strike claiming that they were underpaid. The city then experienced two nights of violence and looting, and three people died. Coolidge ended the violence and restored order by sending in the Massachusetts Militia. His tough response met with widespread public approval and he was re-elected Governor with a record vote.

The way that he dealt with the police strike brought him to national attention and in 1920 the Republican national convention nominated him as Vice-President on the first ballot as the running mate of Warren G. Harding. In the 1920 presidential election, Harding and Coolidge won an overwhelming victory over their Democratic opponents, Governor James M. Cox of Ohio and Assistant Secretary of the Navy, Franklin D. Roosevelt.

As Vice-President, Coolidge was invited to attend Cabinet meetings by President Harding. He was the first Vice-President to do so. In August 1923, he took a vacation to his father's farm in Vermont. On the morning of August 3rd, he was woken to the startling news that President Harding had died. He immediately got dressed and made his way to the dining room where at 2.45am his father, a public notary, administered the presidential oath of office. Never before had the oath been administered by such a low ranking official. It was also the first time that the oath had been administered by a President's father. However, his father only had the legal authority to swear in the state officials of Vermont and so eighteen days later Coolidge had a second oath administered by a Justice of the Supreme Court of the District of Columbia.

Coolidge's Administration 1923 – 1925

Coolidge entered office just as the Teapot Dome scandal and the other scandals of Harding's administration were becoming known to the public. His personal honesty was never questioned and he made no effort to shield the guilty. In 1924 he forced the resignation of the Attorney General, Harry M. Daugherty and other high officials that had been part of the scandals. A former interior secretary, Albert B. Fall, became the first former cabinet member to receive a prison sentence for misconduct in office when he was jailed for his part in the Teapot Dome scandal.

Coolidge declared that "The business of America is business." He pursued a program he called *constructive economy* which supported American businesses at home and abroad. Tariffs were kept high to help American manufacturers and Congress reduced taxes. However, income from taxation increased as the economy grew and the government reduced the national debt by a billion dollars a year. Congress also voted to restrict immigration even further than it had done in 1921. However, the general increase in prosperity was not shared by America's farmers when prices for their goods fell due to global surpluses. Coolidge twice vetoed a bill that would enable the government to buy surplus crops and sell them abroad. He also vetoed a World War One veterans' bonus bill but Congress passed it over his veto.

The 1924 Presidential Election

Coolidge had no important rivals for the Republican presidential nomination in 1924. Charles C. Dawes, Director of the Bureau of the Budget, was nominated for Vice-President. The Democratic nomination for President was John W. Davis, former ambassador to Great Britain, with Governor Charles W. Bryan of Nebraska for Vice-President. Dissatisfied members of both parties formed the Progressive party who nominated Senator Robert L. LaFollette of Wisconsin for President and Senator Burton K. Wheeler of Montana for Vice-President.

The Republicans campaigned under the slogan "Keep Cool with Coolidge," while their opponents highlighted the scandals of the Harding era. In the election, Coolidge won with more than half of the popular vote, gaining 382 seats in the electoral college to 136 for Davis.

Presidential Election of 1924		
Candidate	Popular Votes	Electoral Votes
Calvin Coolidge (Rep.)	15,719,921	382
John W. Davis (Dem.)	8,386,704	136
Robert M. LaFollette (Pro.)	4,832,532	13

On March 4th 1925, Chief Justice William Howard Taft became the first former President to administer the oath of office. Coolidge's inaugural address was also the first to be broadcast by radio. Coolidge suffered a tragedy just after he won the nomination in 1924 when his sixteen-year-old son, also called Calvin, died from blood poisoning that spread from a blister that had developed while he was playing tennis on the White House courts. Two years later, the President's father died.

During his time in the White House, there were some notable foreign policy achievements. In 1923 and 1924, Vice-President Dawes directed an international committee that worked out a way that Germany could pay its reparations from World War One. In addition, relations with Mexico improved when Dwight W. Morrow was appointed ambassador there. He settled some old disputes and obtained valuable concessions from Mexico for American and British owners of oil property. In 1926, US Marines landed in Haiti and helped stabilise that nation's government. However, America did not join either the League of Nations nor the World Court, which held its first session in 1922.

With the country doing well and the President enjoying great popularity it seemed likely that Coolidge would be re-elected in 1928. In the summer 1927, Coolidge and his wife travelled for a summer vacation to the Black Hills of South Dakota. On August 2nd, the day before the fourth anniversary of his presidency, he called newsmen to his office in Rapid City high school. There he handed each reporter a slip of paper which said simply: "I do not choose to run for President in 1928." The announcement caught the nation by surprise as there was no prior indication of his plans. However, he later mentioned in his autobiography that both he and the First Lady found the presidency a strain.

Later Years

After leaving the White House, Coolidge and his wife returned to Northampton. However, they could not enjoy a quiet life due to the steady stream of tourists that visited their house. In 1930 they bought an estate called *The Beeches* with big iron gates to keep visitors at a distance. In 1929 he published his autobiography and became a director of the New York Life Insurance Company. That same year the stock market crashed causing him much distress. He forever wondered if he could have done more to prevent it. On 5th January 1933, he died of a heart attack and was buried next to his son in Plymouth Notch cemetery. His wife died in 1957.

Summary

While he was in office, Calvin Coolidge was admired and respected as President because of his honesty and integrity. The country achieved a new level of prosperity and there were some notable foreign policy achievements. However, historians often blame his policies for the Wall Street Crash and the Great Depression that followed. As a result, he is often ranked near the bottom of all the Presidents.

CHAPTER 31 – HERBERT HOOVER

31ˢᵗ President of the United States 1929 – 1933

Born: *10ᵗʰ August 1874, West Branch, Iowa*

Married: *Lou Henry (1874 – 1944), 10ᵗʰ February 1899*

Number of Children: *Two*

Died: *20ᵗʰ October 1964, New York City*

Final Resting Place: *Hoover Presidential Library, West Branch, Iowa*

Introduction

Herbert Hoover was a successful businessman who was elected as the 31ˢᵗ President of the United States. Before entering the White House, he had worked as an engineer and consultant in the mining industry and became a millionaire. In the First World War he helped thousands of stranded Americans to return to the United States from Europe. He was then appointed as the Head of the United States Food Administration, which ensured that food was produced and supplied to wartime America and Europe. When he became President, the country had 48 states and nearly 126 million people, and enjoyed great prosperity. He was elected with the largest majority in a presidential election up to that time. However, seven months later the stock market crashed and America was swept by the Great Depression. He then became the first President to fight a depression using the full powers of the Federal government. However, in 1932 Franklin Roosevelt defeated him in the presidential election with an even larger majority than that of 1928.

Background

Herbert Hoover was born in West Branch, Iowa, on 10th August 1874. He was the first President to be born west of the Mississippi River. His ancestors had arrived in America from Germany in 1738 and he was one of three children of a blacksmith and dealer in farm equipment. His mother was born in Canada. His father died of typhoid fever when he was six and his mother died of pneumonia when he was nine. He was raised by relatives and had a happy childhood even though he was an orphan. However, he did not live with his brother and sister as he grew up.

In 1885 he went to live with his uncle in Newberg, Oregon where he attended secondary school at Newberg College, a small Quaker academy of which his uncle was principal. In 1888 his uncle opened a real estate office in Salem and Hoover went to work there as an office boy when he was fifteen. In 1890 he became interested in engineering and decided to become a mining engineer. At the age of seventeen he enrolled in the first class of the newly founded Stanford University in Palo Alto, California. He graduated in 1895 and briefly worked as a miner in California.

While he was at Stanford he met Lou Henry, the daughter of a wealthy banker. On February 10th 1899 they married in Monterrey, California. They later had two sons. She was very clever woman who spoke several languages and was interested in science, literature and art. They both received special degrees from Stanford for translating an old book about mining from Latin into English.

In 1896 he began his career as a mining engineer in San Francisco. The following year he joined a company in London that wanted an engineer to manage its gold mines in Australia. Two years later he accepted the post of chief engineer for the Chinese Imperial Bureau of Mines. The Hoovers spent their honeymoon sailing from California to China, where his wife learned to speak Chinese. During the Boxer Rising of 1900, Hoover supervised the construction of defenses for the foreign settlement in Tientsin. During the two months siege of the settlement, he supervised the distribution of food and other supplies.

After the rising, the Chinese government discontinued its Bureau of Mines and Hoover returned to London where he helped to organize a private company to develop the Chinese mines. In 1901, he returned to China as the company's general manager. After a few months he resigned and returned to London as a partner in a firm of mining consultants. In 1908 he established his own engineering firm with a headquarters in London. He reorganized mines in many parts of the world and was a millionaire by 1914.

Entry into Politics

He was in London when the First World war began in 1914. Many Americans were stranded in Europe and the American government asked Hoover to help these people. He organized a committee that helped 112,000 Americans to return home. In August 1914 the U.S. ambassador in London asked him to organize food relief for Belgium. From October 1914 to April 1917, he gathered funds and distributed food which saved many thousands of lives.

When the U.S. entered the war, President Wilson asked Hoover to head the United States Food Administration and he was given broad powers over prices, production and distribution of food. Americans responded eagerly to save food for war-torn Europe. The term "Hooverize" meant saving and doing without various foods. Meatless and wheatless days were observed. When the war ended in 1918, he returned to Europe to direct the feeding of millions of people. He had become internationally famous.

Both parties wanted him to become their presidential candidate in 1919. He declared that he was a Republican but would not stand. In 1921, President Harding named him Secretary of Commerce and he continued to hold this office under President Coolidge. He reorganized the department and expanded its work, again showing his skill as an administrator and planner. He became interested in many activities. He held conferences concerning industrial production, labor relations, child welfare, foreign trade and housing. He brought order to radio broadcasting, promoted commercial aviation and helped end the 12-hour workday in the steel industry.

The Election of 1928

In August 1927, Coolidge announced that he did not "choose to run" for re-election and in February 1928 Hoover became a candidate for the Republican presidential nomination. He was nominated on the first ballot and Senator Charles Curtis of Kansas was nominated for Vice-President. The Democrats nominated Alfred E. Smith of New York for President and Senator Joseph T. Robinson of Arkansas for Vice-President.

In his campaign Hoover spoke about increasing prosperity and many people thought that he would help them to become rich. Smith wanted to end Prohibition and many people opposed him because he was a Catholic. In the election Hoover won 40 out of 48 states, receiving 444 electoral votes to only 87 for Smith.

Presidential Election of 1928		
Candidate	Popular Votes	Electoral Votes
Herbert Hoover (Rep.)	21,429,109	444
Alfred E. Smith (Dem.)	15,005,497	87

After the election Hoover made a goodwill tour of South America, which helped to lay the foundation for Franklin D. Roosevelt's "Good Neighbor Policy."

Hoover's Administration 1929 – 1933

Hoover was inaugurated in 1929. When he entered the White House, he and the First Lady had it redecorated with souvenirs and works of art collected during their travels. When he first became President, America was enjoying great prosperity and he expected this to continue. In his campaign he promised to help the farmers who had not shared in the general prosperity. To fulfil his promise, he called a special session of Congress in April 1929. That June, Congress passed the *Agricultural Marketing Act*. This law established the Federal Farm Board, which promoted farm cooperatives and purchased farm surpluses. Hoover also wanted to raise tariffs on farm products to reduce foreign competition. However, the *Smoot-Hawley Bill*, which he signed, went too far and tariffs were raised on many non-farm products. The increased tariffs seriously damaged America's foreign trade and contributed to the depression.

The United States had been building up to a crash for a long time. Other groups besides farmers had not shared in the general prosperity of the 1920's. In the coal-mining and textiles industries, for example, working conditions were poor and wages low. The economy was also weakened by a widespread buying on credit. Thousands of people had borrowed money to pay for stocks and partly as a result stock prices soared to record heights. Then in October 1929 the stock market crashed and the Great Depression began.

At first, few people thought the depression would affect the whole nation. Many thought the stock market would recover in a few weeks or months but by the end of 1929 the crash had caused losses valued at $40 billion. The value of stocks in the New York Stock Exchange had dropped forty percent and entire fortunes had been wiped out. Thousands of workers lost their jobs. Hoover called businessmen, industrialists, and labor leaders together for conferences. All these groups promised to cooperate to keep wages stable and avoid strikes but economic conditions grew worse. By 1932 twelve million Americans were out of work, about one quarter of the nation's workforce. Factories closed and many banks failed. Thousands lost their homes as they could not afford to keep up the mortgage repayments. Many families lived in clumps of shacks that became known as *Hoovervilles*. Other countries were also affected and could not pay their war debts. At Hoover's suggestion, Congress suspended all these payments.

Hoover was reluctant to interfere with the American economy. He called the depression "a temporary halt in the prosperity of a great people." At first, he depended on business companies and industries

216

to solve their own problems. However, in 1932, at Hoover's request, Congress passed several laws enabling the government to help business. One of these laws set up the *Reconstruction Finance Corporation* (RFC) which loaned money to banks and other firms to keep them from going bankrupt. Altogether, the RFC injected two billion dollars into the U.S. economy. Hoover had believed that the states and local communities should provide relief for jobless workers but it became clear that the unemployed needed much more help. Congress authorized the RFC to lend up to 300 million dollars to the states for relief. Other laws provided credit for homeowners and farmers and improved court practices and bankruptcy procedures. Hoover also supported many public works and conservation programs which helped to provide jobs. During his presidency the Bureau of Reclamation started to build the *Boulder (now Hoover) Dam* on the Colorado River. Three million acres were added to national parks and monuments and enlarged national forests. It built more than 800 public buildings and helped states to build 37,000 miles of major highways

Unemployed workers staged hunger marches and demonstrations in several cities. The most famous was an army of First World War veterans called the *Bonus Expeditionary Force*. The bonus law of 1924 had given every veteran a certificate that was payable in 1945 but now the veterans wanted the bonus to be paid immediately and the House of Representatives passed a bill to meet their demand. In June 1932, 15,000 veterans from many states marched on Washington DC to bring pressure on the Senate to pass the bill. However, the Senate defeated the bonus bill. Hoover opposed the bill as he did not believe it was financially sound and sent troops to drive the veterans out of Washington DC.

When it came to foreign policy matters, under Hoover the U.S. moved towards cooperation with other nations on such problems as disarmament. In the London Naval Treaty of 1930, the U.S., Britain and Japan agreed to limit the number of their fighting ships. He proposed a reduction in land weapons but other countries would not cooperate. Hoover also worked to improve relations with Latin America. He withdrew American marines from Nicaragua where they had been helping to maintain peace since 1912. He reached an agreement with Haiti to withdraw American troops in 1934 where they had been since 1915 to end a series of revolutions. In 1931 Japan invaded Manchuria, an action that was condemned by the League of Nations. Hoover declared that the U.S. would not recognize territorial gains made in violation of the Kellogg Peace Pact.

Election of 1932

The Republicans realized that they had little hope of winning the 1932 election. They renominated Hoover and Vice-President Curtis but did not support the candidates vigorously. The Democrats nominated Governor Franklin D. Roosevelt of New York for President with Speaker of the House John N. Garner of Texas for Vice-President. The Democrats attacked Hoover's leadership during the depression and Roosevelt called for a "new deal" for the American people. He promised to balance the budget, bring relief to the unemployed, help farmers, and end Prohibition. In the election, Roosevelt carried 42 out of 48 states and won the electoral vote by 472 to 59.

During Hoover's last four months in office, bank failures and unemployment increased. In February 1933, the *lame duck amendment* – Amendment 20 to the Constitution – provided that a President's term of office should end on January 20th instead of March 4th. This became law in October 1933 and Hoover was the last "lame duck" President.

Later Years

After leaving the Presidency he spent time travelling, speaking and writing. He continued to develop the Hoover Institution on War, Revolution and Peace. He and his wife moved from California to New York. She died there on 7th January 1944. He published several books and organized relief for Finland in their war against Russia in 1940. After World War Two, Truman appointed him Chairman of the Famine Emergency Commission and he went to Europe where he reported on relief needs. In 1947 he became Chairman of the Hoover Commission and his proposals to streamline government and cut costs were adopted. By 1961 he was the director or trustee of nine private educational, scientific, and charitable institutions. He gave all his government income and pensions to charity. In 1962 the Herbert Hoover Library was dedicated in West Branch. He published three volumes of memoirs. He lived longer after leaving the White House than any other former President up to that time. When he died on October 20th 1964 at the age of 90 in New York City and the country mourned him as a truly great American. He was buried near his birthplace in West Branch.

Summary

Herbert Hoover was one of the most talented and accomplished men ever to become President of the United States. However, his reputation and ranking among the Presidents has been badly affected by the Wall Street Crash and subsequent Great Depression. He did great work providing famine relief for in Europe but did not respond as effectively to the suffering of Americans that lost the jobs and homes when the nation's economy slumped.

CHAPTER 32 – FRANKLIN D. ROOSEVELT

32ⁿᵈ President of the United States 1933 – 1945

Born: January 30ᵗʰ 1882, Hyde Park, New York

Married: Anna Eleanor Roosevelt (1884 – 1962), 17ᵗʰ March 1905

Number of Children: Six

Died: 12ᵗʰ April 1945, Warm Springs, Georgia

Final Resting Place: Springwood, Hyde Park, New York

Introduction

Franklin Delano Roosevelt was the longest-serving President in American history spending twelve years in the White House. He was the only President to be elected four times. He led the country through its greatest economic crisis and its worst foreign war. The first half of his Presidency was spent attempting to resolve the issues created by the Great Depression. However, when the Second World War broke out in 1939, this became the President's chief concern for the remainder of his term. America then became the most powerful country on earth with a population of 140 million people. During these crises, he became a popular and unifying leader. His *fireside chats* made him the first President to become part of people's everyday life and he was affectionately known by his initials, *FDR*.

When he became the seventh President to die in office in April 1945, he was mourned all over the world.

Background

Franklin Delano Roosevelt was born on January 30th 1882 on his father's estate in Hyde Park, New York. His ancestor, Klaes Martensen van Roosevelt, was a Dutch landowner who settled in New York (then called New Amsterdam) in the 1640s. Van Roosevelt was also the ancestor of President Theodore Roosevelt. Franklin and Theodore Roosevelt were fifth cousins. Franklin's father was the wealthy vice-president of a railway company and his mother also came from a wealthy family. He was privately tutored until the age of 14 when he entered Groton School in Massachusetts, from which he graduated in 1900. He then enrolled at Harvard University where he majored in history, graduating in 1903. The following year he enrolled at the Columbia University Law School but left before receiving his degree. He spent the next three years working as a clerk for a law firm in New York City but had little enthusiasm for the work. On March 17th 1905 he married his distant cousin, Eleanor Roosevelt. They had six children, two of whom later served in the U.S. House of Representatives.

Entry into Politics

Roosevelt joined the Democratic party because his father had been a Democrat. In 1910, state Democratic leaders invited him to stand for the New York Senate and he succeeded in winning a seat that had been held for many years by the Republicans. In 1912, he supported Woodrow Wilson in the presidential election. Wilson defeated Theodore Roosevelt and in 1913 he appointed Franklin Assistant Secretary of the Navy. In 1914 Roosevelt ran for the U.S. Senate but lost. During World War One he became a national figure whose many naval projects helped America and her allies to achieve victory. In 1920 he was nominated as Democratic candidate for Vice-President as the running mate to Governor James M. Cox of

Ohio as it was felt he would appeal to eastern voters. They campaigned on a platform that called for American membership of the League of Nations but were easily defeated by Senator Warren G. Harding of Ohio and Governor Calvin Coolidge of Massachusetts.

In 1921, tragedy struck when Roosevelt contracted polio and lost the use of his legs. However, regular exercises and swimming helped him to regain partial use of them. He dealt with his disability so successfully that many Americans never realized that he was paralyzed. He refused to retire from politics and in 1924 made a spectacular return when he made a speech at the Democratic national convention nominating Governor Alfred E. Smith of New York for President. In 1928, again with Roosevelt's support, Smith won the Democratic nomination for President and in return supported Roosevelt's bid to run for Governor of New York. Although Smith lost to Herbert Hoover, Roosevelt defeated his opponent, Republican Albert Ottinger, the Attorney General of New York. He was in office when the Wall Street Crash led to the Great Depression and he took steps to bring relief to the unemployed. In 1930 he was re-elected with a state record majority of 725,000 votes.

Election of 1932

Roosevelt was widely respected for his work as Governor and was popular with voters. In 1932 he sought the Democratic nomination for President and in a radio nationwide radio address said that there should be an economic program to address the problems being experienced by the "forgotten man," the average American. At the Democratic national convention, he was nominated on the fourth ballot. When he flew to Chicago to make his acceptance speech, it was the first time a nominee had done so at a national convention. John Nance Garner of Texas, the Speaker of the U.S. House of Representatives, was nominated for Vice-President. The Republicans renominated President Herbert Hoover and Vice-President Charles Curtis. In the campaign, Roosevelt visited 38 states showing that he was physically capable of being President. He promised to provide

222

relief to farmers and the unemployed and to end Prohibition. In the election, he received 472 electoral votes to 59 for Hoover.

Presidential Election of 1932		
Candidate	Popular Votes	Electoral Votes
Franklin D. Roosevelt (Dem.)	22,815,785	472
Herbert Hoover (Rep.)	15,759,266	59
Norman M. Thomas	884,649	0

Shortly after the election, on 15th February 1933, a mentally ill bricklayer, Guiseppe Zangara, tried to assassinate Roosevelt in Miami. The shots missed the President but killed the Mayor of Chicago, Anton J. Cernak. Zangara was executed on 20th March 1933.

Roosevelt's First Administration 1933 – 1937

Roosevelt was inaugurated on 4th March 1933. This was the last time that the inauguration took place in March. Under Amendment 20 to the Constitution, all subsequent inaugurations took place in January. His cabinet included Frances Perkins as Secretary of Labor, the first woman to be named to a Cabinet post.

Roosevelt took office during the midst of the Great Depression. Thousands of unemployed workers stood in bread lines to receive food. Many people had lost their homes and many more were about to lose them because they could no longer afford to pay their mortgages. Just before he took office a financial panic caused more than 5,000 banks out of business as people withdrew their money. On 6th March, Roosevelt declared a "bank holiday." All banks were closed until the Treasury could examine their books. Those found in good financial condition were to be supplied with money by the Treasury. Those banks in doubtful condition were to remain closed until they could be put on a sound basis. As a result, many badly operated banks were permanently closed. The President's action restored confidence and ended the banking crisis. People did not want to withdraw their money from a bank they knew was sound.

Roosevelt called a special session of Congress which came to be known as the "Hundred Days." On 9th March 1933 he began to submit new bills aimed at reform and recovery. Many of these bills were approved with large majorities. Important laws passed in this time included the *Agricultural Adjustment Act (AAA),* the *Tennessee Valley Authority (TVA) Act,* and the *National Industrial Recovery Act (NIRA).* On 12th March, Roosevelt gave the first of his *fireside chats,* addressing the nation by radio to explain what action he had taken and what he was planning in the future. The President called his reform program *The New Deal,* and several agencies were created to provide relief to the unemployed. The *Civil Works Administration (CWA)* supplied funds to states and cities to fund public works such as roads, bridges and schools. The *Civilian Conservation Corps (CCC)* gave training and work to young men that helped with flood control, forestry and soil conservation. Other legislation passed in the first term included the 21st Amendment in December 1933 which ended Prohibition. In 1935 the *Social Security Act* provided unemployment relief and old-age assistance. Legislation was also passed to help the oil and railroad industries.

Roosevelt said that his foreign policy at this time was that of a *good neighbor.* He promoted good relations with the countries of Latin America. In 1934 the government repealed the Platt Amendment of 1901 which gave the U.S. the right to intervene in the affairs of Cuba. American occupation forces were withdrawn from some countries in the Caribbean and long-standing dispute with Mexico concerning oil was settled. Trade agreements were signed with Canada and countries in South America. In 1934, Roosevelt became the first President to visit South America when he arrived in Cartagena, Colombia. He later visited Argentina and Uruguay.

Relations with Russia had been broken off following the Russian Revolution in 1917. In November 1933 the U.S. recognized the Soviet government of Russia leading to the restoration of diplomatic relations.

Election of 1936

Roosevelt was renominated for President by acclamation at the Democratic national convention in Philadelphia in 1936. They also re-nominated Vice-President Garner. The Republicans nominated Governor Alfred M. Landon of Kansas for President and Frank Knox, publisher of the Chicago Daily News, for Vice-President. Roosevelt's campaign stressed the progress that he had made in fighting the depression and returning the country to prosperity. He won the election by a landslide receiving 523 electoral votes to 8 for Landon and carried every state except for Maine and Vermont.

Presidential Election of 1936		
Candidate	Popular Votes	Electoral Votes
Franklin D. Roosevelt (Dem.)	24,751,597	523
Alfred M. Landon (Rep.)	16,697,583	8
William Lemke (Union)	892,267	0

Roosevelt's Second Administration 1937 - 1941

Roosevelt began his second administration in March 1937. A number of distinguished visitors stayed at the White House with the Roosevelts during this time. In 1939, King George VI and Queen Elizabeth became the first British Monarchs to visit the United States and stayed at the White House as guests of the President. In the Second World War, British Prime Minister Sir Winston Churchill frequently stayed there and had a map room on the second floor. Wartime security arrangements included the installation of machine guns on the roof and an air-raid shelter in the basement. During Roosevelt's time in the White House, the West Wing was enlarged and a new Cabinet Room was added. The East Wing was also enlarged and remodeled.

225

Domestic issues had dominated Roosevelt's first term whereas international issues were to dominate the remainder of his presidency. In the 1930's the Japanese pursued a very aggressive policy in China. They invaded the country and created a puppet state called Manchukuo in Northern China. Roosevelt refused to recognize Manchukuo and demanded compensation when the Japanese sank an American gunboat *Panay* in 1937. Roosevelt recognized that Japan was a danger to world peace and tried to strengthen the army and navy.

At this time most Americans wanted to avoid becoming involved in foreign wars. This was reflected in the *Neutrality Acts* passed by Congress between 1935 and 1937. On 1st September 1939, Nazi Germany attacked Poland and the Second World War began. The Nazis subsequently attacked Denmark, Norway, Belgium, Luxembourg, the Netherlands, France and Great Britain. Only Great Britain did not fall to the Germans. Roosevelt wanted to give "all aid short of war" to the countries fighting Germany and the other Axis powers, namely Italy and Japan. In 1939, Congress amended the Neutrality Act so that America could supply arms to the countries fighting the Axis. However, American ships could not be used to carry weapons. In November 1941, the act was further amended so that American ships could carry guns into the war zones.

In 1940, Roosevelt appointed two Republicans to his Cabinet in an attempt to unite the country. Henry L. Stimson became Secretary of War and Frank Knox became Secretary of the Navy.

Election of 1940

In 1940, The Democrats renominated Roosevelt for a third term. Henry A. Wallace, the Secretary of Agriculture, was nominated for Vice-President. The Republicans nominated businessman Wendell L. Wilkie of Indiana for President and Senator Charles L. McNary of Oregon for Vice-President. The American public believed that Roosevelt's experience was needed to deal with the difficult international situation. In the election, he received 449 electoral votes to 82 for Wilkie. Roosevelt carried 38 of the 48 states.

226

Presidential Election of 1940		
Candidate	Popular Votes	Electoral Votes
Franklin D. Roosevelt (Dem.)	27,243,466	449
Wendell L. Wilkie (Rep.)	22,304,755	82

Roosevelt's Third Administration 1941 – 1945

In January 1941, Roosevelt made a speech defining the *four freedoms*: freedom of speech, freedom of worship, freedom from want and freedom from fear. When Roosevelt began his third term, America was already providing massive support to Great Britain, the only country then still fighting against Nazi Germany. In March 1941, Congress passed the *Lend-Lease Act* which authorized the government to supply arms to any country fighting the Axis. It was partly due to American support that Britain did not fall to her enemies. Roosevelt built a very strong relationship with the British Prime Minister, Sir Winston Churchill. In August 1941, the two leaders met on a cruiser anchored off Newfoundland. There they adopted the *Atlantic Charter*, a pledge that they would not seek territorial or other gains, to respect the right of each country to choose its own government, to guarantee freedom of the seas, and to conduct peaceful world trade.

During 1940 and 1941, America's relations with Japan became increasingly tense. The Japanese agreed a mutual aid pact with Nazi Germany and Italy in 1940 and pursued an aggressive policy in Southeast Asia. America responded with trade sanctions. On 7th December 1941, Japanese planes made a surprise attack on the U.S. Pacific Fleet while it was anchored in Pearl Harbor. The next day the President addressed Congress and called the attack "a day that will live in infamy." The U.S. declared war on Japan. Four days later, on December 11th 1941, Germany and Italy declared war on America. The U.S. then declared war on those two countries.

America now faced a large-scale war in both Europe and Asia and a decision had to be made where to strike first. In December 1941, the President's British ally, Sir Winston Churchill, travelled to Washington D.C. Both men agreed that Germany was the most powerful and dangerous enemy and should be defeated first. Roosevelt suggested that the alliance that fought against the axis powers should be called the *United Nations*. This alliance later formed the basis for the peacetime United Nations organization established in 1945.

At first, the war continued to go badly for the United Nations. The Germans had invaded the Soviet Union in 1941 and by 1942 had advanced as far as the river Volga deep inside Russian territory. Their forces had also advanced across North Africa. Meanwhile, the Japanese had made quick advances in Southeast Asia and the Pacific. In November the allies invaded North Africa and began to liberate the territory occupied by the Germans. In May 1943, all German forces in Africa surrendered.

During the war Roosevelt frequently left the United States to confer with the other Allied leaders. He was the first President to leave the country in wartime. In early 1943 he met with Churchill in Casablanca, Morocco, and both men agreed that they would only accept the *unconditional surrender* of the Axis powers. Later that year, Roosevelt travelled to Tehran, Iran, to meet with Churchill and the leader of the Soviet Union, Joseph Stalin. The leaders formed what became known as the *Big Three*. They agreed that the war against Germany should be fought on more than one front. In the summer of 1943, the Allies invaded and liberated Sicily and followed this by an invasion of Italy. As a result, Italy surrendered. In June 1944 the Allies invaded Normandy in France and began the liberation of Western Europe. It was the largest landing operation in history.

The Election of 1944

Roosevelt stood for election for the fourth time because he felt that it would not be in America's best interests to change leader during the middle of a war. He easily won renomination even though many senior Democrats felt that he would not live through a fourth term. They nominated Senator Harry S Truman of Missouri for Vice-President. The Republicans nominated Governor Thomas E. Dewey of New York for President and Governor John W. Bricker of Ohio for Vice-President. They claimed that no man should be President for 16 years. They also claimed that the President was in poor health. However, the Democrats said that America should not "change horses in mid-stream." In the election, Roosevelt won a clear victory. He carried 30 of the 48 states and received 432 electoral votes to 99 for Dewey.

Presidential Election of 1944		
Candidate	Popular Vote	Electoral College
Franklin D. Roosevelt (Dem.)	25,602,505	432
Thomas E. Dewey (Rep.)	22,006,278	99

Roosevelt's Fourth Administration 1944 – 1945

Roosevelt began his fourth term in poor health. In February 1945 he met with Churchill and Stalin in a conference at Yalta, Russia. They agreed their plans to defeat Germany and to create a peacetime *United Nations Organization*. The Russians also agreed to entered the war against Japan after the defeat of Germany. However, after the conference Roosevelt became increasingly concerned about the Russian's attitude and behavior.

In March 1945 the President travelled to Warm Springs, Georgia, where he planned to have a short rest. However, on April 12th he collapsed at his desk and he died a few hours later of a cerebral hemorrhage. He was buried at Hyde Park, New York. Millions of people all over the world mourned his passing.

Summary

Along with George Washington and Abraham Lincoln, Franklin Delano Roosevelt is often regarded as one of the three greatest Presidents in American history. His attempts to resolve the economic crisis were already proving successful when America entered the Second World War. America then played a leading role in helping the United Nations achieve victory against the axis powers. Although Roosevelt passed away before the final victory was won, America had already become the richest and most powerful country in the world. His personal courage at living with the effects of polio remains inspirational.

CHAPTER 33 – HARRY S. TRUMAN

33ʳᵈ President of the United States 1945 – 1953

Born: 8ᵗʰ May 1884, Lamar, Missouri

Married: Bess Wallace (1885 – 1982), 28ᵗʰ June 1919

Number of Children: One

Died: 26ᵗʰ December 1972, Kansas City, Missouri

Final Resting Place: Harry S. Truman Presidential Library and Museum, Independence, Missouri

Introduction

Harry S. Truman was the seventh Vice-President to become President upon the death of the current office-holder. He had been Vice-President for only 83 days when President Franklin D. Roosevelt died on 12ᵗʰ April 1945. At that point he was mainly known for his work serving as the chairman of a wartime Senate committee that saved millions of dollars by investigating military contracts. Shortly after he became President, the allies won the Second World War against Nazi Germany in Europe. However, the war continued against Japan in Asia. Truman then took one of the most difficult decisions ever taken by one man – to authorize that use of the powerful new atomic bomb against targets in mainland Japan to bring the war to an end. However, with peace came further problems. The American economy had to be reorganized from a wartime to a peacetime basis. The *Cold War* began as the Soviet Union supported Communist subversion and aggression in the war-torn countries of Europe and Asia. In 1949, The United States became a founding member of the *North Atlantic Treaty Organization (NATO)*. In 1950, Truman sent U.S. forces to South Korea to prevent that country being over taken by Communist North Korea.

Background

Harry S. Truman was born on May 8th 1894 in Lamar, Missouri, the eldest three children of a farmer. His parents named him Harry in honor of his uncle, Harrison Young. They chose a middle initial "S" in honor his grandfathers, Solomon Young and Anderson Shippe Truman. Harry went to elementary school and high school in Independence, Missouri. He wanted to go to the United States Military Academy at West Point but his vision was not good enough to meet army standards. After graduating from high school in 1901, he went to work as a timekeeper for a construction crew on the Santa Fe Railroad. He later worked in a mailing room of the *Kansas City Star* and as a clerk and a bookkeeper in two Kansas City Banks. He moved to Grandview in 1906, a few years after his grandfather's death, and operated the family farm until 1917.

When United States entered World War 1 in 1917, Truman helped organize a field artillery regiment. He joined Missouri National Guard in 1905 where he became a Lieutenant. He then won promotion to Captain while serving in France with the 35th division where he commanded an artillery battery. He was discharged as a Major in 1919, and later rose to Colonel in the reserves. On June 28th 1919, six weeks after he returned home, he married his childhood sweetheart Elizabeth "Bess" Virginia Wallace, the daughter of an Independence farmer. They had met at Sunday School when he was about 6 years old and she was about five. They had one child, Mary Margaret, who became a concert soprano and had a brief career on stage, television, and radio. Later in 1919, Truman opened a men's clothing store with his friend Eddie Jacobson. However, the business failed during a business depression that began in 1921. Truman then worked about 15 years to repay the store's debts.

Entry into Politics

Discouraged by the failure of the store, Truman decided to seek a career in politics. He received help from friends

who belonged to the political organization of "Big Tom" Prendergast, the Democratic Party boss of Kansas City. Prendergast led one of the largest political machines in the United States. He decided that Truman could win votes because of his farm background, his war record, and his friendly personality. Prendergast supported Truman in his campaign for election as county judge of Jackson County. Truman won the election and served from 1922 to 1924. Truman then attended the Kansas City School of Law during the mid-1920s, but did not obtain a degree. He served a presiding county judge from 1926 to 1934. During this period Truman won a reputation for honesty and efficiency. He supervised projects financed by more than 60 million dollars in tax funds and bond issues.

In 1934, again with the Prendergast's support, Truman was elected to United States Senate. As a member of the Senate Interstate Commerce Committee, Truman directed an investigation of railroad finances. He won re-election in 1940 even though Prendergast had gone to prison for fraud and tax evasion. The outbreak of World War Two in Europe led a large increase in the nation's defense spending. Truman urged the Senate to set up a committee to investigate waste and corruption in military expenditure. The Senate set up such a committee in 1941 and Truman was named Chairman. The group soon became known as the Truman Committee and their investigation of waste and inefficiency in war production may have saved the government a billion dollars.

In 1944 many senior Democrats believed that President Roosevelt would not live through a fourth term in the White House and that that the man they chose for Vice-President would probably succeed to the presidency. Truman's reputation and strong voting record helped him to emerge as a compromise candidate in a tight contest for the nomination and he was selected on the 2nd ballot. In that November's presidential election, Roosevelt and Truman comfortably defeated their Republican opponents. During the 83 days that Truman spent as Vice-President, his most important act was to break a Senate tie by voting to continue the lend-lease program.

Truman's First Administration 1945 to 1949

Late in the afternoon of April 12th 1945 Truman was suddenly summoned to the White House where Eleanor Roosevelt informed him that the President had died. He took the oath of office at 7.09pm that evening. When Truman became President, the allies were close to achieving victory in Europe and Germany surrendered on 7th May 1945. The following day, which also was the President's 61st birthday, was proclaimed as *VE Day (Victory in Europe Day)*. In July, Truman travelled to Potsdam in Germany to meet with the Prime Minister of Great Britain, Sir Winston Churchill, and the Premiere of the Soviet Union, Joseph Stalin. While he was in Potsdam, Truman then received secret word that allied scientists had successfully tested an atomic bomb for the first time. He then had a very difficult decision to make. The bomb could be used to bring the war to a close but would kill thousands of people. Alternatively, if the war continued and allied forces had to invade Japan then even more people may die. Truman decided that using the bomb would save more lives than it would take and so authorized its use against targets in Japan. On 6th August 1945, the first atomic bomb was dropped on the Japanese city of *Hiroshima*. Three days later a second atomic bomb was dropped on the city of *Nagasaki*. The following day, Japan opened peace negotiations and the war came to an end on the 14th August.

Truman believed that President Roosevelt's *New Deal* policies had worked well for America. He therefore proposed a similar program called the *Fair Deal* which would expand social security, boost the minimum wage, improve the rights of minorities, and increase investment in scientific research and energy projects. However, in 1946 the Republicans gained control of Congress and many of Turman's proposals were then blocked. A commission was established to study ways of improving government efficiency and Truman named former President Herbert Hoover to head it. However, in 1947, Congress passed the *Labor Management Relations Act*, also known as the *Taft-Hartley Act*, over the President's veto. Congress did approve Trumans plan to unify the armed forces under a single Secretary of Defense.

Once the Second World War had ended, the Soviet Union began to support Communist subversion and aggression in the war-torn countries of Europe and Asia. The *Cold War* developed between the Soviet Union and the democracies of the West as Communists gained control over one nation after another in Eastern Europe. On 12th March 1947, Truman announced what became known as the *Truman Doctrine* which guaranteed American aid to any free nation resisting Communist sabotage or aggression. The Truman Doctrine was then extended by the *Marshall Plan* which was outlined by the Secretary of State, George C. Marshall, in 1947. Under this plan, the war-damaged nations of Europe received grants from the United States which aided their economic recovery. The plan was rejected by the Communist nations in Eastern Europe but sixteen other countries accepted it and received grants totaling thirteen billion dollars. By 1950, the economies of the countries that had received Marshall Aid had expanded beyond their pre-war levels. In 1948, the Soviet Union blockaded the allied zones of occupation in West Berlin in an attempt to take control of the whole city. However, the United States and Britain launched a massive airlift to keep their zones supplied with food and energy and in 1949 the Soviet Union lifted the blockade.

Election of 1948

Truman was nominated on the first ballot at the Democratic Party National Convention and he selected Senator Alben W. Barkley of Kentucky for Vice-President. The Republicans again nominated Dewey for President and chose governor Earl Warren of California as his running mate. Two other parties also fielded candidates in the election. The Progressive party was formed from a group of liberal democrats and nominated former Vice-President Wallace for President. The Dixiecrat party was formed from Southern democrats who opposed a strong civil rights program and nominated Governor Strom Thurmond of South Carolina for President. The election of 1948 seemed certain to bring victory to the Republicans given that they faced a sharply divided Democratic party. Every public opinion poll predicted that Dewey would win by a landslide. However, Truman fought an energetic campaign travelling 31,000 miles and making 350 speeches. He attacked the Republican Congress for doing "nothing" and calling it "the worst in my memory." In the election, Truman achieved one of the greatest upsets in political history carrying twenty-eight states to sixteen for Dewey and four for Thurmond.

Presidential Election of 1948		
Candidate	Popular Vote	Electoral College
Harry S Truman (Dem.)	24,105,695	303
Dewey (Rep.)	21,969,170	189
Strom Thurmond (Dixie.)	1,169,021	39
Wallace (Pro.)	1,156,103	0

Truman's Second Administration 1949 – 1953

The structural part of the White House had become dangerously weak and engineers had to make extensive repairs. The rebuilding began late in 1948 and the Truman moved to Blair House. They lived there until March 1952. On November the 1st 1950, two Puerto Rico nationalists tried to invade Blair house and assassinate the President. They killed one secret service guard and wounded another. One of the gunners was killed and the other captured. Truman commented that "The president has to expect those things." He kept all his appointments that day and took his usual walk the following morning

In the Spring of 1949 the United States, Canada, Great Britain, France and eight other nations signed the North Atlantic Treaty, which formed a military alliance called *NATO*. They agreed that an attack on one member would be considered as an attack on all the other members. Other countries later joined NATO. General Dwight D. Eisenhower was appointed the first Supreme Commander of NATO and the armed forces of western Europe were grouped under his command. In 1951, Truman asked Congress to set up a new foreign aid program for countries threatened by Communism in Southeast Asia. Congress then established the *Mutual Security Administration* to provide aid that strengthened the military defenses in many countries.

On 25th June 1950, Communist forces from North Korea invaded South Korea and began to advance quickly. Truman decided to intervene without waiting for approval from the United Nations and sent American ships and planes that helped to save the independence of South Korea. On 27th June the U.N. authorized other countries to send forces to help join the U.S. and South Korean units when North Korea ignored a demand to withdraw. On 30th June Truman ordered ground forces to South Korea. General Douglas MacArthur took command of all UN forces in Korea and his troops brought most of Korea under UN control by October 1950. However, later that month troops from Communist China entered the war on the side of the North and began to recover lost ground. MacArthur wanted to attack Chinese Communist bases in Manchuria but Truman believed that the fighting must be confined to Korea and not allowed to spread into a possible global war. In April 1951 Truman dismissed MacArthur after the General made several public statements criticizing this policy. A peace settlement that ended the war in Korea was not concluded until after Truman had left office.

A Democratic-controlled Congress had been elected in 1948 but Truman soon found it almost as uncooperative in domestic affairs as the preceding Republican-controlled Congress had been. Most of the President's domestic proposals were defeated by a combination of Southern Democrats and conservative Republicans. Truman also became concerned by possible Communist infiltration into the government and set up a Federal Board to investigate the loyalty of government employees. The trials of Alger Hiss and Ethel and Julius Rosenberg revealed that spies had stolen secret information and given it to Russian agents.

On 29th March 1952, Truman announced that he would not seek re-election having already served nearly two terms. The Democrats then nominated Governor Adlai E. Stephenson of Illinois for President and Truman campaigned on his behalf. However, in November 1952 Stephenson lost the presidential election to Dwight D. Eisenhower

Later Years

Truman left office on 20th January 1953 and retired to his home in Independence. There he continued his active interest in politics and in the Democratic Party. He published the two volumes of his memoirs, *Years of Decisions* in 1955 and *Years of Trial and Hope* in 1956. Late in 1972, Truman became gravely ill and entered hospital on 5th December suffering from severe lung congestion. He died there on 26th December 1972 and was buried in the courtyard of the Harry S. Truman Library in Independence, Missouri.

Summary

Sir Winston Churchill once described Harry Truman as the man that "saved Western civilization." During the eight vital years of his presidency, America had led the United Nations to victory in the Second World and then began the long defense of the world's democratic nations in the Cold War. Stability had been brought to Western Europe by the Truman Doctrine, the creation of NATO and the Marshall Plan. An honest and straightforward man, Truman's brave and decisive foreign policy earns him a high ranking among the Presidents even though his success in domestic matters was rather   limited.

CHAPTER 34 – DWIGHT D. EISENHOWER

34ᵗʰ President of the United States 1953 – 1961

Born: 14ᵗʰ October 1890, Denison, Texas

Married: Mary "Mamie" Doud (1896 – 1979), 1ˢᵗ July 1916

Number of Children: Two

Died: 28ᵗʰ March 1969, Washington D.C.

Final Resting Place: Dwight D. Eisenhower Presidential Library Museum and Boyhood Home, Abilene, Kansas

Introduction

Dwight D. Eisenhower was a hero of the Second World War that became the 34ᵗʰ President of the United States in 1953. He was the first Republican President for nearly twenty years. At that time America was a wealthy superpower with a population of more than 180 million people. America led the free western world while the Communist Eastern Bloc was dominated by a rival superpower, the Soviet Union. Americans were very concerned by the possibility of nuclear war and of Communist infiltration in the United States. During his administration, Eisenhower worked hard to achieve world peace. The war in Korea was brought to a close and America supported the North Atlantic Treaty Organization (NATO) and the

South East Asia Treaty Organization (SEATO). In 1958, the National Aeronautics and Space Administration (NASA) was set up to respond to the early Soviet lead in the Space Race. At home, Americans enjoyed great prosperity and the President supported *Civil Rights* for African-Americans.

Background

The third of seven sons, Dwight David Eisenhower was born in Denison, Texas, on October 14th 1890. His German and Swiss ancestors had migrated to America in the 1730's to seek religious freedom. When he was two years old the family moved to Abilene, Kansas, where his father worked as a mechanic in a creamery. After he left High School, Eisenhower entered West Point in June 1911. He graduated 61st in a class of 164 in 1915 and was posted as a Second Lieutenant to Fort Sam Houston, near San Antonio, Texas. On July 1st 1916 he married Mary "Mamie" Dowd, the daughter of a wealthy meat-packer and was promoted to First Lieutenant on his wedding day. They later had two sons. In 1968 their grandson married Julie Nixon, the younger daughter of Richard Nixon.

Eisenhower trained tank battalions during and after the First World War. In 1918 he won the Distinguished Service Medal for his work as commander of the tank training center at Camp Colt, in Gettysburg, Pennsylvania. From 1922 to 1924 he served as an executive director of Camp Gaillard in the Panama Canal Zone and then attended the Command and General Staff School in Fort Leavenworth, Kansas. In 1926 he graduated first from a class of 275. Two years later he graduated from Army War College in Washington D.C. He then held various posts until 1933 when he was appointed as an aide to Douglas MacArthur, then Chief of Staff of the U.S. Army. When MacArthur went to the Philippines in 1935, Eisenhower accompanied him as his assistant and established the Philippine Air Force and Philippine Military Academy.

When the Second World War began, he was a little-known Lieutenant Colonel based near San Francisco. In March 1941 he became a full Colonel and three months later was made Chief of

Staff of the Third Army with a headquarters in San Antonio, Texas. In September 1941 he was promoted to Brigadier General. On 12th December 1941, five days after Pearl Harbor, Marshall appointed Eisenhower to the army's War Plans Division. In March 1942 he was promoted to Major-General and became head of the Operations Division of the War Department. There he drew up plans to unify all American forces in Europe under one commander. Three days after submitting his plan Eisenhower was named Commanding General of American forces in Europe.

In June 1942, Eisenhower set up his headquarters in London and began planning the transfer of two million American troops to Europe. In July, he was promoted to Lieutenant General. That summer he planned the first major Allied offensive, *Operation Torch*. The plan was to land in French North Africa and drive out German and Italian forces. He was named commander of the Allied invasion forces and on 8th November 1942 the allies landed in Algeria and Morocco. By May 1943 they had succeeded in liberating North Africa. In February 1943, he became a full general and turned his attention to planning the allied invasion of Sicily and Italy. In August 1943, the allies occupied Sicily and in September they invaded Italy. Rome was captured on 4th June 1944.

Eisenhower then joined the planning of Operation Overlord, a cross-channel invasion of Normandy in France. He was named as the Supreme Commander of the Allied Expeditionary Force. D-Day originally set for Monday the 5th of June. However, it was postponed by poor weather for 24 hours. Then at 6:30am on 6th June 1944, the first troops landed and by nightfall the allies had established a firm bridgehead in France. The allied armies then advanced across Western Europe and forced the surrender of Nazi Germany on 7th May 1945.

Eisenhower was promoted to General of the Army in December 1944 and then in November 1945 he replaced General Marshall as the Army Chief of Staff. In 1948 he retired from active duty and became the president of Colombia University. He also wrote his memoirs, *Crusade in Europe*. In December 1950, NATO appointed him as the Supreme Commander in Europe and he tried to unify many armies into one force in order "to preserve the peace and not to wage war."

Entry into Politics

After his successful military career, both parties sought to make Eisenhower a presidential candidate. He selected the Republicans and in June 1952 left the army without pay or benefits to seek the presidential nomination. The Republican national convention nominated him for President on first ballot with Senator Richard M. Nixon of California nominated as Vice-President. The Democrats nominated Governor Adlai E. Stephenson of Illinois for President and Senator John J. Sparkman of Arkansas as Vice-President. Eisenhower called his campaign a crusade "to clean up the mess in Washington" and in the election he received more votes than any previous candidate. Eisenhower won over 33 million votes to 27 million votes for Stephenson. In the electoral college Eisenhower received 442 votes to 89 for Stephenson.

Presidential Election of 1952		
Candidate	Popular Vote	Electoral Votes
Dwight D. Eisenhower (Rep.)	33,778,963	442
Adlai E. Stevenson (Dem.)	27,314,992	89

Eisenhower's First Administration 1953 – 1957

Once he took office, Eisenhower set up a staff system based on that of the army. Eisenhower made each member of the Cabinet responsible for an area of government affairs and appointed Sherman Adams as *chief of staff* to oversee them. Eisenhower called his legislative program *Modern Republicanism*. Several weeks after he took office, the Department of Health, Education and Welfare was created. His administration strengthened welfare programs and gave more authority to the states. The tax system was given a thorough overhaul and the social security system was broadened. The minimum wage was increased to one dollar per hour. In 1954, urged by Eisenhower, Congress passed a series of internal security laws which limited the legal rights of the Communist Party. Congress also investigated Communist infiltration in the government.

Eisenhower used his first term of office to promote world peace. On 27th July 1953, a truce was signed to end the war in Korea. In December 1953, the President proposed that the nations of the world pool their knowledge and materials to use atomic power for peaceful purposes. This led to the creation of the *International Atomic Energy Agency (IAEA)* in 1957 when 62 countries ratified its charter. Eisenhower also took the lead in creating the *Southeast Asia Treaty Organization (SEATO)* in 1954 to resist Communist aggression in Southeast Asia. However, it proved ineffective and was dissolved in 1977. In July 1955, the leaders of Great Britain, France, Russia and the United States met at a summit in Geneva. Eisenhower proposed an *open skies* plan to allow an inspection of each other's military bases. The Russians rejected this plan along with other Western proposals.

Eisenhower suffered several illnesses during his first term of office. In September 1955 he suffered a heart attack while on vacation in Denver. He did not return to his desk in Washington until December. In 1956 a disorder of the small intestine led to an emergency operation. However, he recovered rapidly. Then on 25th November 1957 he suffered a mild stroke but again quickly regained full health.

Election of 1956

Eisenhower was renominated by acclamation at the Republican national convention in 1956. Vice-President Nixon was also re-nominated for Vice-President. The Democrats again nominated Adlai E. Stevenson for President with Senator Estes Kefauver of Texas as his running mate. The President's health became an issue during the election campaign. Stevenson called him a "part time President" and raised doubts that Eisenhower would survive a second term. Eisenhower responded by ignoring his health and pointing out the peace and prosperity that America now enjoyed under his leadership. In the election, Eisenhower and Nixon won by an even greater landslide than in 1952. They received 457 votes in the electoral college to 73 for Stevenson. However, the Democrats won majorities in both houses of Congress.

Presidential Election of 1956		
Candidate	Popular Votes	Electoral Votes
Dwight D. Eisenhower (Rep.)	35,581,003	457
Adlai E. Stevenson (Dem.)	25,738,765	73

Eisenhower's Second Administration 1957 – 1961

On 19th June 1955, Eisenhower held the first ever televised presidential news conference. In his second term he had to deal with America's growing domestic problems. In September 1957, he sent troops to Little Rock, Arkansas, to enforce school integration after Governor Orval E. Faubus had defied a 1954 Supreme Court order to end the segregation of black and white pupils in public schools. On 4th October 1957, the Soviet Union took the lead in the *Space Race* when it launched the first artificial satellite, *Sputnik*. They then launched a second satellite, *Sputnik II*, on 3rd November. The United States sent up its first satellite, *Explorer 1*, on 31st January 1958. The Soviet lead in space technology concerned the public and in July 1958 Congress set up the *National Aeronautics and Space Administration (NASA)* to coordinate the American space exploration program. Also in 1958, Sherman Adams had to resign after a congressional investigation revealed that he had accepted bribes from a Boston businessman while serving as an assistant to the President. In 1957 the economy entered a recession but then began to recover in 1958. In the congressional elections of 1958, the Democrats retained control of both houses and so Eisenhower continued to find it difficult to win support for much of his program.

244

Foreign affairs were a source of great concern during his second term. A series of crises in the Middle East led the President to propose what became known as the *Eisenhower Doctrine*. This doctrine pledged U.S. help to any nation in the Middle East that was fighting against Communist aggression. In July 1958, the doctrine was used to send troops to Lebanon to support the government there against rebel forces. In August 1958, China's communists began shelling the Nationalist-held Quemoy Islands. The President ordered the U.S. Seventh Fleet to help convoy Nationalist supplies from Taiwan to the islands. The Communist attacks died down in October 1958. In September 1959, the Soviet Premier Nikita S. Khrushchev visited the United States. A return visit was planned for Eisenhower to attend a second summit conference. However, in May 1960 the Russians shot down an American U2 spy plane over Soviet territory. Eisenhower admitted the flights had been going on for four years and Khrushchev angrily withdrew his invitation for the President's visit. In 1959, Fidel Castro became the premier of Cuba. In 1960 he charged that the U.S. embassy in Havana was the center of "counter-revolutionary activities" and seized all the property in Cuba that belonged to American companies. On January 3rd 1961, Eisenhower broke off diplomatic relations with Cuba. One achievement in foreign relations, however, was the completion of an agreement with Canada in 1959 to create the *St. Lawrence Seaway* which opened the interior of North America to ocean-going ships.

Later Years

Eisenhower was the first president affected by 22nd Amendment to the Constitution which limited a President to two full terms. He left office in January 1961 and retired to his farm in Gettysburg. His health gradually declined and in 1965 he suffered two mild heart attacks. In 1968 he suffered another heart attack and was admitted to hospital. There he suffered three more heart attacks and undertook surgery on his intestines. He then developed pneumonia and died of heart failure on 28th March 1969. He was buried at the Dwight D. Eisenhower Presidential Library Museum and Boyhood Home, Abilene, Kansas.

Summary

Dwight D. Eisenhower was a hero of the Second World War who became the first Republican President for nearly twenty years. During his time in office, he had to recover from several major illnesses but was still an effective leader that made difficult decisions. At home he presided over a great period of prosperity and promoted equal rights for African-Americans. Overseas he strove for world peace and challenged the Soviet lead in the Space Race. He was a friendly, likeable man that was popular all over the world. For these reasons he ranks highly among the Presidents.

CHAPTER 35 – JOHN F. KENNEDY

35th President of the USA 1961 – 1963

Born: 29th May 1917, Brookline, Massachusetts

Married: Jacqueline Lee Bouvier (1929 – 1994), 12th September 1953

Number of Children: Four

Died: 22nd November 1963, Dallas, Texas

Final Resting Place: Arlington National Cemetery, Washington D.C.

Introduction

John Fitzgerald Kennedy was the youngest man ever elected President. He claimed to be the first leader of a new generation of Americans and said that he would lead the country towards *New Frontiers*. He won the 1960 presidential election after a series of close television debates with his Republican opponent, Richard Nixon. As President, he committed the country to landing a man on the moon before the end of the decade. In 1962, risking a war, he forced the Soviet Union to withdraw their nuclear missiles from Cuba. However, after two years and ten months in office, he was shot while visiting Dallas and died in hospital. His death was mourned around the world and his funeral was attended by world leaders and members of royalty. He was the President at the time of great prosperity and optimism. America then had more than 190 million people and launched her first astronauts into space in 1961.

Background

John Fitzgerald Kennedy was born on May 29th 1917 in Brookline, Massachusetts, the second of nine children of a self-made millionaire who had served as Chairman of the Securities and Exchange Commission and as US ambassador to Great Britain. His great-grandfather had moved to Boston from Ireland and his grandfather had served in the U.S. House of Representatives. Two of his brothers, Robert and Edward (Ted), later served in the U.S. Senate.

Kennedy grew up in smart neighborhoods in Brookline and New York City, and attended elementary schools in Brookline and Riverdale. At the age of 13 he was sent to Canterbury School in New Milford, Connecticut, and then transferred to the Choate Academy in Wallingford, Connecticut, the following year.

After graduating in 1935, he briefly attended Princeton University before entering Harvard in 1936 where he majored in government and international relations. He spent the spent the spring and summer in Europe where he travelled from country-to-country interviewing politicians and statesmen just before the outbreak of the Second World War in September 1939.

Back at Harvard he wrote his senior thesis explaining why Britain had not been ready for war and this was later published as a best-selling book called "Why England Slept." In 1940 he graduated cum laude and then enrolled in Stanford University graduate business school. However, he dropped out six months later and spent time travelling around South America.

Kennedy then enlisted as a seaman in the U.S. Navy and after the Japanese attack on Pearl Harbor in 1941 was assigned to a patrol torpedo (PT) boat squadron. On 2nd August 1943, while patrolling off the Soloman islands, his craft was cut in two by a Japanese destroyer. Two men were killed and, after spending the night clinging to wreckage, he helped the remaining ten survivors to reach a nearby island. He spent five hours towing a wounded crewman ashore even though he had an injured back. The men were then rescued on 7th August. Kennedy later received the Navy and Marine Corps Medal for his heroism and leadership, and the Purple Heart for being wounded in combat.

Entry into Politics

The Kennedy family thought that his older brother, Jack, would be the brother that entered politics while John became a writer or a teacher. However, in 1944 Jack was killed was killed in action while serving in England.

It was then that John decided to enter politics and in 1946 he began his political career when he successfully ran for the U.S. House of Representatives. There he supported President Harry S. Truman's social welfare programs. He was re-elected in 1948 and 1950. In 1952 he ran for the U.S. Senate and beat the experienced Republican, Henry Cabot Lodge Jr. On September 12th 1953, he married Jacqueline "Jackie" Lee Bouvier, the daughter of a wealthy Wall Street broker. They later had three children but the youngest was born prematurely and died when two days old.

During his time in the Senate, Kennedy sat on the Senate Labor Committee and the Government Operations Committee. He worked for moderate legislation to end alleged corruption in labor unions. In 1956, Kennedy attempted to win the Democratic nomination for Vice-President. However, he lost to Senator Estes Kefauver of Tennessee.

While serving in the Senate, Kennedy wrote a book called "Profiles in Courage," about some of the brave deeds performed by U.S. Senators. In 1957, he received the Pulitzer Prize for Biography for this book.

The Election of 1960

Kennedy started to prepare his candidacy for the presidency in 1956. Some Democrats saw his youth, family wealth and relative inexperience in international affairs as drawbacks. He was also a

Roman Catholic. Kennedy thought that the key to the nomination was to win as many state primary elections as he could as this would prove he could win the presidency. He entered and won primaries in seven states. At the Democratic national convention in Los Angeles, Kennedy won the nomination on the first ballot. At his request, Senator Lyndon B. Johnson of Texas was nominated for Vice-President.

The Republicans nominated Vice-President Richard M. Nixon for President and Henry Cabot Lodge, Jr., then U.S. delegate to the UN, as his running mate. The campaign was close and hard-fought but his strong performances in the four televised debates helped Kennedy to gain an advantage. This was the first time that two presidential candidates had argued the campaign issues face-to-face and voters were impressed by Kennedy's mature poise and clear answers. While Nixon ran chiefly on the record of the Eisenhower administration, Kennedy charged that under the Republicans the U.S. had lost ground to Russia in the Cold War. He promised to lead Americans towards a *new frontier*.

In the election, Kennedy received just 120,000 more popular votes than Nixon. However, he won a clear majority in the electoral college, receiving 303 votes to 219 for Nixon. Senator Harry F. Byrd of Virginia received 15 electoral votes.

Presidential Election of 1960		
Candidate	Popular Votes	Electoral Votes
John F. Kennedy (Dem.)	34,226,731	303
Richard M. Nixon (Rep)	34,108,157	219
Harry F. Byrd (Independent)	*	15

Kennedy's Administration 1961 – 1963

Kennedy was inaugurated as President in January 1961. After entering the White House, he began his domestic program known as

The New Frontier. In March 1961 he created the *Peace Corps* which sent thousands of Americans abroad to help people in developing nations to raise their standard of living. In April 1961, Congress approved his plan to provide aid to economically depressed areas. In May 1961, they approved an increase in the hourly wage from $1 to $1.25. In September 1962, Congress passed the President's *Trade Expansion Act* which gave Kennedy the power to cut tariffs so the U.S. could trade freely with the European Common Market.

He further tried to help business by increasing tax benefits for companies investing in new equipment and by introducing a tax cut to boost consumer spending. However, Congress also defeated Kennedy's attempts to create a new Cabinet-level Department of Urban Affairs and to introduce medical care for the aged.

The major domestic issue during the Kennedy Administration concerned equal rights for African-Americans. In 1961, a group of *freedom riders* entered Montgomery, Alabama, by bus to test the local segregation laws. When violence erupted, the Attorney General, Robert F. Kennedy, sent U.S. marshals to the city to restore order. In 1962, the President sent 3,000 troops to Oxford, Mississippi, to quell the rioting that took place when James Meredith became the first African-American to enroll at the University of Mississippi. In 1963, racial protests and demonstrations took place all over the United States and the President had to use the Alabama National Guard to enforce integration in that state's schools and universities. In August 1963, 200,000 people staged a *Freedom March* in Washington D.C. to demonstrate their demands for equal rights for African-Americans. Kennedy requested sweeping *civil rights* legislation to desegregate schools and give African-Americans access to restaurants and hotels.

In the midterm elections, the Democrats gained four seats in the Senate and only lost two seats in the House. This was only the third time that century that the party in power increased its representation in Congress in a mid-term election.

The President faced several challenges in foreign affairs. On 17th April 1961, Cuban rebels landed in the Bay of Pigs to overthrow

Fidel Castro, the Communist-supported dictator. The invasion ended in disaster and, as it had been planned by the United States, Kennedy accepted the blame. In October 1962, another Cuban crisis erupted when the U.S. found that the Russians had placed nuclear missiles on the island capable of hitting American cities. Kennedy ordered the U.S. Navy to *quarantine* (blockade) Cuba. The Navy was ordered to turn back all ships delivering Russian missiles to Cuba. For a tense week, the world waited on the brink of war. Russian Premier Nikita S. Khrushchev then ordered all the Soviet offensive missiles to be removed and Kennedy lifted the quarantine.

Another challenge came in Berlin. At the end of the Second World War the city had been divided into American, British, French and Russian zones of occupation. The Russian zone became East Berlin while the other zones formed West Berlin, which was isolated completely within Russian-held Communist East Germany. In 1961, Russia threatened to hand control over the western nation's air and land supply routes to West Berlin over to East Germany in an effort to drive them out. However, the western nations said that they would oppose any threat to the freedom of West Berlin. In August 1961 the crisis in Berlin deepened when East Germany's Communist government built a wall between East and West Berlin to prevent people fleeing to the West. Kennedy increased America's military strength and made a visit to West Berlin in the summer 1963 to reassure them of America's commitment to their freedom.

Another trouble spot was Southeast Asia. Kennedy sent 17,000 U.S. military advisers to South Vietnam, Thailand and Laos in response to a Communist threat.

In September 1961, the Russians resumed testing nuclear weapons in defiance of a ban that had lasted three years. Shortly afterwards, the Americans also resumed testing. However, in July 1963, Russia, the United States and Great Britain signed a treaty banning atomic testing in the atmosphere, outer space and under water. Testing underground was still permitted. The treaty was also signed by many countries that did not have nuclear weapons and was approved by the Senate.

Assassination

In November 1963 Kennedy travelled to Dallas with his wife, the Vice-President and Mrs. Johnson. His aim was to heal a split in the Texas Democratic party before the 1964 presidential campaign in which Kennedy planned to run for a second term. The party left Washington D.C. on 21st November and travelled to San Antonio, Houston and Fort Worth. The following morning, they arrived in Dallas after a short flight from Fort Worth. A motorcade took them through the streets of the city from the airport to the Dallas Trade Mart where they were scheduled to have lunch. Kennedy sat in the back seat of an open-air limousine with his wife while the Governor of Texas, John B. Connally, sat with his wife in a seat in front of the President. Secret Service agents followed in the car behind, with Mr. and Mrs. Johnson in a third car behind that. They were greeted by cheering crowds of thousands of people that lined the streets and waved from the sidewalks. As the car made its way through Dealey Plaza, three shots rang out from the sixth floor of the Texas Schoolbook Depository. Bullets struck the President in the head and neck and one injured Governor Connally in the back. The limousine raced to Parklands Hospital but Kennedy died at 1pm without regaining consciousness. Governor Connally later made a full recovery. The party returned to Washington that afternoon and Johnson took the oath of office on Air Force One.

Witnesses reported hearing the shots being fired from the Texas School Book Depository but when police entered the building, they could not find the gunman. They began to look for an employee called Lee Harvey Oswald who was said to have left the building just after the shooting. At 1.15pm on 22nd November he is said to have shot a Dallas policeman, J.D.Tippit, while resisting arrest. A short time later he was arrested in a theatre and charged with the murders of Kennedy and Tippit. He was a former U.S. Marine that had married a Russian wife and had once tried to become a citizen of the Soviet Union. He was a committed Communist and supported Fidel Castro's regime in Cuba. Police found a rifle in the School Book Depository with his palm prints on it. There was evidence that he had purchased it from a mail order firm. After two days of questioning, police were in the process of moving him from the city jail to the county jail when a Dallas nightclub owner, Jack Ruby (formerly Rubinstein) stepped out of the crowd and shot Oswald in front of live television news cameras. Oswald was rushed to Parklands Hospital where he died at 1.07pm, 48 hours after the President's death. The Warren Commission, headed by Chief Justice Earl Warren, investigated the assassination and in 1964 reported that Oswald had acted alone. However, many Americans still believe that they have not been told the full truth about Kennedy's murder.

Kennedy's funeral took place in Washington on 25h November and was attended by representatives from over 90 countries. He was buried in Arlington National Cemetery and Mrs. Kennedy lighted an eternal flame to burn over his grave.

Summary

John F. Kennedy was the youngest man to be elected President and the youngest to die in office. He was also noteworthy for being the first President to be a Roman Catholic. As the first President to be born in the twentieth century, he claimed to be leader of a "new generation." During his short time in office, he promoted improved civil rights for African-Americans and presided over increased prosperity at home. In 1962, he bravely confronted the Soviet Union and forced the withdrawal of their nuclear missiles from Cuba. The Test Ban Treaty began a period of "thaw" in the Cold War. For all these reasons, Kennedy is often ranked in the top ten Presidents.

CHAPTER 36 – LYNDON BAINES JOHNSON

36ᵗʰ President of the United States 1963 – 1969

Born: 27ᵗʰ August 1908, Stonewall, Texas

Married: Lady Bird Taylor (1912 – 2007), 17ᵗʰ November 1934

Number of Children: Two

Died: 22ⁿᵈ January 1973, Stonewall, Texas

Final Resting Place: Johnson Family Cemetery, Stonewall, Texas

Introduction

Lyndon Baines Johnson became the 36ᵗʰ President of the United States following the murder of John F. Kennedy. He led the country through troubled times. America became involved in a full-scale war in Vietnam and the country was rocked by violent protest both against the war and the draft. There was also widespread unrest and rioting as African-Americans sought to enjoy equal rights and opportunities with Americans of European descent. The Civil Rights leader, Martin Luther King, was murdered in 1968 as was the Democratic politician, Robert Kennedy, while he campaigned for the presidential nomination. In March 1968, Johnson shocked the country by declining to run for a second term. He hoped that this would help to restore unity to the nation. At this time, America was the richest and most powerful country in the world with a population exceeding two hundred million people. The wealth and strength of the United States was demonstrated when the country took the lead in the Space Race and American astronauts were the first to fly around the moon in December 1968.

Background

Lyndon Baines Johnson was born on 27th August 1908 in a farmhouse near Stonewall, Texas. He was the eldest of five children of a farmer and schoolteacher, who had served five terms in the Texas House of Representatives. In 1930 he graduated from Southwest Texas State Teachers College and then taught public speaking and debate in in Sam Houston High School in Houston. On 17th November 1934 he married Claudia Alta (Lady Bird) Taylor and they later had two daughters.

Entry into Politics

Johnson entered politics in 1931 when he campaigned for Democrat Richard M. Kleberg who was attempting to enter the House of Representatives. In August 1935, President Franklin D. Roosevelt appointed Johnson the Texas state administrator of the National Youth Organization (NYA). In 1937 he ran for Congress and won election to the U.S. House of Representatives with twice as many votes as his nearest opponent. He was re-elected in 1938 and 1940. In 1941, he ran for a vacant seat in the U.S. Senate but was narrowly defeated by Governor W. Lee O'Daniel. When the United States entered World War Two in December 1941, he was the first Congressman to go into uniform and joined as a Lieutenant Commander in the U.S. Navy. He was a awarded a Silver Star for gallantry by General Douglas MacArthur. He was re-elected to the House in 1942 and was ordered to return to Washington.

In 1948, after the war, Johnson again ran for the U.S. Senate and this time was successful. In 1951, the Democratic Senators elected Johnson as their whip (assistant leader) and he tried to ensure that party members were present when a bill came up for a vote. He campaigned for Governor Adlai E. Stevenson in the election of 1952 but the Republicans won both the presidency and the Senate.

Johnson was then elected minority leader by Democrats in the Senate. At the age of 44 he was the youngest man ever chosen as Senate leader by either party. In 1954, he was re-elected and the Democrats won control of both houses of Congress. In January 1955, he became majority leader in the Senate and ensured the smooth running of the legislative process. In 1957, he sponsored the first civil rights bill in 80 years. He also took an interest in space exploration and established and chaired the Senate Aeronautical and Space Committee. He sponsored the law that led to the creation of the *National Aeronautics and Space Administration (NASA)* in 1958.

In 1960 Johnson ran for the Democratic presidential nomination but he was defeated on the first ballot by Senator John F. Kennedy. With 761 votes required to win the nomination, Kennedy won 806 and Johnson 409. However, Kennedy asked Johnson to be his running mate believing that would widen his appeal to the voters in the South. In the presidential election of November 1960, Kennedy and Johnson narrowly defeated the Republican team of Vice-President Richard Nixon and Henry Cabot Lodge, Jr., of Massachusetts.

As Vice-President, Johnson took a more active role in the government than any of his predecessors. He served as Chairman of the National Aeronautics and Space Council, the Peace Corps, National Advisory Council, and the President's Committee on Equal Employment Opportunity. He also served on the National Security Council. He often took overseas trips to represent the President and visited West Berlin shortly after the construction of the Berlin Wall in 1961 to re-assure the citizens there of America's continuing support.

President 1963 – 1965

On November 22nd 1963, Kennedy and Johnson visited Dallas in Texas. As Kennedy was riding through the city in an open-topped car he was shot by an assassin and later died in hospital. Governor John B. Connally of Texas, who was riding in the same car as Kennedy, was wounded. Johnson was riding two cars behind the President and was not hit. His bodyguard from the Secret Service lay over him like a human shield until the threat had passed. One hour and thirty-nine minutes later, at 2.39pm, Johnson was sworn in as the 36th President of the United States aboard Air Force One at Love Field in Dallas. Johnson stood next to Kennedy's widow, Jackie Kennedy, who was still wearing a dress splattered with her husband's blood, as U.S. District Court Judge Sarah T. Hughes administered the oath of office. He was the first Southerner to become President since Andrew Johnson had succeeded Abraham Lincoln in 1865. The plane then flew back to Washington where Johnson addressed the nation asking for their support.

As President, Johnson had many severe problems both at home and abroad. In America racial tensions were high and many people were unemployed. In Vietnam, Communist rebels fought troops supported by the United States. The Cold War with the Soviet Union kept the world in danger of a nuclear war. Democratic governments in Latin America were also threatened by Communists.

Johnson's experience helped the country recover from the shock of Kennedy's assassination. Stock prices which had fallen sharply at the news of the President's death soon recovered in a sign of confidence in Johnson. The new President pushed hard for the legislation that had been proposed by Kennedy. These included a new civil rights bill and a tax cut. Johnson also proposed a national *War on Poverty*, to create jobs in deprived areas. All these proposals were approved by Congress. The new civil rights law guaranteed equal job opportunities for African-Americans all as well as access to all hotels, restaurants and other businesses that serve the public.

In April 1964 Johnson played a key role in settling a serious labor dispute between the railroads and the union men who ran the trains. As a result of his intervention the dispute was resolved without a strike. In terms of foreign policy, Johnson maintained Kennedy's commitments to South Vietnam and West Berlin. He eased tension with Panama after anti-American riots broke out in the canal zone.

The Election of 1964

In 1964, Johnson easily won nomination for his first full term. He chose Senator Hubert H. Humphrey of Minnesota as his running mate. The Republicans nominated Senator Barry M. Goldwater of Arizona for President and Representative William E. Miller of New York for Vice-President. Johnson won the election by a landslide, receiving 486 electoral votes to 52 for Senator Goldwater. He carried 44 states as well as the District of Columbia.

Presidential Election of 1964		
Candidate	Popular Votes	Electoral Votes
Lyndon B. Johnson (Dem.)	42,995,259	486
Barry M. Goldwater (Rep.)	27,204,571	52

Johnson's Administration 1965 – 1969

During his full term the economy boomed. Johnson described many of his program's using the term the *Great Society*. These programs included continuing the *War on Poverty*, improving education, providing for the elderly, and aiding urban areas. Aided by Democratic majorities in both houses, he was very successful in getting his plans passed by Congress. These included proposals to increase federal aid to education, improve road safety, establish both the Department of Housing and Urban Development and the Department of Transportation, and set up Medicare, a health insurance plan for the elderly.

Congress also passed important new civil rights legislation. Voting rights for African-Americans were guaranteed by a new law passed in 1965. Among other things, the law outlawed literacy tests as a voting requirement. *The Civil Rights Act* of 1968 aimed at ending racial discrimination in the sale or renting of houses of apartments. A new housing law was also passed in 1968 that provided over $5

259

billion of federal funds to help the needy buy houses and rent apartments. In 1966, Johnson appointed the first African-American to the cabinet when he made Robert C. Weaver Secretary of Housing. In 1967, Johnson appointed Thurgood Marshall to the Supreme Court of the United States, the first African-American to become a Supreme Court Justice.

In the White House, Johnson worked with great energy and became known as the "Whirlwind President." On 6th August 1966, his first daughter, Luci, married her husband while her father was in office, the first to do so since Eleanor Wilson in 1914. Her first child, Patrick, was born on 21st June 1967. Then on 9th December 1967, his second daughter, Lynda, married her husband in the East Room of the White House. Her first child, Lucinda, was born on 25th October 1968.

However, the Vietnam War soon became Johnson's chief problem. When he first became President, the U.S. had 16,300 troops in Vietnam acting as military advisers to the South Vietnamese government. In August 1964, torpedo boats from North Vietnam attacked U.S. Navy destroyers in the Gulf of Tonkin. Johnson responded by ordering American planes to bomb North Vietnam's torpedo boat bases. The war then rapidly escalated and in 1965 Johnson ordered the first U.S. combat troops into South Vietnam to protect American bases and stop Communist forces from overrunning the country. By 1968, more than 500,000 U.S. troops were based in South Vietnam.

With casualties and the cost of the war mounting, the conflict in Vietnam increased unrest and racial tension in America. Violent demonstrations and riots took place throughout the country. In early 1968, North Vietnamese troops launched the *Tet Offensive* and heavy fighting took place across the South. Throughout the month of February all the major cities of South Vietnam became battle zones and even the U.S. Embassy in Saigon was attacked. Although the offensive was defeated, peace seemed further away than ever. Many people began to question Johnson's policies and running of the war and his popularity began to drop. Senators Eugene McCarthy and Robert F. Kennedy, who both opposed U.S. involvement in the

Vietnam War, announced that they would stand against Johnson for the Democratic presidential nomination in 1968. In the evening of Sunday 31st March 1968, Johnson made a live television address in which he announced a reduction in the bombing of North Vietnam. This announcement paved the way for peace talks later that year. However, Johnson then shocked the nation when he said: "I shall not seek, and I will not accept, the nomination of my party for another term as your President."

Johnson hoped that his announcement would restore civil peace and national unity. However, the country remained a troubled one. On 4th April 1968, the Civil Rights leader, Martin Luther King, was shot and killed in Memphis, Tennessee. Severe rioting then took place in major cities across the country including Washington D.C. and 40 people died. In another tragedy, on 6th June 1968, Senator Robert F. Kennedy was shot and killed while campaigning for the Democratic nomination. Vice-President Hubert Humphrey was later nominated as the Democratic candidate for President but he lost the election of November 1968 to the Republican candidate, Richard Nixon.

Later Years

Johnson attended the inauguration of President Nixon in January 1969 and then retired to his ranch in Stonewall, Texas. In 1971 he published his memoirs. In April 1972, he suffered a heart attack and slowly recovered on his ranch. However, on 22nd January 1973 he suffered a further heart attack and died. He was buried in the family cemetery on the ranch.

Summary

Lyndon Baines Johnson became President in tragic circumstances and united the country during a time of grief and worry. In 1964 he was elected President with sixty-one percent of the popular votes, the largest share in history. During his presidency there were notable achievements in civil rights, education, and space travel. However, America's involvement in the Vietnam War divided the country and was a key reason that he chose not to run in the 1968 election. Historians generally rank him in the middle of all the Presidents.

CHAPTER 37 – RICHARD M. NIXON

37th President of the United States 1969 – 1974

Born: 9th January 1913, Yorba Linda, California

Married: Thelma Catherine (Pat) Ryan (1912 – 1993), 21st June 1940

Number of Children: Two

Died: 22nd April 1994, New York

Final Resting Place: Richard Nixon Presidential Library and Museum, Yorba Linda, California

Introduction

Richard Nixon was a former Vice-President who was elected as the 37th President of the United States. Before he entered the White House, Nixon had also served in the U.S. Navy, the U.S. House of Representatives and the U.S. Senate. He was inaugurated as the President in the same year that American astronauts first walked on the surface of the moon. By this time, the population of the United States had surpassed two hundred million people and the country was by far the richest and most powerful in the world. His first term of office was considered to be very successful and he improved relations with China and Russia. In 1972 he was re-elected by a landslide. He then took steps to end the involvement of the United States in the Vietnam War and secure the release of American prisoners-of-war. However, he was accused covering up his involvement in a burglary of the Democratic Party headquarters in the Watergate complex in Washington D.C. and, in order to avoid certain impeachment, he became the first President ever to resign from office in August 1974.

Early life

Richard Milhous Nixon was born on 9th January 1913 in Yorba Linda, California, a village thirty miles (48km) southeast of Los Angeles. He was the second of five sons of a farmer and laborer, Francis Anthony Nixon, who would later open a store and gasoline station in Whittier, California. Nixon attended elementary schools in Yorba Linda, Whittier and Fullerton before attending High School in Whittier. He grew up a Quaker and attended, Whittier College, which was a Quaker Institution. When he graduated in 1934, he won a scholarship to the Duke University School of Law in Durham, North Carolina. He graduated third in his class of forty-four in 1937. He then became a lawyer in a firm in Whittier and taught a law course at Whittier College, where he became a member of the Board of Trustees at the age of 26. On 21st June 1940 he married Thelma Catherine Ryan, who was nicknamed Pat, and they later had two daughters. In 1968, their younger daughter, Julie, married David Eisenhower, the grandson of the former President. In the Second World War, Nixon served as an officer in the U.S. Navy and was promoted to the rank of lieutenant commander before it ended in 1945.

Entry into Politics

In 1946 Nixon defeated Democrat, Jerry Voorhis, to win a seat in the U.S. House of Representatives. There he sat on a committee that laid the groundwork for the Marshall Plan and other U.S. aid programs. He helped to write the Taft-Hartley Act, which set up controls over labor unions. He was also a member of the House Committee on Un-American Activities. The question of communists in the government was a big issue at the time and Nixon was brought to national prominence when the committee successfully brought charges of spying against Alger Hiss, a former State Department official. In 1950 he successfully ran for the U.S. Senate where he served on the Labor and Public Welfare Committee.

Vice-President 1953 – 1961

In 1952, he was nominated for Vice-President at the Republican National Convention to run with General Dwight D. Eisenhower. In the election they defeated their Democratic opponents, Governor Adlai E. Stevenson of Illinois, and Senator John J. Sparkman of Alabama.

As Vice- President, Nixon took a greater role in the executive branch of government than any of his predecessors. He stepped in to keep the wheels of government running smoothly when Eisenhower suffered a heart attack in 1955, a further illness in 1956 and a stroke in 1957.

In the 1956 election, Eisenhower defeated his Democratic opponents, Adlai Stevenson and Senator Estes Kefauver of Tennessee. As Vice-President, Nixon frequently represented the United States abroad and visited nearly sixty countries. In July 1959, he visited Moscow where he publicly argued about foreign policy with Premier Nikita Khrushchev while touring an exhibit of a model home in what became known as the *kitchen debate*.

Defeat by Kennedy 1960

In 1960 the Republican National Convention nominated Nixon for President on the first ballot with Henry Cabot Lodge Jr., the American ambassador to the United Nations, as his running mate. The Democrats nominated Senator John F. Kennedy of Massachusetts for President and Senator Lyndon B. Johnson of Texas for Vice-President. In a close and hard-fought campaign,

Kennedy argued that Republican methods had slowed U.S. economic growth while Nixon showed that the economy was growing at a satisfactory rate. Nixon and Kennedy took part in four debates which were broadcast on television and radio. These "great debates" were the first time in the history of America that the two presidential candidates had argued campaign issues face-to-face.

Nixon lost to Kennedy in one of the closest ever elections. Out of nearly 69 million votes cast, Kennedy won by just 119,450 votes. Nixon carried 26 states to 22 for Kennedy, but Kennedy received 303 electoral votes to Nixon's 219. Senator Harry F. Byrd of Virginia received 15 electoral votes.

In 1961, Nixon returned to practicing law in California. In 1962 he ran for governor of California but he lost to Democrat Edmund G. (Pat) Brown by about 300,000 votes. He then moved to New York and became a partner in a Wall Street law firm.

In the 1964 presidential election, Nixon campaigned for the Republican candidate, Senator Barry M. Goldwater of Arizona. However, in the election Goldwater was defeated by a large margin by President Lyndon B. Johnson. In 1966, Nixon again campaigned vigorously for Republican candidates in the congressional elections and received much credit when the Republicans gained 47 seats in the House and three in the Senate that had been held by the democrats.

The 1968 Election

In February 1968, Nixon announced that he would be a candidate for the Republican presidential nomination. He appealed to both liberal and conservative Republicans and won a series of primary elections by large margins. His main opponents for the nomination were Governors Nelson Rockefeller of New York and Ronald Reagan of New York. However, at the Republican convention in Miami, Nixon won the nomination on the first ballot. Nixon's choice of running mate, Governor Spiro T. Agnew of Maryland, was nominated for Vice-President.

266

President Johnson had announced that he would not seek re-election and so the Democrats nominated Vice-President Hubert Humprey for President with Senator Edmund S. Muskie of New York as his running mate. Governor George C. Wallace of Alabama and retired General Curtis E. LeMay ran as the candidates of the American Independence Party.

Nixon announced that his main goal as President would be to end the Vietnam War. He said that other countries should be encouraged to take over from the United States for preserving world peace. He also promised to strengthen law enforcement in the U.S.

In the election Nixon defeated Humphrey by more than 800,000 votes. He won 301 electoral votes to 191 for Humphrey and 46 for Wallace.

Presidential Election of 1968		
Candidate	Popular Votes	Electoral Votes
Richard M. Nixon (Rep)	31,710,470	301
Hubert H. Humphrey (Dem)	30,898,055	191
George C. Wallace (Ind)	9,446,167	46

Nixon's First Administration 1969 – 1973

Nixon was inaugurated on 20th January 1969. In his inaugural address he said that America would seek to make peace in Vietnam. Peace talks had begun in 1968 and continued in Paris. However, little progress was made. Nixon then began a program of *Vietnamization* by which American combat troops were gradually withdrawn from Vietnam while South Vietnamese troops were trained to take their place. The first American troops were withdrawn in July 1969. However, the following year U.S. troops invaded Cambodia to attack North Vietnamese supply lines there. Nixon claimed the invasion would shorten the war but many people felt it would expand it. Many people wanted U.S. involvement to end immediately and protests and demonstrations swept the country. At Kent State University, Ohio, National Guardsmen fired into a crowd of demonstrators killing four students.

Nixon knew that achieving peace in Vietnam would depend on improving relations with China and Russia, the Communist countries that were supporting North Vietnam. In 1969, he removed some restrictions on travel to China by American citizens. He also encouraged re-opening trade between the two countries which had ceased during the Korean War (1950 – 1953). In 1971 he approved the export of certain goods to China. In February 1972 he became the first U.S. President to visit China, staying for seven days. In May 1972, he visited Russia for nine days where he signed an agreement with the Soviet leader, Leonid Brezhnev, to limit the production of nuclear weapons. However, that same year, Nixon ordered a blockade of North Vietnam to cut off its war supplies from Russia and China. North Vietnamese ports were mined and her road and rail links to China were bombed.

In terms of domestic policy, Nixon proposed a series of reforms which he called the *New Federalism*. The reforms stalled in Congress due to Democratic opposition. However, Congress did pass several important new laws. In 1969, they passed Nixon's proposal to establish a lottery system for the military draft. They also reformed federal tax laws which cut taxes for individuals but increased them for oil companies. In 1970, they passed the 26th *Amendment* to the U.S. Constitution (ratified in 1971) which set the voting age to 18 for all elections. In 1972, Congress passed Nixon's proposal for a *revenue-sharing* plan by which billions of dollars in federal tax revenues were shared with state and local governments.

Inflation became a concern during Nixon's first term and in 1971 he attempted to address it by establishing a Pay Board to stop inflationary salary and wages increases and a Price Commission to regulate pay and rent increases. By 1972 the rate of inflation had slowed and the economy had grown. One of the most debated issues of his first term was his proposal to establish an anti-ballistic missile (ABM) system called *Safeguard*, to protect American bomber and missile bases from enemy attack. Critics said that that it would cost too much money, would step up the arms race with the Soviet Union, and would not work. However, the Senate approved the construction of two ABM bases in 1972. One key domestic achievement was the desegregation of schools in the South. Another came in 1970, when Nixon set up the *Environmental Protection Agency* to tackle the increased pollution of the air, land and water.

During Nixon's presidency, America also became the first and only country to send astronauts to the moon. In July 1969, astronauts Neil A. Armstrong and Edwin E. (Buzz) Aldrin became the first men to walk on the lunar surface and Nixon congratulated them from a special telephone connection in the White House. A total of twelve U.S. astronauts landed on the moon between 1969 and 1972.

The 1972 Election

Nixon and Agnew easily won re-nomination at the 1972 Republican national convention in Miami Beach. The Democrats nominated Senator George S. McGovern of South Dakota for President with Sargent Schriver, former director of the Peace Corps, as his running mate. In the election, Nixon won by a landslide receiving seventeen and half million more votes than McGovern, the widest margin of any presidential election up to that time. Nixon won 520 electoral votes to Mc Govern's 17. John Hospers of the Libertarian Party won one electoral vote.

Presidential Election of 1972		
Candidate	Popular Votes	Electoral Votes
Richard M. Nixon (Rep.)	46,740,323	520
George S. McGovern (Dem.)	28,901,598	17
John Hospers (Lib.)	3,673	1

Nixon's Second Administration 1973 – 1974

On 27th January 1973, the United States signed an agreement with North Vietnam to stop fighting immediately and start exchanging prisoners. In March, the U.S. completed its troop withdrawal. Nixon's chief foreign policy adviser, Henry A. Kissinger, secretly assured the leaders of South Vietnam that the U.S. would use "full force" to aid them should the Communists violate the agreement. Fighting continued in Vietnam but without the participation of U.S. troops. Later that year, Kissinger succeeded William P. Rogers as Secretary of State.

In January 1973, Nixon ended the draft and the military became an all-volunteer force. However, during 1973 Nixon's relations with the Democratic-controlled Congress became increasingly strained. He refused to spend billions of dollars of Federal projects that they approved because he said it was wasteful. They forced him to end the U.S. bombing of Cambodia which he said was necessary to prevent a Communist take-over of that country. They refused to provide funding beyond 15th August 1973, the first time Congress had ever denied funds for U.S. combat operations in a war. They also overrode his veto of a resolution that limited presidential war powers. The *War Powers Resolution* gave Congress the power to halt the use of any U.S. armed force that the President had ordered into combat abroad.

In 1973, the country was affected by the return of high inflation and from shortages of gasoline. In 1974, Congress approved Nixon's proposal to establish a *Federal Energy Commission* to deal with the energy shortage.

The Watergate Scandal

On 17th June 1972, burglars broke into the Democratic Party headquarters in the Watergate building complex in Washington DC. Several burglars were arrested in the break-in and it was found that they were employees of Nixon's 1972 re-election committee. In 1973, evidence was uncovered that linked top White House aides with either the break-in or a later attempt to hide information related to it. Nixon claimed that he had no part in the break in or the attempt to cover it up. He promised a full investigation and in May 1973 Archibald Cox, a professor from the Harvard law School, was appointed to head it.

In July 1973, a Senate investigating committee learned that Nixon had secretly made tape recordings of his conversations in the White House since 1971. When the Senate committee asked the President for access to the tapes that they thought would aid their investigation he refused arguing that he had a right to maintain the confidentiality of his private conversations. In August, Cox and the committee filed a petition in court to obtain the tapes. U.S. District Court Judge John J. Sirica ordered Nixon to provide the tapes to him so that he could review them. Nixon appealed the order but the U.S. Court of Appeals supported Judge Sirica.

On October 19th, Nixon offered to supply summaries of the tapes to Cox. However, Cox refused arguing that the summaries would not be accepted as proper evidence in court. Nixon then had Cox fired and he was replaced by a noted Texas attorney, Leon Jaworski. Nixon's actions resulted in a move for his impeachment. Meanwhile, that same month, Vice-President Agnew resigned after Federal investigators uncovered evidence that he had accepted illegal payments while in office both in Maryland and as Vice-President. Nixon appointed House Minority Leader Gerald R. Ford as Agnew's successor and he became Vice-President on December 6th 1973.

The Impeachment Hearings began before the House Judiciary Committee in October 1973. The committee issued subpoenas (legal requests) to obtain the tapes but Nixon still refused to hand them over. In July 1974, the committee finished reviewing evidence and voted to recommend three articles of impeachment against the President. The first article charged that Nixon obstructed justice by delaying the investigation into the Watergate burglary. It also accused Nixon of attempting to hide the identities of the people who ordered the burglary. The second article of impeachment charged that Nixon had abused presidential powers and third accused him of disobeying subpoenas.

On August 5th, Nixon released the records of the taped White House conversations. However, these showed that on 23rd June 1972, six days after the burglary, he had approved a Watergate cover-up. This new evidence damaged his Nixon's case and Republican congressional leaders warned him that he now faced almost certain impeachment by the House of Representatives and removal by the Senate. On 8th August Nixon announced his resignation as President to the American public live on television. It was the first time a U.S. President had resigned from office. Nixon's resignation became effective at noon on 9th August and Vice-President Ford was sworn in as the 38th President of the United States.

Although the impeachment proceedings ended, Nixon still faced prosecution in the courts for his role in the Watergate cover-up. On September 8th, however, President Ford granted Nixon a federal pardon for all crimes that he may have committed while serving as President.

Later Years

After leaving the White House, Nixon returned to his home in San Clemente, California. In 1977, he admitted that he had "let down the country" in a televised interview with talk-show host David Frost. In 1978 he published his memoirs and later also published further books. In 1990, the Richard Nixon Library and Museum was opened in Yorba Linda, California. Pat Nixon died in June 1993 and left him grief-stricken. On 18th April 1994, he suffered from a stroke and died four days later. He was buried next to his wife at the Richard Nixon Presidential Library.

Summary

In many ways, Richard Milhous Nixon was one of America's most successful Presidents. He won a decisive victory in the 1968 election and a landslide in 1972. He desegregated schools, ended the war in Vietnam and improved relations with China and the Soviet Union. However, he attempted to cover up several serious crimes committed by his supporters, including a burglary of the national headquarters of the Democratic party. When this was exposed in the *Watergate Scandal*, he was the first and only President ever to resign from office. For this reason, he is ranked lowly among all the Presidents.

CHAPTER 38 – GERALD FORD

38ᵗʰ President of the United States 1974 – 1977

Born: 14ᵗʰ July 1913, Omaha, Nebraska

Married: Betty Bloomer (1918 – 2011), 15ᵗʰ October 1948

Number of Children: Four

Died: 26ᵗʰ December 2006, Rancho Mirage, California

Final Resting Place: Gerald R. Ford Presidential Museum, Grand Rapids, Michigan

Introduction

Gerald Ford came the President of the United States on the 9ᵗʰ August 1974 following the resignation of Richard Nixon, who left the White House to avoid certain impeachment. It was the only time a Vice-President became President following the resignation of the Chief Executive. America celebrated two hundred years of independence while Ford was in the White House. The United States had grown from a series of small colonies to become a global superpower with 220 million people. However, it was not a happy time for the country. Ford had to deal with the divisions created by the Watergate scandal as well as high inflation and unemployment. Between 1965 and 1973, thousands of Americans had died trying to prevent communist North Vietnam taking over the non-communist

South. However, in April 1975 the communists won the Vietnam War and the whole country fell into their hands.

Background

Gerald Rudolph Ford was born in Omaha, Nebraska on July 14th 1913. He was originally named Leslie Lynch King after his father, who ran a wool business. When he was two years old his parents divorced and his mother then took him to Grand Rapids, Michigan, where she had friends. In 1916 she married Gerald Rudolph Ford, who owned a small print company in the city. Ford adopted her son and gave him his name. Ford grew up with three younger half-brothers. His real father also remarried and had three children.

As a child Ford received good grades at school and excelled at sports, particularly American football. He joined the scouts and became an *Eagle Scout*, the highest rank. After attending high school in Grand Rapids, he entered the University of Michigan in 1931 and graduated in 1935. In 1938 he entered Yale Law School and received his degree in 1941.He was admitted to the Michigan bar later that year.

In December 1941, the United States entered World War Two and Ford volunteered for the U.S. Navy. He served in the Pacific on an aircraft carrier, the USS Monterrey. He was discharged as Lieutenant Commander in 1946. On October 15th 1948 he married Elizabeth "Betty" Bloomer, the daughter of a machinery salesman. They later had four children.

Entry into Politics

After the war, Ford resumed his law career in Grand Rapids. At the same time, he became active in a local Republican reform group. In 1948 he challenged U.S. Representative Bartel J. Junkman in the Republican primary election. Junkman believed that America should stay out of world affairs whereas Ford held the opposite view. Ford won the primary and then beat his Democratic opponent, Fred Barr, in the election that November. He was subsequently re-elected a further twelve times.

In Congress, Ford gained a reputation as a hard-working and loyal Republican and an expert in military affairs. In 1963 he was elected Chairman of the Republican Conference of the House, his first leadership role in the House. In November 1963 he sat on the Warren Commission which investigated the assassination of President Kennedy. In 1965 he was chosen as House Minority Leader. There he opposed many of President Johnson's social programs as costly and unnecessary as well as the war in Vietnam. In 1968 Republican Richard Nixon was elected President but the Democrats still controlled both houses of Congress. Ford won some support there for Nixon's policies concerning Vietnam and inflation.

Vice-President 1973 – 1974

In 1972 President Nixon and Vice-President Spiro T. Agnew won re-election by a landslide. However, in 1973, federal investigators uncovered evidence that Agnew had accepted bribes. As a result of these investigations, Agnew resigned on October 10th 1973. Ford was nominated as Vice-President by Nixon. However, procedures established by the 25th amendment in 1967 meant that approval was required by both houses of Congress. Previously, vacancies had remained unfulfilled until the next election. The Senate approved Ford's appointment by 92 to 3 votes and the House approved it by 387 to 35 votes. Ford was then sworn in as 40th Vice-President on December 6th 1973.

Shortly before Ford became Vice-President, the House of Representatives had begun impeachment proceedings against Nixon because they believed he was hiding evidence of the Watergate scandal. The *Watergate Scandal* shook public faith in Nixon, even though he insisted he had no part in it. Ford went on a nation-wide speaking tour and expressed his faith in Nixon. By mid-1974 he had visited forty states and made several hundred public appearances.

In July 1974, the House Judiciary Committee recommended that Nixon be impeached. It voted to adopt three articles of impeachment for adoption by the full House of Representatives. The first accused the President of interfering with justice by acting to hide evidence about the Watergate burglary from federal law-enforcement officials.

The second charged that Nixon had abused Presidential powers. The third charged that Nixon had illegally withheld evidence from the judiciary Committee. Ford continued to defend Nixon saying that he had not committed an impeachable offence and predicted that the House of Representatives would not impeach Nixon. On 5th August 1974, Nixon released transcripts of taped White House conversations that clearly supported the first article and immediately he lost all remaining support in Congress. Nixon was warned he faced certain impeachment and removal from office by Republican leaders in both houses. Nixon resigned and at noon on the 9th August 1974 Ford took the oath of office as 38th President of the USA in the East room of the White House. Ford became the only President in the nation's history not to have been elected to either the presidency or the vice-presidency.

Ford's Administration 1974 – 1977

At the start of his Administration, Ford kept all of Nixon's cabinet members. He nominated Nelson A. Rockefeller, former governor of New York, as Vice-President and both houses confirmed it. The new President was challenged by soaring inflation and a lack of public confidence in the government. Inflation was causing hardship, especially to the poor and elderly. Sharp price increases also threatened a business slump. Public faith in government was at its lowest level for years due to the Watergate scandal. The impeachment crisis had also slowed the work of many government agencies and created confusion about government policies.

Ford had strained relations with the Democratic-controlled Congress. He vetoed more than fifty bills, believing they would increase the rate of inflation and Congress passed few of his major proposals. His early popularity was damaged when on 8th September 1974 he pardoned Nixon for all federal crimes he might have committed while in office. The pardon angered millions of Americans but Ford said he did it to end division within the nation and "heal the wounds that had festered too long." Many people believed the government should have brought Nixon to trial and had enough evidence to do so. Others felt that the pardon should only have been granted once he had admitted his involvement in the Watergate Scandal

Eight days after he had pardoned Nixon, Ford announced an *Amnesty Program* to draft dodgers and deserters from the period of the Vietnam War. The program required most of these men to work public service jobs for up to two years. About 22,000 of approximately 106,000 eligible men applied for amnesty under the program. Of those that did not apply, most objected to the work requirement

At the beginning of his Presidency, Ford called inflation the nation's "public enemy number one." With congressional approval, he established the *Council on Wage and Price Stability* to expose any inflationary wage and price increases. Ford also proposed tax increases for corporations, families and individuals but dropped these plans in late 1974 as a recession took hold. He then introduced legislation to create public service jobs for the unemployed and to lower federal income taxes. Congress passed both measures. Early in 1975, inflation slowed and the economy showed signs of recovery. However, by May nine percent of workforce had no jobs, the highest rate of unemployment since 1941. Unemployment dropped slowly during the recovery and by October 1976 it stood at eight percent.

The President survived two attempted assassinations which occurred in California in September 1975. The first one took place in Sacramento on 5th September when Lynette Alice Frome, a follower of convicted murderer Charles Manson, pointed a pistol at Ford but a Secret Service agent grabbed it before it was fired. The second took place in San Francisco on September 22nd when Sara Jane Moore fired a shot at Ford but missed. She was associated with groups protesting U.S. government policies. Both women were convicted of attempted assassination of a President and sentenced to life imprisonment.

In foreign affairs, Ford relied on the guidance of Henry Kissinger, the Secretary of State, who had also been Nixon's chief foreign policy advisor. Ford worked to continue improving relations with China and the Soviet Union. The first foreign crisis for the new President occurred in August 1974 when Turkish troops invaded Cyprus and took control of a large part of the island. Ford took no action to stop the Turks. In 1975 Ford and Kissinger helped Egypt and Israel to settle a territorial dispute that arose from their war in 1973.

Between 1965 and 1973, thousands of Americans had fought and died to prevent South Vietnam from being conquered by Communist North Vietnam. However, on 30th April 1975, North Vietnamese troops succeeded in capturing Saigon and the long Vietnam War ended. Shortly afterwards, the neighboring country of Cambodia was also overtaken by Communist troops leading to the deaths of millions of people. Just before the end of the war, Ford asked Congress to approve emergency aid totaling seven hundred million dollars to save South Vietnam but his request was rejected. Ford then arranged for the evacuation of refugees from South Vietnam and about approximately one hundred thousand went to live in the United States. In May 1975, Cambodian Communists seized an American merchant ship, the *Mayaguez*, in the Gulf of Siam. Ford sent two hundred Marines to the area and they quickly recaptured the ship and freed its 39 crew members.

The 1976 Election

Former governor Ronald Reagan of California challenged Ford for the Republican nomination for President in 1976. They fought a close, bitter contest but Ford narrowly won on first ballot. Senator Robert J. Dole of Kansas was nominated for Vice-President. Their Democratic opponents were Governor Jimmy Carter of Georgia and Senator Walter Mondale of Minnesota. Ford wanted to pursue policies he said had led to the recovery. Carter said that Ford had mismanaged the economy and contributed to the high rate of unemployment. They took part in the first series of nationally

279

televised debates since Kennedy and Nixon in 1960. In the election, Carter won the popular vote and 297 electoral votes to Ford's 240. However, Ford won 27 states to Carter's 23 as well as the District of Columbia. Reagan won one electoral vote.

Later Years

After he left the White House, Ford retired to Rancho Mirage in California. He remained active in politics and was considered for Ronald Reagan's running mate in 1980. He became a popular public speaker and was the author of several books including his memoirs, *A Time to Heal*, in 1979. In 1982, the Gerald R. Ford Presidential Museum opened in Grand Rapids, Michigan. In 1999, he was awarded the Presidential Medal of Freedom by President Bill Clinton. He died in 2006 and was buried in the grounds of the Gerald R. Ford Presidential Museum.

Summary

Gerald Ford was a decent, friendly man with a well-deserved reputation for honesty. He seemed exactly the right man to take over as President from the disgraced Richard Nixon. However, his attempt to unite the country and put to an end the nightmare of the Watergate Scandal by pardoning Nixon was ill-judged and divisive. He also failed to effectively deal with America's economic problems including increasing inflation and high unemployment. In 1975, South Vietnam fell to the Communists, something which thousands of Americans had died trying to prevent between 1964 and 1973. When America celebrated her bicentenary in 1976, she did so as a troubled, divided and defeated country. Ford only served a short term and is often ranked in the middle of all the Presidents.

CHAPTER 39 – JAMES E. CARTER

39ᵗʰ President of the United States 1977 – 1981

Born: 1ˢᵗ October 1924, Plains, Georgia

Married: Rosalynn Smith (1927 – 2023), 1ˢᵗ July 1946

Number of Children: Four

Introduction

Jimmy Carter became the 39ᵗʰ President of the United States after defeating Gerald Ford in the election of 1976 even though he was almost unknown at the start of that year. His decency, honesty and centrist positions carried him through the primary elections and into the White House. Prior to entering politics, Carter had served in the U.S. Navy and then managed the family's peanut farm. He won a seat in the Georgia Senate and was then elected as Governor of Georgia. As President of the United States, he faced tough problems at home and abroad. He had to tackle inflation, high oil prices and rising unemployment. In 1979, the Soviet Union invaded Afghanistan and Iranian revolutionaries took Americans hostage in Tehran. A disastrous rescue attempt failed to secure the release of the hostages in 1980 and they remained in captivity for the remainder of his term. Carter's achievements in office include restoring diplomatic relations with China and helping to negotiate a peace agreement between Egypt and Israel.

Early Life

James Earl Carter Junior was born on 1st of October 1924 in Plains, Georgia, the eldest of four children of a farmer and small businessman. His mother was a registered nurse. He went to school in Plains and then entered Georgia Southwestern College in Americus in 1941. He then entered the Georgia Institute of technology the following year. In 1943 he was appointed to U.S. Naval Academy in Annapolis, Maryland where he graduated 5th out of 820. On 1st July 1946, he married Rosalynn Smith, also from Plains and the daughter of a garage mechanic. Until her death in November 2023, his marriage to Rosalynn was the longest of any President's at 77 years and 135 days. While in the navy he served on battleships and submarines. He left the navy in 1953 and returned to Plains. His father had died so he took over the family farm and peanut warehouse. He devoted much time to his business and to civic affairs where he was opposed to racial segregation in his local church.

Entry into Politics

In 1962 he was elected to state senate and was re-elected in 1964. While in the senate he worked hard for reforms in education. In 1966, he was a candidate for the Democratic nomination for Governor of Georgia but he was defeated in the primary election. From 1966 to 1970 he worked hard to increase his understanding of George's problems.

1970 he stood for Governor again and this time won it. He began his term in January 1971 and used his time in office to carry out critical reforms to make state government more efficient. He showed great concern for racial equality and created many job opportunities for African-Americans in state government. During his time in office, the number of African-American state employees increased by forty percent.

Election of 1976

During his term as Governor, Carter began to consider running for president in 1976. He thought public would support a leader from outside Washington D.C. He offered bold new solutions to the country's problems.

In December 1974 he announced his candidacy for the 1976 Democratic presidential nomination. He was still unknown outside Georgia and as late as Octoberhe was not mentioned in an opinion poll that ranked potential contenders. However, from January 1976 there was a whirlwind rise prominence. He received the most votes in the Iowa caucus, the first contest to elect delegates. In February, he won his first presidential primary election in New Hampshire against ten other candidates including governor George Wallace. In March, Carter beat Wallace in the Florida primary and opinion polls now put him in the lead for the nomination. The public liked that he was from outside Washington and had no ties to special interest groups. He offered to restore morale leadership after Watergate. People did not like how Ford had pardoned Nixon.

At the Democratic National Convention in New York City, Carter easily won on first ballot. Senator Walter Mondale of Minnesota was nominated for Vice-President. The Republicans nominated Gerald Ford for President and Senator Robert J. Dole of Kansas as Vice-President.

In his campaign, Carter promised to develop a national energy policy and to increase federal spending to reduce unemployment. Ford argued that Carter's policies would lead to an increase in inflation. For most of the campaign, Ford trailed behind Carter in the polls and he did not help his cause when, with the Cold War at its height, he made an embarrassing gaffe in a live televised debate in which he claimed that the Soviet Union did not dominate eastern Europe.

In the election Carter received more 40 million popular votes to 39 million for Ford, which led to 297 votes for Carter in the electoral college to 240 for Ford.

Presidential Election of 1976		
Candidate	Popular Votes	Electoral Votes
James E. Carter (Dem.)	40,825,839	297
Gerald R. Ford (Rep.)	39,147,770	240
Ronald W. Reagan (Ind.)	*	1

Carter's Administration 1977 – 1981

Carter was inaugurated on 20th January 1997. During his time in office, his nine-year-old daughter, Amy, attended to local schools and would bring friends home to the White House. Carter's first major decision as President was to pardon the draft evaders of the Vietnam war.

Other early actions included lowering federal income taxes, stopping production of the B1 bomber, consolidating federal agencies that duplicated services, and establishing a new executive department, the *Department of Energy*.

During the first year of his presidency the economy grew and unemployment fell. However, in 1978 soaring inflation became a major problem. That same year, Congress approved his national energy program designed to reduce U.S. oil imports. A tax was imposed on vehicle owners that used an excessive amount of gasoline. However, oil imports remained at a high level and inflation grew worse. In 1979, continuing high inflation and gasoline shortages affected his performance rating. In July 1979, he asked his cabinet to resign. He then made six changes in the hope of strengthening his administration. He also appointed Harrison Jordan to the newly-created role of White House Chief of Staff.

In March 1980, he announced a new program to fight inflation. This included cuts in federal government spending, a tax on imported oil, and voluntary restraints on wages and prices. The use of credit cards and other types of consumer credit was restricted. However, inflation stayed above fifteen percent, and in July 1980 only twenty-one percent of Americans approved his performance, the lowest score on record.

In foreign affairs, the U.S. Senate ratified two treaties concerning the Panama Canal, which had been controlled by the U.S. since its construction. According to one treaty, Panama would gain control of the canal on 31st December 1999, and in the other treaty, that the United States would be given the right to defend it. In 1978 Carter arranged meetings with the leaders of Israel and Egypt to agree a peace treaty which was adopted in 1979. The treaty brought a lasting peace between the two and is sometimes regarded as Carter's biggest achievement in office.

Also in 1979, the U.S. established full diplomatic relations with China. That same year the second round of the Strategic Arms Limitation Talks led to the *SALT II* treaty with the Soviet Union which limited the use of nuclear weapons. However, late in 1979 the Soviet Union invaded Afghanistan and this caused their relations with America to plunge to the lowest level for several years. At Carter's urging, the U.S. boycotted 1980 summer Olympics and the Senate postponed ratifying the SALT II treaty.

In February 1979, the Shah of Iran, Mohammed Raza Pahlavi, was overthrown. He had already left the country and in October 1979 entered the USA for medical treatment. In November, Iranian revolutionaries took over U.S. embassy in Tehran and began to hold sixty-six American citizens as hostages. The revolutionaries wanted to exchange them for the Shah. However, Carter refused and responded by cutting off diplomatic relations and banning imports from Iran. In April 1980, he authorized a rescue attempt. However, this failed when three out of eight helicopters to be used in the mission broke down in a sandstorm. The mission was cancelled but then a fourth helicopter crashed into a transport plane causing an explosion which killed eight people. The Secretary of State, Cyrus Vance, who had opposed the mission, resigned and was replaced by Edward Muskie of Minnesota. The Shah died in Egypt in July 1980 but the hostages were held until the 20th January 1981, the day Carter left office.

The Election of 1980

In 1980, Carter was challenged for the Democratic presidential nomination by Senator Edward Kennedy of Massachusetts. Early polls put Kennedy a long way head of the President but Carter's handing of the Iranian hostage crisis helped him to regain popularity. At the Democratic National Convention in New York City, Carter won the nomination on the first ballot. Mondale was once again nominated as his running mate. The Republicans nominated the former Governor of California, Ronald Reagan, for President with the former U.S. ambassador to the United Nations, George Bush, for Vice-President. Representative John B. Anderson of Illinois and his running mate, Governor Patrick Lucey of Wisconsin, ran as independent candidates.

In the campaign, Carter stressed his achievements in office, which included the peace treaty between Egypt and Israel, while Reagan claimed that that the President had failed to deal effectively with the nation's problems such as high inflation and unemployment. Reagan won the election by a wide margin with 44 million votes to Carter's 35 million. Reagan won forty-four states gaining 489 electoral votes while Carter won six states and the District of Columbia leading only 49 electoral votes.

Later Years

After he left the White House, Carter enjoyed the longest life and the longest post-presidency of any former President. He remained active in politics and diplomacy, undertook charity work, promoted peace and human rights, wrote several books, and established a presidential library, which was dedicated in 1986. In 1982 he published his first memoirs, *Keeping Faith*. In 2002 he won the Nobel Prize for Peace for setting up the Carter Center for Human Rights. In 2015, he published his second memoirs *A Full Life*.

Summary

Jimmy Carter was a decent, honest and charming man whose determination and skill helped him achieve a remarkable rise to the White House. However, as President he proved incapable of effectively solving the country's problems. At home, inflation and unemployment remained high while abroad, his attempts to free American hostages in Iran led to disaster. He did have some noteworthy achievements in office, however. He negotiated a peace agreement between Israel and Egypt as well as establishing diplomatic relations with China. He has generally been ranked low among the Presidents. However, the American public recognize that his post-Presidency period was an accomplished one.

CHAPTER 40 – RONALD W. REAGAN

40ᵗʰ President of the United States 1981 – 1989

Born: 6ᵗʰ February 1911, Tampico, Illinois

Married: (1) Jane Wyman (1917 – 2007), 25ᵗʰ January 1940, divorced 1948 (2) Nancy Davis (1921 – 2016), 4ᵗʰ March 1952

Number of Children: Five (1) Three with Jane (2) Two with Nancy

Died: 5ᵗʰ June 2004, Los Angeles, California

Final Resting Place: Ronald W. Reagan Presidential Library, Simi Valley, California

Introduction

Ronald Reagan became the 40ᵗʰ President of the United States when he defeated Jimmy Carter in the election of 1980. Before entering the White House, he had been a well-known film actor and a Governor of California. When he became President, the United States was a rich and powerful country with nearly 227 million people. However, Reagan had severe problems to deal with at both home and abroad. On the day he became President, Iranian revolutionaries released all the American hostages that they had held for more than a year. The Cold War was at its height and the Soviet Union was attempting to subdue Afghanistan. The U.S. economy was affected by severe inflation and high unemployment. In 1981 the President survived an attempt on his life. Reagan recovered to become one America's most successful and popular Presidents. Tax cuts helped to revive the economy while high military spending and the Strategic Defense Initiative put the Soviet Union on the back foot. Reagan was re-elected with a landslide in 1984 and his second term was noted for improved relations with the Soviet Union and a tough stance against the growing menace of international terrorism.

Background

Ronald Wilson Reagan was born in Tampico, Illinois, on 6th February 1911. He was the second of two sons of a travelling shoe salesman. His father moved the family from town to town as he searched for work and the Reagans lived in several small towns in western Illinois. In 1920, his family settled in Dixon, which Reagan thereafter regarded as his home town. In 1928 he graduated from Dixon High School and enrolled in Eureka College near Peoria where he majored in economics and sociology. After graduation he worked as a radio announcer in Iowa and enlisted as a reserve officer in the U.S. cavalry.

However, Reagan had always been interested in acting and in 1937 he arranged a screen test with Warner Brothers in Hollywood. They offered him a contract as a film actor paying two hundred dollars per week. He made his first film, *Love is in the Air*, that year and made a total of 52 until his last film, *Hellcats in the Navy*, in 1957. His best film is considered to be *Kings Row*, which was made in 1942. That same year he entered the U.S. Army Air Force but was disqualified from combat because of poor eyesight. He then spent the rest of the Second World War in Hollywood where he helped to make training films. In December 1945 he was discharged with the rank of captain.

In 1947 he became president of the Screen Actors Guild (SAG), a union that represented film performers. He was elected for five consecutive terms until 1952. During that time, he helped to remove suspected Communists from the film industry. He served a sixth term in 1959 to 1960 during which time he led a successful strike against the movie studios which won payments to actors from sales of their old films to television. From 1954 to 1962 he hosted "The General Electric Theatre," a weekly dramatic series on television. He also starred in some of the episodes and toured the country as a public relations representative of General Electric. Between 1962 and 1965 he hosted and performed in a western series called "Death Valley Days" and made commercials for a maker of cleaning products.

On 25th January 1940 he married actress Jane Wyman, who he had met while they were appearing in films for Warner Brothers. They had two children but divorced in 1948. In 1951 he met actress Nancy Davis while working as president of SAG and they married on the 4th March 1952. They had three children.

Entry into Politics

Reagan's parents had benefitted from Franklin D. Roosevelt's "New Deal" and were Democrats. Reagan was originally a Democrat like his parents but, convinced that the Federal government was stifling economic growth, became a Republican in 1962. In 1964 he made a stirring televised speech on behalf of the Republican presidential candidate, Barry Goldwater, attacking high taxes, wasteful government spending and soaring welfare costs. He stressed that the United States was not doing enough to prevent the Soviet Union from attempting to dominate the world. Goldwater lost by a landslide but the Republicans had identified Reagan as a politician of the future.

In 1966, Reagan ran for Governor of California and defeated the incumbent Democrat, Pat Brown, by more than a million votes. As Governor, he tackled the budget deficit that he had inherited from his predecessor, made improvements to higher education, and reformed welfare. He was re-elected in 1970. Boosted by his success as Governor, Reagan made his first bid for the presidential nomination in 1968 but was not successful. In 1976, he narrowly lost the nomination to incumbent President, Gerald Ford.

Election of 1980

In November 1979, Reagan announced his candidacy for the presidential election of 1980. Six other Republicans also sought the nomination but Reagan achieved a huge lead in the polls. In February and March 1980, he won 20 of the first 24 primaries to be held and the other candidates withdrew from the race. In July 1980 he easily won the party's nomination on the first ballot at the Republican National Convention in Detroit. At his request, the former U.S. Ambassador to the U.N., George H. W. Bush, was nominated for Vice-President. The Democrats renominated President Jimmy Carter, with Walter F. Mondale for Vice-President. Representative John B. Anderson of Illinois ran as an independent candidate with former Governor Patrick J. Lucey of Wisconsin as his running mate. In the campaign, Reagan claimed that Carter had not dealt with inflation and unemployment effectively and said that he would stimulate the economy by cutting federal taxes. In the election, Reagan won by a wide margin. He received nearly 44 million votes to 35 million for Carter and won 44 states while Carter won six states and the District of Columbia. In the electoral college, Reagan won 489 votes to 49 for Carter and zero for Anderson.

Presidential Election of 1980		
Candidate	**Popular Votes**	**Electoral Votes**
Ronald W. Reagan (Rep.)	43,904,153	489
James E. Carter (Dem.)	35,483,883	49
John B. Anderson	5,720,060	0

Reagan's First Administration 1981 – 1985

Reagan was inaugurated on 20th January 1981. On the day that he became President, the Iranian government released the American hostages that it had held in Teheran for 444 days. Reagan's objectives for his first term were to revitalize the economy, reduce taxes, balance the federal budget, reduce the size and scope of the federal government, rebuild the military, and confront the Soviet Union from a position of strength. In February 1981, he announced his economic proposal to cut taxes, reduce federal spending but increase funds for defense. In March he asked Congress to approve a budget that would spend $695.3 billion but make cuts to two hundred programs.

On 30th March 1981, Reagan was leaving a hotel in Washington D.C. when he was shot in the chest and severely wounded. The surgeons removed the bullet and he made a full recovery. He told the doctors that were about to operate on him: "I hope you are all Republicans." Three other people were also struck by bullets including Reagan's press secretary, James S. Brady, who was badly wounded and later died. John W. Hinckley, Jr., of Evergreen, Colorado, was charged with the shooting. However, he was found not guilty for reason of insanity and confined to a hospital.

As Reagan recovered, his approval ratings soared and he pressed his economic program. In August 1981, Congress had approved nearly all his proposed cuts in taxes and government spending. Later that year the economy plunged into recession. This led to a fall in government tax revenues which, together with an increase in defense spending, led to a soaring budget deficit. Reagan supported the moves of the Federal Reserve Chairman, Paul Volcker, to use high interest rates to curb inflation and crush the recession. Unemployment rose but inflation subsided. In the first quarter of 1983, the economy grew dramatically and the recession ended. That July, a further tax cut came into effect. America would enjoy economic growth for the remainder of Reagan's term in office.

Reagan wanted to increase America's military strength so that he could negotiate arms reductions with the Soviet Union from a position of strength. In 1983 he called the Soviet Union the "evil empire." However, in his first term, the Soviet Union was led by a succession of hardline Communist leaders who refused to negotiate with him. On 23rd March 1983, Reagan announced a new proposal that he hoped would give America the advantage in the Cold War. Known as the "Strategic Defense Initiative" (SDI) or the "Star Wars

Program," it consisted of a defense system that would protect America from attacks by Soviet ballistic missiles. The proposed system would use both ground and space-based weapons, including lasers and particle-beam weapons, to destroy Soviet missiles before they could hit their targets in the U.S.

During Reagan's term of office, the United States had to deal with increasing international terrorism. In August 1982, U.S. troops were sent to Beirut to act as part of multi-national peace-keeping force with European allies following an invasion of Lebanon that summer by Israeli forces who were attempting to drive out Palestinian guerillas. On April 18th 1983, an Iranian-backed terrorist organization called Islamic Jihad (meaning "Holy War"), carried out a suicide bombing of the U.S. embassy killing 63 people as well as the bomber. Then early on the Sunday morning of October 23rd 1983, another suicide bomber smashed a truck full of explosives into the compound containing the barracks of the U.S. peace-keepers and detonated an explosion that caused the four-story building to collapse killing more than 220 U.S Marines.

While America was still coming to terms with the huge casualty list in Beirut, more than three thousand miles away, an American force of 7,600 troops invaded the Caribbean Island of Grenada. On October 19th 1983, Prime Minister Maurice Bishop was overthrown in a coup and murdered. Reagan was concerned that the new regime would take hostage the six hundred American medical students on the island creating a situation not dissimilar to that had faced by President Carter in Iran. The President was also concerned by a large Soviet and Cuban military build-up in Grenada and ordered the invasion which took place on 25th October, just two days after the bombing of the barracks in Beirut. Two days of fighting resulted in an American victory with only light casualties. Democracy was restored and free elections were held in 1984.

Election of 1984

Reagan announced his candidacy for the Presidency on 27th June 1984. In August he accepted the nomination against only token opposition at the Republican national convention in Dallas. Once again, George H.W. Bush was nominated as his running mate. The Democrats nominated former Vice-President Walter Mondale from Minnesota with Geraldine Ferraro, a Representative from New York, as his running mate. Reagan's campaign was helped by the withdrawal of U.S. troops from the Lebanon in February 1984 which eliminated a potential political liability for him. His campaign made very effective use of a television commercial which began with the words "It's morning again in America," and explained that the improvements in the economy were due to Reagan's policies. The President asked how anyone would want to return to the policies of the Democrats which had led to economic problems. Mondale attempted to make an issue of Reagan's age (he was already 73) and it was true that the President seem to fluff his lines during the first presidential debate. However, in the second debate Reagan said to great applause "I will not make age an issue of the campaign. I am not going to exploit, for political purposes, my opponent's youth and inexperience." In the election, Reagan won by a landslide carrying every state except for Mondale's home state of Minnesota. He received 525 votes in the electoral college to just 13 for Mondale.

Presidential Election of 1984		
Candidate	Popular Votes	Electoral Votes
Ronald Reagan (Rep.)	54,455,075	525
Walter Mondale (Dem.)	37,577,185	13

Second Term 1985 – 1989

In Reagan's second term the economy continued to expand but so did the budget deficit and national debt. Income and prosperity levels reached a new high. However, during his second term, the administration was criticized for a weak response to the acquired immunodeficiency syndrome (AIDS) pandemic, which had spread across America since 1981, and also for weak sanctions aimed at ending the apartheid regime in South Africa.

In the second term, Reagan once again had to deal with the increasing problem of international terrorism. Since taking power in Libya in 1969, Muammar Gaddafi had supported anti-western acts of terrorism around the world. In March 1986 there was a brief naval engagement in the Gulf of Sirte when Gaddafi's Libyan jets made a hostile approach on the U.S. carrier fleet. Shortly afterwards, on 5th April 1986, Libyan agents detonated a bomb in a discotheque in West Berlin used by U.S. troops. Two American soldiers and one Turkish civilian were killed. Reagan responded by ordering a series of airstrikes against ground targets in the Libyan cities of Tripoli and Benghazi. The attacks were carried out in the early hours of 15th April by F-111 airplanes flying from bases in England as well as A6 jets flying from carriers in the Mediterranean and killed up to 75 people. Reagan said that the attacks would halt Gaddafi's "ability to export terrorism." However, on 21st December 1988, a Libyan terrorist exploded a bomb on board a Pan Am 747 flying over Scotland. The airplane crashed on to the town of Lockerbie. All 259 people on board the flight were killed along with eleven on the ground. The terrorist responsible later served a long prison sentence in Scotland and the Libyan government paid compensation to the families of the victims.

During Reagan's presidency the Soviet Union had no less than four different leaders – Leonid Brezhnev (d. 1982), Yuri Andropov (d. 1984), Konstantin Chernenko (d. 1985) and Mikhail Gorbachev. When Gorbachev became the leader of the Soviet Union in March 1985, he was very much focused on reform. The country had a stagnant economy and found it difficult to finance her large military. It would be impossible for the Soviet Union to also finance her own "Star Wars program" and so Gorbachev was very concerned by the advantage that the SDI gave to America. On the other hand, Reagan supported the reforms in the Soviet Union, which he hoped would lead to the end of Communism. In November 1985, Reagan met Gorbachev at a summit in Geneva, Switzerland, which led to an improvement in relations between the two countries. In October

1986, the two men held their second summit at Reykjavik in Iceland where they nearly reached an agreement on bilateral nuclear disarmament. However, the talks collapsed when Reagan refused to abolish the SDI program.

In December 1987, Gorbachev visited the United States and made a good impression on the American people. While in Washington both he and Reagan signed the Intermediate Nuclear Forces Treaty (INF), which was the first treaty of the Cold War which reduced the number of nuclear weapons rather than just stabilize their numbers. The INF abolished all ground-launched ballistic and cruise missiles with ranges of 500km to 5500km (310 miles to 3420 miles). The Treaty paved the way for better relations and for further agreements to reduce nuclear arms. In May 1988, Reagan went to Moscow where he and Gorbachev held their fourth summit at the Kremlin Palace. The improved relationships between the two countries led to better cooperation on international issues and increased trade. When Reagan left office there was optimism in Europe that reforms would take place across the Eastern Bloc. In 1987, Reagan had visited Berlin and made a speech asking Gorbachev to "tear down this wall." Shortly after he left office, the Berlin Wall was dismantled and the Iron Curtain was swept aside.

In the final years in office, the reputation of Reagan's presidency became tarnished by what became known as the *Iran-Contra Affair*. In 1986 it was learned that members of his National Security Council had engineered secret arms sales to Iran, which was then fighting a bloody war with Iraq, in an ill-conceived attempt to win the release of Americans held hostage in the Lebanon. This was in violation of the administration's own arms embargo. Some of the proceeds had then been funneled to Contra rebels fighting the Marxist government in Nicaragua, which the CIA and Department of Defense had been prohibited from doing by Congress since 1982. In November 1986, the transactions were exposed in a Lebanese magazine and Congress set up the Tower Commission to investigate them. In February 1987, the Commission confirmed that the administration had traded arms for hostages and sent the proceeds to the contras. However, there was no evidence that the President knew that the proceeds of the arm sales had been diverted to the Contras. Nevertheless, the credibility of the administration had been tarnished.

Later Years

Reagan left office in January 1989 and handed the presidency to his favored successor, George H.W. Bush. During his time in office, he had the highest approval rating of any President since Franklin D. Roosevelt forty-four years before. In 1994, he announced he was suffering from Alzheimer's Disease. He died on 5th June 2005 and was mourned around the world.

Summary

Ronald Reagan was a former film actor that became a popular and well-regarded President. He was twice elected to the White House with landslide victories and his tax cuts helped to lead to increased prosperity, with falling levels inflation and unemployment. He dealt effectively with foreign policy problems and there was an improvement in relations with the Soviet Union. By the time Reagan left office, the end of the Cold War was in sight. Although his reputation has been affected by the Iran-Contra Affair, he still enjoys one of the highest rankings of all the Presidents.

CHAPTER 41 – GEORGE H.W. BUSH

41ˢᵗ President of the United States 1989 – 1993

Born: 12ᵗʰ June 1924, Milton, Massachusetts

Married: Barbara Pierce (1925 – 2018), 6ᵗʰ January 1945

Number of Children: Six

Died: 30ᵗʰ November 2018

Final Resting Place: George H.W. Bush Presidential Library and Museum, College Station, Texas

Introduction

George Herbert Walker Bush became the 41ˢᵗ President of the United States after winning the election of 1988. He had previously served as the U.S. ambassador to the United Nations, the Head of the CIA and as Vice-President to Ronald Reagan. He became the President at a time when the U.S. population surpassed 250 million people and America was the wealthiest country in the world. As President, he is best known for bringing the Cold War to a successful close. One Eastern European country after another made the peaceful transition from Communist dictatorship to democracy. In 1989, the Berlin Wall ceased to divide the city and Germany was reunified in 1990. The following year the Soviet Union disintegrated into fifteen separate republics. Bush also sent U.S. forces to depose Panama's General Noriega in 1989 and to lead the liberation of Kuwait from Iraqi occupation in 1991. However, Bush lost popularity as the U.S. economy faltered and he felt forced to break his promise not to raise taxes. In 1992, Republican support was divided by an independent conservative candidate, Ross Perot, and the charismatic Democratic challenger, Bill Clinton, defeated Bush in that year's presidential election.

Background

George Herbert Walker Bush was born on 12th June 1924 in Milton, Massachusetts. He was the son of a wealthy investment banker who later became a U.S. Senator for Connecticut. His eldest son, George Walker Bush, became the 43rd President of the United States. They were only the second father and son to become President of the U.S. after John Adams (second) and John Quincy Adams (sixth). George H.W. Bush was also the father of Jeb Bush, the Governor of Florida, who ran for the Republican presidential nomination in 2016.

Bush was raised in a wealthy family and was privately educated at the Phillips Academy Andover. He then joined the U.S. Navy and qualified as one of its youngest pilots. In the Second World War he saw action against the Japanese in the Pacific where he piloted torpedo-bombers flying from aircraft carriers. In September 1944, he was shot down and survived in a life raft until rescued by a U.S. submarine. On 6th January 1945 he married Barbara Pierce, whose ancestor Franklin Pierce had been the 14th President of the U.S.A. They enjoyed a marriage lasting 72 years and had six children.

Entry into Politics

After the war, Bush attended Yale University where he graduated with a degree in economics. After college, he moved with his family to Texas where he worked in the oil business. By the age of 40 he was a millionaire. His first political role was as the Republican Party Chairman in Harris County, Texas. In 1966 he was elected to the U.S. House of Representatives where he served two terms. In 1970 he ran unsuccessfully for a seat in the U.S. Senate. However, in 1971 President Nixon appointed him the U.S. ambassador to the United Nations. This was the first of several high-ranking positions that he held in the Nixon and Ford administrations. He later served as chairman of the Republican National Committee, the U.S. ambassador to China in 1974, and the director of Central Intelligence in 1976.

In 1980 he ran for the Republican presidential nomination and became the main challenger to Ronald Reagan. Although Bush was defeated, Reagan invited him to become his vice-presidential running mate. Reagan felt that Bush offered vast experience in foreign policy and would attract support with his moderate views. Bush spent eight years as Vice-President as Reagan was elected by large majorities in both 1980 and 1984. During this time, Bush travelled widely and expanded his foreign policy experience.

The Election of 1988

In 1988, Bush ran for President offering a continuation of the Reagan years. He did not propose any radical changes or sweeping new legislation but promised "a kinder and gentler nation." He selected Senator James (Dan) Quayle from Indiana as his vice-presidential running mate and they were formally nominated at the Republican convention in New Orleans in August. The Democrats nominated the governor of Massachusetts, Michael Dukakis, for President and Senator Lloyd Bentsen of Texas for Vice-President.

After an acrimonious campaign, Bush won the election by a landslide carrying 40 states to ten states and the District of Columbia for Dukakis. Bush received more than 400 votes in the electoral college, the last time this has been achieved. It was also the last time that the Republicans won the popular vote three times in a row. However, in elections held at the same time, the Democrats retained control of both houses of Congress.

Presidential Election of 1988		
Candidate	Popular Votes	Electoral Votes
George H. W. Bush (Rep.)	48,886,097	426
Michael Dukakis (Dem.)	41,809,074	111

Bush was the first serving Vice-President since Martin Van Buren 150 years before to become President through his own election.

Bush's Administration 1989 – 1993

Bush was sworn in as President on 20th January 1989. In his inaugural speech he claimed that the era of the dictator was over. Many of the key events of his presidency concerned matters in foreign policy.

Bush became President at a time of momentous change in Europe. The *Iron Curtain* which had divided the continent between the democratic countries in the west and the Communist dictatorships in the east began to be swept aside as one country after another in Eastern Europe began to reform. The leader of the Soviet Union, Mikhail Gorbachev, made the decision not to intervene militarily in these countries to reimpose Communism effectively abandoning what was known as the *Brezhnev Doctrine*. In June 1989, the Solidarity trade union won a partially free election which led to the peaceful fall of Communism in Poland. That same month, Hungary began to dismantle her portion of the Iron Curtain and opened the border with Austria. This gave people living in Eastern Europe a route to freedom in the West and led quickly to the disintegration of the Eastern Bloc. Many of the people who travelled West came from East Germany where the most visible symbol of the Iron Curtain, the Berlin Wall, had prevented East-West movement since August 1961. Following mass demonstrations across the country, East German border guards cut crossing points into the wall on 9th November, and it was completely dismantled shortly after. Communist governments also fell in Bulgaria, Czechoslovakia and Romania.

The potential for reuniting East and West Germany was discussed at a summit in Malta in December 1989. Russia, France and Britain had reservations but both President Bush and Chancellor Kohl of West Germany were keen that it should happen. After extensive negotiations, Germany was officially reunified in October 1990. Gorbachev also agreed that Germany could join NATO. However, although Gorbachev did not intervene in the changes taking place in

Eastern Europe, he did suppress movements for change within the Soviet Union. Bush took no action when Russian troops invaded Lithuania in January 1991 to suppress a nationalist movement. In August 1991, Gorbachev's leadership of the Soviet Union was fatally undermined when hardline Communists launched a coup in Moscow. Although the coup it led to the dissolution of the Soviet Union in December 1991. What used to be called the Union of Soviet Socialist Republics (USSR) was replaced by fifteen independent Republics of which the largest was Russia. When Bush met the new leader of Russia, Boris Yeltsin, they agreed to further reduce nuclear weapons following the Strategic Arms Reduction Treaty (START 1) previously agreed with Gorbachev in July 1991.

While the Cold War was ending in Europe, Bush also had to face challenges closer to home. In May 1989, the anti-Communist leader of Panama, Manuel Noriega, annulled the results of a democratic election in which his opponent, Guillermo Endara, had been elected. Bush was concerned by the status of the Panama Canal and responded by sending 2,000 troops to the Panama Canal Zone which the United States had the legal right to defend. In December 1989, Panamanian troops shot a U.S. serviceman and Bush ordered a full-scale invasion of Panama called *Operation Just Cause*, which began on December 20th. American troops quickly occupied the capital, Panama City, and Noriega surrendered on the 3rd January 1990. Twenty-three Americans died in the operation and nearly four hundred were injured. Noriega was transported to the United States where he was convicted of trafficking drugs and racketeering in April 1992 and imprisoned with a 40-year sentence. However, the United Nations condemned the invasion as a violation of international law.

Bush faced another difficult challenge when on the 2nd August 1990 the Iraqi dictator, Saddam Hussein, launched an invasion of neighboring Kuwait. The country was quickly occupied and Iraqi troops perpetrated a large number of atrocities against the civilian population. Occupation of Kuwait meant that Hussein now controlled a quarter of the world's oil reserves and Bush was concerned that his troops may try and invade Saudi Arabia, which would give him control of another quarter. When Hussein ignored a UN resolution to withdraw, Bush imposed sanctions and began to build a multi-national coalition. Initially the aim of the coalition was to prevent the invasion of Saudi Arabia, an operation known as *Desert Shield.* However, Congress approved the use of force to remove Iraqi troops from Kuwait and Hussein was given until the 15th January 1991 to withdraw. When he failed to do so, the coalition began an operation called "Desert Storm" to liberate Kuwait. The campaign began on 16th January with the bombing of targets in Iraq and Kuwait. Hussein then responded by launching Scud missiles against Israel and Saudi Arabia. On 23rd February, American troops spearheaded a ground invasion which successfully evicted all Iraqi forces from Kuwait within four days. A ceasefire was arranged on the 3rd March. Given the large forces involved, allied casualties were relatively light. Three hundred American troops were killed along with sixty-five from other coalition countries. In March 1991, Bush enjoyed an approval rating of eighty-nine percent, at the time the highest in history.

As 1991 progressed, the American people became less concerned by Bush's successful handling of foreign affairs and more concerned by the state of the economy. In 1990 the American economy slipped into recession for the first time since 1982 and unemployment rose. At the same time the federal deficit increased by $220 billion and in October 1990 Bush was forced to break his promise not to raise taxes when he increased the top rate for America's highest earners. This damaged his standing both with conservatives and the public. His standing was also affected when he was taken ill and fainted while attending a dinner with the Prime Minister of Japan in January 1992.

Bush was renominated for President in the election of 1992, once again with Dan Quayle as his running mate. The Democrats nominated the Governor of Arkansas, Bill Clinton, for President with Senator Al Gore of Tennessee as his running mate. Clinton successfully made an issue of the faltering economy and offered the country "a new beginning." Bush did not help his cause when he looked at his watch while the recession was being discussed during a presidential debate. He was also poorly helped by his Vice-President who made a series of embarrassing gaffes. In June 1992, Quayle visited a school in Trenton, New Jersey, where he publicly and incorrectly altered a twelve-years-old pupil's spelling of "potato" to "potatoe". The entry into the election of an independent candidate, Texan billionaire Ross Perot, also drew votes from Bush. In the election, Bush gained 168 votes in the electoral college to 310 for Clinton.

During his last months in office, Bush agreed to sign the *North American Free Trade Agreement(NAFTA)* with Canada and Mexico in December 1992. He also committed U.S. troops to a peace-keeping mission in the East African country of Somalia. Bush left the White House in January 1993.

Later Years

In his later years, Bush supported the political careers of his sons. Jeb Bush became Governor of Florida while George Bush, Jr., served as the Governor of Texas and the 43rd President of the United States. In 2011, President Obama awarded Bush the Presidential Medal of Freedom. Barbara Bush died in April 2018 aged 92. President Bush died on 30th November 2018 at the age of 94 and was buried next to Barbara at the George H.W. Bush Presidential Library in College Station, Texas.

Summary

George H.W. Bush was one of America's most successful foreign policy Presidents. During his administration the Cold War ended and the Iron Curtain was swept aside, and Kuwait was liberated from Iraqi occupation. However, he was not as successful at dealing with America's economic problems and seemed to be out of touch with voters and their concerns. He lost support when he broke his promise not to raise taxes. It is due to his foreign policy achievements that he is usually ranked in the top twenty Presidents.

CHAPTER 42 – BILL CLINTON

42nd President of the United States 1993 – 2001

Born: 19th August 1946, Hope, Arkansas

Married: Hillary Rodham (1947 –), 11th October 1975

Number of Children: One

Introduction

Bill Clinton became the 42nd President of the United States after defeating George H.W. Bush in the election of 1992. Before entering the White House, Clinton had served as Governor of Arkansas. As President he is best remembered for being impeached over the Monica Lewinsky Affair. He was only the second President to be impeached but successfully defended himself against the charges. During in his time in office, America was the richest and most powerful country in the world with a population exceeding 256 million. Clinton used America's strength to promote peace in the Middle East and Northern Ireland. He took military action to defend the people of Kosovo from Serbia and the Kurds in Iraq from Saddam Hussein. He took a tough stance against terrorism in the United States and overseas. In 1996 he became the first Democrat since Franklin Roosevelt to win consecutive presidential elections. During his second term the economy continued the longest period of expansion in history and the budget deficit was eliminated.

Background

Bill Clinton was born on 19th August 1946 in Hope, Arkansas. His name at birth was William Jefferson Blythe III. His father, William Jefferson Blythe Jr., was a travelling salesman who was killed in a road accident three months before he was born. His mother, Virginia Dell Cassidy, later remarried a car dealer, Roger Clinton Jr., and Bill adopted his stepfather's surname.

Clinton attended Hot Springs High School and then studied at Georgetown University, from which he graduated in 1968. He won a scholarship to University College at Oxford University but he left before completing his degree. In 1994, while serving his first term as President of the United States, he received an honorary degree from the University. Returning to America at the time of the Vietnam War, Clinton registered for the draft but was not selected for military service. Clinton then attended Yale Law School and received his degree in 1973. In 1971, he met his future wife, Hillary Rodham Clinton, in the Yale Law Library. They married on October 11th 1975 and had one child, Chelsea Clinton.

Entry into Politics

After graduating from Yale, Clinton briefly taught law at the University of Arkansas. However, Clinton was drawn to a career in politics having been inspired by Martin Luther King's "I have a dream" speech in August 1963 as well as a brief meeting with President John F. Kennedy in the White House that same year. In 1974, he ran for the U.S. House of Representatives but was defeated by the Republican candidate, John Paul Hammerschmidt. In 1976, however, he successfully ran for Attorney General of Arkansas and was then elected the Governor of Arkansas in 1978. Aged only 31, he was one of the youngest Governors in the history of the state.

In 1980, he lost office after being defeated by the Republican challenger, Frank D. White, but was elected for a second term in 1982. He stayed in office for ten years being re-elected for a two-year term in 1984 and for four-year terms in 1986 and 1990. He was still serving as Governor when he ran for President in 1992. During his time as Governor, he took important steps to improve the state's education and economy.

Election of 1992

During the 1980's Clinton became one of the leading Democrats and advocated a more centrist political stance. In 1992 he stood as a candidate for the Democratic Party nomination. He made a poor start after it came to light that he had had an extra-marital affair with Gennifer Flowers, a former employee of the State of Arkansas. However, his fortunes turned when his wife publicly supported him in a television interview and he secured the nomination after winning the primaries in most of the Southern states, New York and California.

At the time of the 1992 election, the Republicans had been in power for twelve years and for twenty of the previous twenty-four years. His Republican rival was George Bush, who enjoyed enormous approval ratings after victory in the Gulf War of 1991. However, during Bush's last year in office his approval ratings declined as the economy worsened and taxes were increased. His vote was also affected by an independent candidate, the billionaire Ross Perot, who ran on a populist platform.

Meanwhile, Clinton emphasized his moderate record as Governor of Arkansas and with his running mate, Tennessee Senator Al Gore, travelled all over America pledging a "new beginning" for the country.

In the election, Clinton carried 32 states as well as the District of Columbia gaining 370 votes in the electoral college, whereas Bush carried only 19 states gaining 168 electoral votes. Clinton won 43 percent of the popular vote to Bush's 38 percent. Ross Perot won nearly 19 percent of the popular vote but did not win any states or votes in the electoral college.

Presidential Election of 1992		
Candidate	Popular Votes	Electoral Votes
William J. Clinton (Dem.)	44,909,326	370
George H.W. Bush (Rep.)	39,103,882	168
H. Ross Perot (Ind.)	19,741,657	0

Clinton's First Term 1993 – 1997

Clinton was inaugurated as the 42nd President of the United States on 20th January 1993. At the time the economy was only beginning to recover from recession and there was a big budget deficit. He attempted to introduce a stimulus package worth sixteen billion dollars to help the inner cities but this was defeated by a Republican filibuster in the Senate. He then announced to Congress that rather than cutting taxes for the middle classes as promised in his election campaign, he would raise taxes in an attempt to close the budget deficit. In August 1993, he signed the Omnibus Budget Reconciliation Act which cut taxes for low-income families and small businesses while raising them for America's wealthiest individuals. Later that year he expanded Earned Income Tax Credits, a subsidy for low-income workers.

During Clinton's term of office, the United States suffered from attacks made by both domestic and international terrorists. On February 26th 1993, little more than one month after Clinton's inauguration, a bomb concealed in a van detonated in a car park under the North Tower of the World Trade Centre which was intended to destroy both skyscrapers. Although it failed to cause the towers to collapse, the bomb killed six people and injured more than a thousand others. An anti-American Islamist terrorist organization called Al Qaeda claimed responsibility. Six terrorists were later convicted and imprisoned. On April 19th 1995, a bomb concealed in a truck was detonated in front of the Alfred P. Murrah Building in Oklahoma City killing 168 people and injuring 680 others. The building housed fourteen federal agencies. The bomb had been planted by two American white supremacists, Timothy McVeigh and Terry Nicholls, who were angry with the way federal law enforcement officers had ended the Waco Siege exactly two years earlier. In that incident the officers tried to force access to a ranch occupied by a religious cult called the Branch Davidians, which then caught fire leading to the deaths of at least 75 people, including 25 children. In August 1998, truck bombs destroyed the American embassies in Nairobi, Kenya, and Dar es Saleem, Tanzania. The two bombs killed more than two hundred people and injured over 5,000 more. Al Qaeda claimed responsibility and the U.S. retaliated by firing cruise missiles at targets in Afghanistan and Sudan.

One foreign policy problem that President Clinton inherited from his predecessor was Somalia. In December 1992, President Bush had sent U.S. troops to Mogadishu to provide humanitarian assistance and help the country to begin to recover from famine and civil war. However, a local warlord, Mohammed Farah Aidid, harassed and killed the peace-keeping forces and humanitarian workers as well as attempting to resist any attempts at reform. On October 3rd 1993, U.S. special forces attempted to capture him in a quick and precise military operation. However, two helicopters were shot down and ground forces were then ambushed as they attempted to reach them. In the battle that ensued, 18 Americans were killed and 84 injured. The bodies of the dead were shown being dragged through the streets on television. Clinton responded by announcing that all American military personnel would be withdrawn from Somalia by the end of March 1994 and the last troops left on March 25th. Clinton's lack of foreign policy experience was exposed and he was criticized for not capturing Aidid.

Iraq, still under the leadership of dictator Saddam Hussein, continued to be a problem throughout Clinton's term of office. In June 1993, the U.S. Navy fired twenty-three Tomahawk missiles at intelligence-related targets in Baghdad after it came to light that the Iraqis had plotted to kill former President George Bush during his visit to Kuwait that April. In October 1994, the Iraqis built up their forces on the border with Kuwait with the view of once again invading and occupying that country. Clinton responded by dispatching 35,000 U.S. troops to the Gulf which not only deterred an invasion but forced the Iraqis to pull their troops back. In September 1996, Clinton ordered another cruise missile strike against Iraq to bring to and end an assault by Iraqi troops on the Kurdish city of Irbil. In December 1998, three days of air attacks forced Saddam Hussein to cooperate with weapons inspectors from the United Nations. The Iraqi leader remained in power, and a dangerous menace, when Clinton left office in January 2001.

In the former country of Yugoslavia, a civil war had raged since 1991 as the nations of Croatia and Bosnia fought to establish their independence from Serbia. It had become the worst conflict in Europe since the Second World War claiming the lives of more than 250,000 people and making more than two million people homeless refugees. In November 1993, representatives of Serbia, Croatia and Bosnia met in Dayton, Ohio, and agreed in principle a peace settlement brokered by Richard Holbrooke, the Assistant Secretary of State of the United States, which brought the conflict to an end. An independent state of Bosnia was created and many refugees could return home. The peace agreement was formally signed in Paris the following month. Clinton committed 20,000 U.S. peace-keeping troops to Bosnia to help enforce the ceasefire. In February 1999, U.S. and NATO air forces attacked Serbia after that country had reneged on an agreement to grant more autonomy to the province of Kosovo. It was reported that Serbian troops had conducted ethnic cleansing in Kosovo and Albania. On June 9th, Serbia agreed to withdraw from Kosovo and the air campaign came to an end. An international peacekeeping force of 50,000 troops helped to enforce the agreement. Clinton was criticized for not making the same commitment to end the civil war in Rwanda, which had cost two million lives.

Clinton did make important contributions towards world peace during his term of office. In Europe he introduced a *Partnership for Peace* program which aimed to build closer ties between NATO and former members of the Warsaw Pact. He committed 100,000 troops towards upholding the peace and security of Europe. In December 1994, he signed the Strategic Arms Reduction Treaty (START I) with the presidents of Russia, Ukraine, Kazakhstan, and Belarus which eliminated 9,000 nuclear warheads. In 1996 the US ratified START II, which further reduced nuclear arsenals. The same year, the U.S. agreed to an international treaty which banned the testing of all nuclear weapons. In 1997, the Senate ratified the *Chemical Weapons Convention* by which the signatory countries agreed not to produce, stock-pile or use chemical weapons.

Clinton also played an important role in promoting peace in the Middle East. In 1993 he presided over a ceremony in Washington in which the Israel Prime Minister, Yitzhak Rabin, and the Chairman of the Palestinian Liberation Organization (PLO) agreed to the Oslo I Accord, which provided for Palestinian self-government in the Gaza Strip and the West Bank. Clinton also then brokered talks between the leaders of Israel and Jordan aimed at ending 50 years of antagonism between the two countries. In November 1995, Clinton became the first President to visit Northern Ireland where he met with leaders of the conflicting Protestant and Catholic communities to encourage them to make peace. He played a key role in the peace process that led to the *Good Friday Peace Accords* in April 1998 that ended many years of violent conflict.

Presidential Election 1996

In the mid-term elections of 1994, the Republicans gained control of both houses of Congress for the first time in forty years. However, by 1996 the growing economy had helped Clinton to make a recovery in the polls.

The Republicans nominated Senator Robert Dole for President with Jack Kemp as his running mate. Dole was already 73 years old and his age became an issue in the election. He promised tax cuts while Clinton claimed that the Republicans would cut spending on popular social security and Medicare programs.

In the election, Clinton won 49 percent of the vote and carried 31 states as well as the District of Columbia. Dole won 41 percent of the vote and carried 19 states. Ross Perot ran as an independent

311

candidate with Pat Chorta as his running mate and won 8 percent of the vote. In the electoral college, Clinton won 379 votes to 159 for Dole. Clinton was the first Democrat since Franklin D. Roosevelt to win re-election for a second term.

Presidential Election of 1996		
Candidate	Popular Votes	Electoral Votes
William Clinton (Dem.)	47,402,357	379
Robert Dole (Rep.)	39,198,755	159
Ross Perot (Ind.)	8,085,402	0

Clinton's Second Administration 1997 – 2001

Clinton began his second term in January 1997 and there were some noteworthy achievements. The economy continued to enjoy the longest period of expansion in history and enabled Clinton to eliminate the budget deficit. He also continued to play a leading role in the Middle East peace process. In October 1998, nine days of talks in rural Maryland led to the *Wye River Memorandum*, agreed with the leaders of Israel and the PLO, by which Israel began to withdraw troops from the West Bank.

However, Clinton's second term is usually associated with the *Monica Lewinsky Affair*, which led to his impeachment. In January 1998 the news broke that Clinton may have had a sexual relationship with a former White House intern named Monica Lewinsky. The couple had an eighteen-month affair between 1995 and 1997 which started when he was 49 and she was 22. He denied the allegations, publicly stating "I did not have sexual relations with that woman, Monica Lewinsky." In July, Lewinsky was granted immunity from prosecution in return for providing testimony to a Grand Jury investigating the relationship. She turned over a blue dress with a semen stain on it which was then matched to Clinton's DNA using a blood sample. The stain contradicted Clinton's claim that he did not have sexual relations with Lewinsky. On 17th August, Clinton admitted to the Grand Jury that he had engaged in an "improper physical relationship" with Lewinsky. That night he delivered a televised address in which he told the nation that his relationship with Lewinsky was inappropriate. The following month, Independent Counsel, Kenneth Starr, issued a report which led to the House of Representatives approving two articles of impeachment, one for "obstruction of justice" and the other for "perjury." After a twenty-one-day trial in the Senate, Clinton was acquitted on February 12th 1999. Neither article received the two-thirds majority vote of the Senators present.

Later Years

Clinton's second term ended in January 2001, when he attended the inauguration of President George W. Bush. After he left office, he continued to play a part in public life and to support charitable causes. He survived quadruple heart by-pass surgery in 2004. That same year he published his memoirs and opened the Bill Clinton Library in Arkansas. In 2008 and 2016 he supported his wife's own bid to become President.

Summary

Bill Clinton had many positive achievements in office. The economy enjoyed an unprecedented period of growth and the budget deficit was removed. America promoted peace moves in the Middle East and Northern Ireland. However, his behavior in the Monica Lewinsky Affair was shameful. But he was neither the first nor the last President to bring scandal and disgrace to the White House. Of more crucial importance, he failed to deal effectively with the growing problem of terrorism and within months of leaving office terrorists would bring death to people of New York and Washington D.C. He is ranked in the middle of all the Presidents.

CHAPTER 43 – GEORGE W. BUSH

43rd President of the United States 2001 – 2009

Born: 6th July 1946, New Haven, Connecticut

Married: Laura Welch (1946 –), 5th November 1977

Number of Children: Two

Introduction

George W. Bush was a successful businessman who was elected as the 43rd President of the United States. He was the son of the 41st President, George H.W. Bush. He was the second President after John Quincy Adams whose father had also been President. Before he entered the White House, Bush had served as the Governor of Texas. In 2000, he won one of the most closely contested elections in American history. He served at a time when America was considered as the world's only *hyperpower* with 290 million people. As President, he had to tackle some of the gravest challenges in the nation's history. On 11th September 2001, attacks by Al-Qaeda terrorists killed nearly 3,000 people in New York, Washington D.C., and Pennsylvania, and led to a long military commitment in Afghanistan. In 2003, American troops spearheaded an invasion of Iraq as part of a war on terror which led to a further long military commitment in that country. Bush was re-elected in 2004 but faced further tough challenges in his second term. In 2005, Hurricane Katrina devastated a large part of the south-eastern United States in one of the worst natural disasters in the nation's history. In 2008, a serious financial crisis led to failures of banks and businesses and a large increase in unemployment. Since leaving office, Bush's presidency had been frequently criticized but there have been no further large-scale terrorist attacks inside the United States.

Background

George Walker Bush was born in New Haven, Connecticut, on 6th July 1946. He was the eldest of six children of the future President of the United States, George Herbert Walker Bush, and his wife Barbara. One of his sisters died of leukemia at the age of four. He attended primary schools in Texas and then entered the Phillips Academy in Andover, Massachusetts, in 1961. Upon graduation he studied at Yale University where he completed a bachelor's degree in History in 1968. He then served in the Air National Guard until November 1974. The following year he completed a master's degree in Business Administration at Harvard University. He then worked in oil industry in Texas. In 1977 he met and married Laura Lane Welch, a former teacher and librarian from Midland, Texas. They had twin daughters in 1981. In 1989 he was part of a consortium that purchased the Texas Rangers baseball team and he served as their managing general partner for the next five years.

Entry into Politics

In 1978 Bush ran for a seat in the U.S. House of Representatives but was unsuccessful. In 1994 he was elected the Governor of Texas promising to improve education, reform welfare and reduce crime. During his first term of office, he was able to introduce tax cuts. In 1998 he was re-elected with sixty-nine percent of the vote. He was the first Governor of Texas to be elected for two consecutive four-year terms. He continued to enjoy high approval ratings and in 1999 decided to seek the nomination for President in the 2000 election.

Election 2000

Bush campaigned in the Republican primaries as a centrist and said that he wanted to cut taxes, improve education, expand the military and aid minorities. He won the nomination comfortably ahead of his main opponent, Senator John McCain of Arizona. Bush named the former White House Chief of Staff and Secretary of Defense, Dick Cheney, as his running mate. The Democrats nominated Senator Al Gore of Tennessee for President and Senator Joe Lieberman of Connecticut for Vice-President. In his campaign, Bush criticized Gore over taxation and gun control. In the election Bush won 29 states including Florida. However, the closeness of the outcome in Florida led to a recount which also went in favor of Bush. Gore then challenged the result in the courts for a month until the Supreme Court stopped a further recount and upheld a previously certified total. Bush therefore won Florida by just 537 votes out of six million cast. As a result of winning Florida's votes in the electoral college, Bush won the election by 271 electoral votes to Gore's 266. Nationwide, however, Bush received 543,895 votes less than Gore and was the first President to win the election with fewer popular votes since Benjamin Harrison in 1888.

Presidential Election of 2000		
Candidate	Popular Votes	Electoral Votes
George W. Bush (Rep.)	50,456,141	271
Al Gore (Dem.)	50,996,039	266
Ralph Nader (Green)	2,882,807	0

Bush's First Term 2001 – 2005

Bush was inaugurated as President on 20th January 2001. His first eight months in office were concerned primarily with domestic matters. In June 2001 he introduced tax cuts of $1.35 trillion dollars. Further tax cuts were introduced in 2003 in a bid to stimulate the economy and create jobs. In terms of domestic policy, Bush signed important laws concerning education, health and abortion. In January 2002, he signed an education reform bill known as the *No Child Left Behind Act* which aimed to improve standards in math and reading.

316

In November 2003 he signed a law which banned late-term abortions. The following month he overhauled Medicare and provided assistance to people in the payment for prescription drugs.

On 11th September 2001, Bush was visiting a school in Florida when news arrived of an event that became the turning point of his presidency. Just before nine o'clock in the morning, a Boeing 767 crashed into the North Tower of the World Trade Centre. At first it looked like a terrible accident but shortly afterwards a second Boeing 767 crashed into the South Tower. Both airplanes had been hijacked by terrorists from Al Qaeda and then deliberately flown into the Twin Towers. Both towers then collapsed within one hour trapping and killing thousands of people. Meanwhile, a third hijacked airplane, a Boeing 757, crashed into the Pentagon, which partly collapsed. Another 757 was then crashed in rural Pennsylvania after passengers bravely tried to recover control of the plane from the hijackers. They prevented the plane being crashed into either the White House or Capitol. The attacks were the most devastating acts of terrorism in history killing nearly three thousand innocent people, injuring perhaps as many as 25,000 more and damaging or destroying more than $10 billion of property. All nineteen of the hijackers died in the attacks. One week later – and probably not connected – deadly anthrax spores were sent in a series of letters to senior government figures infecting seventeen people and killing five. Bush responded by creating the *U.S. Department of Homeland Security* and signing the *USA PATRIOT Act* which authorized detention without trial, increased surveillance, and tougher penalties. His approval rating soared to ninety percent, the highest in history.

The terrorist attacks had been planned in Afghanistan where the Al Qaeda terrorist organization was sheltered by the unpleasant Taliban regime. When the Taliban refused to hand over Osama Bin Laden and other Al Qaeda leaders, Bush launched an invasion of Afghanistan to depose the Taliban, drive out the terrorists and capture Al Qaeda's leaders. This was the first part of a *war on terror* and commenced on October 7th 2001 when America and Britain initiated a bombing campaign. By November 13th, troops from the Northern Alliance had captured the capital, Kabul, and the U.N.

were able to install a transitional administration under Hamid Karzai. However, Osama Bin laden escaped and managed to evade capture for ten years until he was killed by US Navy SEALS in 2011. Although driven from power, the Taliban regrouped and Bush had to send further troops to Afghanistan in 2007. It was the beginning of a long commitment which did not end until the last U.S. troops were withdrawn in 2021, nearly twenty years after the terrorist attacks in New York and Washington.

In his State of the Union address in January 2002, Bush said that Iraq was part of an "axis of evil" that supported terrorist acts and posed a threat to the United States by possessing weapons of mass destruction (WMD). He later accused the Iraqi leader, Saddam Hussein, of constructing nuclear, biological and chemical weapons and then concealing them from the inspectors of the United Nations (UN). In late 2002 and early 2003 he urged the UN to enforce the disarmament of Iraq. The UN sent inspectors into Iraq to determine if Iraq had developed WMD but were not given time to complete their inspections before Bush ordered an invasion of the country. Bush constructed an alliance of twenty nations which he called "the coalition of the willing" and on 20th March 2003 their forces invaded Iraq from the south. The Iraqi army was defeated quickly and Baghdad fell on 9th April. Saddam was removed from power and went into hiding. On 1st May Bush announced that the mission in Iraq had been accomplished and that major combat operations were over. However, no evidence was ever found that Iraq had possessed WMD and they did not use them in the war. Bush's critics accused him of exaggerating the threat posed by Iraq and said that the war had been fought so that he could gain control of Iraq's oil as well as to settle his family's feud with Hussein. The initial success of the war briefly increased Bush's popularity in the United States. However, in the wake of the war the U.S. and allied forces faced a growing insurgency from sectarian groups, and large numbers of American troops had to stay in the country. In January 2005, free elections were held in Iraq for the first time in fifty years and led to the election of a new President and Prime Minister. A new constitution was adopted in October 2005 with widespread support across Iraq. Hussein was captured in December 2003, put on trial for crimes against humanity, and executed by hanging in December 2006.

Election 2004

Bush stood for re-election in 2004 and did not face a challenge from within his own party. In September 2004 he accepted the nomination at the Republican national convention in New York City and once again chose Dick Cheney as his running mate.

The Democrats nominated Senator John Kerry of Massachusetts for President with Senator John Edwards of North Carolina as his running mate. The main focus of the election was Bush's foreign policy and, in particular, his handling of the war on terror and the invasion of Iraq. The most important domestic issues debated concerned the economy, jobs, healthcare, abortion and same-sex marriage.

The result of the 2004 election was not as close as that of 2000. Bush carried 31 states gaining 286 votes in the electoral college, whereas Kerry carried only 19 states as well as the District of Columbia, gaining 252 electoral votes. Bush won nearly 51 percent of the popular vote to Kerry's 48 percent.

Presidential Election of 2004		
Candidate	Popular Votes	Electoral Votes
George W. Bush (Rep.)	62,040,610	286
John Kerry (Dem.)	59,028,444	252

Bush's Second Administration 2005 - 2009

Bush began his second term in January 2005. He planned further tax cuts and health reforms. However, his second administration was soon beset with serious problems. In late August 2005, Hurricane Katrina formed in the Atlantic and began to devastate the Gulf Coast of the United States. Bush declared a state of emergency in Louisiana on 27th August and then in Mississippi and Alabama the following day. On 29th August, the hurricane made landfall and devastated New Orleans. The levees that kept back the waters of Lake Pontchartrain and the River Mississippi were breached and the city was flooded catastrophically. Bush declared a major disaster in Louisiana and authorized the use of federal funds to assist in the recovery effort. However, over the next week it became clear that the government's response was inadequate as one the nation's worst ever natural disasters unfolded. Bush responded to mounting criticism by claiming full responsibility for the federal government's failures in its handling of the emergency. However, Bush's support never fully recovered from his perceived poor handling the disaster.

In September 2008 the Lehman Brothers bank suddenly collapsed leading not only to an international banking and financial crisis but also the worst global recession since the Great Depression of the 1929. The causes of the crisis were the bursting of the US housing bubble, excessive risk-taking by global financial institutions and predatory lending targeting low-income sub-prime home buyers. Soaring oil prices were also partly to blame. In America, GDP contracted by 8.4% and unemployment swiftly reached 11%, its highest level for 25 years. By the end of 2008, more than 2.6 million jobs had been lost. As businesses failed and people lost their jobs, they could no longer afford to repay their mortgages and so were evicted from their homes. The recession started in America and then spread to the rest of the world. Bush signed a $170 billion stimulus package. However, the crisis was a key reason that the Democrats were able to win the White House in the election of November 2008.

Later Years

Bush left Washington D.C. after the inauguration of Barack Obama in January 2009 and returned to Texas. After leaving office he largely stayed out of the public eye. In 2010 he published his memoirs, *Decision Points*. He had surgery to clear a blocked artery in 2013. He supported his brother's bid for the Presidency in 2016 and led the mourning at his father's funeral in 2018. In January 2021 he joined other former Presidents in condemning the violence at the U.S. Capitol.

Summary

George W. Bush faced a bigger range of challenges than many of his immediate predecessors. Terrorism, wars, natural disasters, and an economic crisis made his presidency a difficult one. It is widely felt that he dealt well with the aftermath of the terrorist attacks in 2001 but poorly with effects Hurricane Katrina and the global financial crisis. Many Americans are now of the opinion that the war in Afghanistan was justified but the war in Iraq was not. The failure to find weapons of mass destruction in Iraq damaged the reputation and standing of the President and his country. As a result, he is ranked lowly among the Presidents.

CHAPTER 44 – BARACK OBAMA

44ᵗʰ *President of the United States 2009 – 2017*

Born: 4ᵗʰ August 1961, Honolulu, Hawaii

Married: Michelle LaVaughn Robinson (1964 –), 3ʳᵈ October 1992

Number of Children: Two

Introduction

Barack Obama was a human rights lawyer and teacher that was elected as the 44ᵗʰ President of the United States. Before he became President he had served in the Illinois Senate and the U.S. Senate. He won the 2008 election with a majority of the popular votes promising to reform healthcare and end the war in Iraq. As an African-American, voters hoped that he would lead them into a future where race was no longer important. Shortly after he entered the White House, he won the Nobel Prize for Peace. During his first term he took action to restore the economy after the financial crisis of 2008. In 2011, U.S. Navy SEALS succeeded in killing Osama Bin Laden, the architect of the 9/11 terrorist attacks. In 2012, Osama was re-elected for a second term with another majority of the popular votes. In his second term he had to deal with important foreign policy challenges in Afghanistan and the Middle East and took steps to promote economic growth, tackle climate change and improve women's rights. During his presidency, the nation continued to be the world's only hyperpower and had a population of nearly 320 million people.

Background

Barack Hussein Obama II was born on August 4th 1961 in Honolulu, Hawaii. He is the only President born outside the contiguous United States. His American mother, Ann Dunham, was born in Wichita, Kansas, and was of British and Irish descent. His African father, Barack Obama Snr., came from Kenya. Obama Jr.'s parents divorced when he was two years old and he grew up with his mother. In 1965, she married an Indonesian, Lolo Soetoro, and the family moved to Jakarta. Obama was educated at several schools in Indonesia before returning to Honolulu in 1971 to live with his grandparents. There he graduated from a private high school in 1979 and moved to Los Angeles to attend Occidental College. In 1981 he transferred to Columbia University in New York City where he studied political science and English literature. He graduated in 1983 and then worked as a financial researcher and writer for the Business International Corporation. He then briefly worked as a project coordinator for the New York Public Interest Research Group. In 1985 he moved from New York to Chicago where he worked as a community organizer. In 1988 he enrolled at the Harvard Law School where he became the president of the Harvard Law Review. He graduated in 1991 and then accepted a position at the University of Chicago law School where he taught constitutional law until 2004. He also worked as a human rights lawyer. In June 1989, Obama met Michelle Robinson when he was employed as a summer associate at the Chicago law firm of Sidley Austin. They got married on 3rd October 1992 and later had two daughters.

Entry into Politics

Obama had early experience of politics in 1992 when he directed Illinois' *Project Vote*, a campaign which aimed to register more African-American voters. In 1996 he was elected to the Illinois Senate where he worked to reform healthcare laws, reform welfare and increase tax credits for low-income workers. He was re-elected in 1998 and 2002. In 2000 he made an unsuccessful bid to be elected to the U.S. House of Representatives. However, when Obama won the primary election for a seat in the U.S. Senate in 2004, the Democratic Party recognized him as a rising star and he was asked to deliver the keynote address at the 2004 Democratic National Convention. That November he was elected to the U.S. Senate with a landslide. His 70 percent share of the vote was the largest for a Senate candidate in the history of Illinois. While in the Senate he sat on the Senate Foreign Relations Committee and chaired the subcommittee on European Affairs. In November 2008, Obama resigned his seat in the Senate to focus on his transition period for the presidency.

Presidential Election 2008

On the 10th February 2007, Obama announced his candidacy for the presidential election in 2008 in front of the Old State Capitol building in Springfield, Illinois. This was the same building where Abraham Lincoln delivered his famous speech in 1858 saying that: "A house divided cannot stand." Lots of candidates entered the primary elections but after the early contests the field narrowed to Obama and Senator Hilary Clinton. After a tight race, Obama received enough votes to win the nomination and Clinton conceded and endorsed him in June 2008. In August 2008, Obama announced Senator Joe Biden of Delaware as his running mate. The Republicans nominated Senator John McCain of Arizona for President and Governor Sarah Palin of Alaska for Vice-President. In the campaign, Obama promised to reform healthcare, increase energy independence, and end the war in Iraq. The Republican campaign was negatively affected by the national financial crisis which broke in September 2008 and by Palin's evident lack of experience. In the election, Obama received 52.9 percent of the popular vote to McCain's 45.9 percent and won a clear majority in the electoral college by 365 votes to 173 for McCain. Obama was only the third Senator to move directly to the White House after Warren G. Harding and John F. Kennedy and was the first African-American to be elected President.

Presidential Election of 2008		
Candidate	Popular Votes	Electoral Votes
Barack Obama (Dem.)	69,498,516	365
John McCain (Rep.)	59,948,323	173

Obama's First Administration 2009 – 2013

Obama was inaugurated as President on 20th January 2008. Many Americans hoped that the election of an African-American as President would heal the country's racial divisions and there was optimism that America would become a "post-race" society. Later that year, Obama would win the Nobel Prize for Peace for "his extraordinary efforts to strengthen international diplomacy and cooperation between peoples." One of Obama's first acts as President was to close the detention center at *Guantanamo Bay* in Cuba where individuals considered to be a threat to the United States were held in controversial conditions. On 29th January 2008, Obama signed his first bill, the *Lilly Leadbetter Fair Pay Act*, which aimed to address the gap in pay earned by men and women. With the nation's economy badly affected from the effects of the financial crisis and recession, he attempted to save and create jobs and to provide relief to those suffering by approving the *American Recovery and Reinvestment Act* 2009. The following year, Obama addressed the causes of the financial crisis by announcing the Volcker Rule which aimed to restrict American banks from making speculative investments that would not be in the best interests of their customers. He also extended tax cuts in a bid to grow the economy.

Obama also took action to address the issues that he had raised during his campaign to be President. In March 2010, Congress passed the *Patient Protection and Affordable Care Act*, dubbed "Obamacare" by the U.S. media, which improved access, affordability, and quality of healthcare. The same month, Obama addressed the issue of increasing energy independence when he announced that he would approve exploration for oil and gas in the

Gulf of Mexico and off the coast of Virginia, which had previously been banned. At the start of his term of office, Obama announced that U.S. combat operations in Iraq would end within 18 months. All troops were then withdrawn before the end of 2011.

During his first term, Obama also supported bills to reform education, tackle hate crimes and improve gun control. He increased funding for space exploration and repealed the military's "Don't Ask, Don't Tell" policy, which allowed people to openly be gay, lesbian, and bisexual while serving in the U.S. Armed Forces.

In March 2011, the CIA reported to the President that they had received intelligence that the architect of the 9/11 terrorist attacks, Osama Bin Laden, was hiding-out in a large compound near Abbottabad, a suburban area 35 miles (56 km) from Islamabad in Pakistan. Obama authorized a precision raid by U.S. Navy Seals and on the 1st May 2011, twenty-four SEALS undertook *Operation Neptune's Spear* and descended on the compound in two Black Hawk helicopters. In a brief firefight, Bin Laden was killed and his body subsequently identified by analyzing his DNA. The U.S. Navy buried him at sea several hours later. The raid was very successful. There were no American casualties and lots of intelligence was recovered in the form of papers, computer drives and compact disks. When Obama announced the success of the mission to the country that evening it led to spontaneous celebrations and large crowds gathered at the White House, at Ground Zero (formerly the site of the World Trade Center) and in Times Square.

Another success was the signing in February 2011 of a new nuclear arms treaty with Russia, called New START (for Strategic Arms Reduction Treaty), which sought to reduce the number of nuclear weapons and improve relations with Russia.

In early 2011 a series of protests and uprisings occurred in the Arab world with the aim of achieving political and economic change. These protests occurred in several countries in North Africa and the Middle East and were collectively known the "Arab Spring." In Libya, the dictator Muammar Gaddafi reacted to these protests with a violent crackdown that showed no mercy towards the rebels. The international community called for the establishment of a no-fly zone over the country to try and curb military action against civilians. On March 18th Obama ordered U.S. airstrikes against Libya to enforce a no-fly zone and protect civilians. The following week, NATO took over leadership of the effort and continued for the next seven month. Then on October 20th 2011, NATO jets attacked a Libyan military convoy in which Gaddafi was travelling. The dictator sought refuge first in a house and then in a drainpipe. However, he was captured by rebel ground forces and shot dead soon after. His death failed to bring peace and stability to the country and Obama's critics said that he had to take responsibility for the political and financial cost of the operation.

Presidential Election 2012

As the incumbent President, Obama was unopposed in the Democratic primaries and was formally nominated at the Democratic National Convention in Charlotte, North Carolina. Vice-President Joe Biden was once again nominated as his running mate.

The Republicans nominated the former Governor of Massachusetts, Mitt Romney, for President and Representative Paul Bryan of Wisconsin for Vice-President.

In the election, Obama received 51.1 percent of the votes cast, making him the first Democratic President since Franklin D. Roosevelt to twice win the majority of the popular votes. He won a clear majority in the electoral college with 332 votes to 206 for Romney.

Presidential Election of 2012		
Candidate	Popular Votes	Electoral Votes
Barack Obama (Dem.)	65,915,795	332
Mitt Romney (Rep)	60,933,504	206

Obama's Second Administration 2013 – 2017

During his second administration Obama took action to keep the economy growing, address climate change and improve women's rights. In January 2013 he signed the *American Taxpayer Relief Act* which cut taxes for most Americans while raising them for the highest earners. The following year he raised the minimum wage from $7.25 to $10.10 for all workers on federal contracts. In November 2013 he signed an order which detailed how the United States would take action to tackle climate change. Two years later he introduced the *Clean Power Plan* to reduce carbon pollution from existing power plants. He sought to provide increased protection for women by approving the *Violence Against Women Reauthorization Act* in 2013 to reduce violent crimes.

During his second term, Obama faced foreign policy challenges in Afghanistan, Iran, Iraq and Syria. Obama reasoned that Afghanistan was the country from which a terrorist attack against the United States would most likely be launched. In February 2009, he increased troop levels there to assist is stabilizing the country. Later that year, further troops were deployed and the total number of U.S. troops in Afghanistan eventually rose to 68,000. Although this number was later reduced, in October 2015 he announced that U.S. troops would have to stay indefinitely due to the country's poor security situation. In Iran, the government was secretly trying to build nuclear weapons. In 2012, the U.S. government froze Iranian assets in response to what Obama called "deceptive practices." In 2015, Iran agreed not to acquire nuclear weapons in return for the lifting of sanctions. In Iraq and Syria, a militant terrorist organization called Islamic State of Iraq and Syria (ISIS) took control of large parts of territory in both countries and massacred thousands of people living there. In 2014 Obama sent ground troops to Iraq and led allies in launching airstrikes against targets in ISIS-held territory. In Syria a bloody civil war raged as President Assad cracked down on dissent to his rule. In August 2013, his forces his forces launched a chemical weapons attack on rebel-held areas around the Syrian capital Damascus. Obama considered military action but this was avoided when Syria agreed to give up its chemical weapons and join the Chemical Weapons Convention. One foreign policy success in his second term was an improvement in relations with Cuba. In March 2016 he became the first sitting U.S. President to visit Cuba since 1928.

Later Years

Obama left the White House in January 2017 when he attended the Inauguration of President Donald J. Trump. He has remained active in national politics and campaigned on behalf of Democratic candidates in presidential elections. In 2021, construction began on his presidential library in Chicago.

Summary

Barack Obama was one of America's most inspirational Presidents. He succeeded in becoming President even though, like many other African-Americans, he was challenged by racism and discrimination. He was the first Democrat since Franklin Roosevelt to win consecutive presidential elections with a majority of the popular vote. His achievements in office include restoring America's prosperity and confidence after the financial crisis as well as eliminating Osama Bin Laden. He won the Nobel Peace Prize and agreed an arms reduction treaty with Russia. He is often ranked in the top twenty Presidents.

CHAPTER 45 – DONALD J. TRUMP

45th President of the United States 2017 – 2021

Born: 14th June 1946

Married: (1) Ivana Marie Zelnickova (1949 – 2022), 9th April 1977, divorced 1993 (2) Marla Maples (1963 –) 20th December 1993, divorced 1999 (3) Melania Knaus (1970 -), 22nd January 2005

Number of Children: Five (1) Three with Ivana (2) One with Marla (3) One with Melania

Introduction

Donald Trump is a well-known businessman and television personality that was elected as the 45th President of the United States. Before entering the White House, he had operated a variety of different businesses and had hosted a television show called "The Apprentice." He was the only President not to have served in neither the military nor in a political office before becoming President. He won the election of 2016 against Hilary Clinton with only a minority of the popular votes and then led a controversial administration that withdrew from a number of important international agreements, and attempted to deport illegal immigrants and ban Muslims from entering the United States. During his term of office, more than a million Americans died from the COVID pandemic, which overtook the Civil War as the biggest tragedy in the nation's history. Trump became the first President to face two separate sets of impeachment charges. In 2019 he successfully defended himself against charges that he abused his power and obstructed Congress. In 2021 he was charged with citing an insurrection after allegedly encouraging his supporters to storm the Capitol building to prevent Congress from certifying the results of the 2020 presidential election which he claimed that he had only lost to Joe Biden because of fraud. He only narrowly avoided impeachment and left office a few weeks later. He refused to attend his successor's inauguration and has remained a controversial figure stating that he plans to run for President again in 2024.

Background

Donald John Trump was born the fourth of five children on 14th June 1946 in the borough of Queens, New York City. His father was a real estate developer and was descended from German immigrants. His mother was an immigrant from Scotland. He was privately educated at Kew Forest School and New York Military Academy before enrolling at Fordham University in 1964. Two years later he enrolled at the Wharton School of the University of Pennsylvania where he graduated with a degree in economics in 1968. While in college he received a student deferment which exempted him from service in the Vietnam War. He later received a medical deferment which permanently disqualified him from military service.

He married his first wife, Czech model Ivana Zelníčková, in 1977 and they had three children. They divorced in 1992 after Trump had an affair with the actress Marla Maples. Trump then married Maples in 1993 but they divorced in 1999. Trump married his third wife, Slovenian model Melania Knauss, in 2005 and they have one son. She became the second foreign-born First Lady after Louisa Catherine Adams, the wife of the sixth President, John Quincy Adams. Melania became an American citizen in 2006.

After leaving university, Trump began a long career as a businessman operating hotels, casinos and airlines. Between 1996 and 2015 he was wholly or partly owner of the Miss Universe pageants and received a star on the Hollywood Walk of Fame for his work in producing them. He wrote a number of books concerning business or financial topics and appeared in cameo roles in films and television shows. From 2004 to 2015, Trump was co-producer and host of reality shows *The Apprentice* and *The Celebrity Apprentice*. Contestants on The Apprentice would compete a year of well-paid employment within his organization while in The Celebrity Apprentice well-known people would compete to win money for charities.

Entry into Politics

Before running for President in 2016, Trump had not taken a serious part in politics. He did not run for any local or state office and frequently changed his political affiliation. In the 2000 presidential election he ran as a candidate for the Reform Party but withdrew from the race after the early primaries. He considered running as a Republican in the 2012 election but then announced that he would not run and endorsed Mitt Romney. Trump would later become the only President who neither served in the military nor held any government office prior to becoming President.

Election of 2016

In June 2015, Trump announced that he would be a Republican candidate in the 2016 Presidential election. At first political analysts did not take his claim seriously but he quickly rose to the top of the opinion polls and became the front runner. The Republicans fielded a record seventeen candidates including governor Jeb Bush of Florida, the brother of former President George W. Bush. However, Trump had established a double-digit lead even before the televised debates, which he dominated, and went on to win 41 states. By March 2016 he was the presumptive Republican nominee. Trump selected Indiana governor Mike Pence as his vice-presidential running mate in mid-July, and the two were officially nominated at the 2016 Republican National Convention.

The Democrats nominated Secretary of State, Hilary R. Clinton, as their candidate for President with Senator Tim Kaine of Virginia as her running mate. Trump's campaign became known for its many provocative statements and frequent changes of position. He promised to "Make America Great Again'" and pledged to invest in infrastructure, repeal the Affordable Care Act, renegotiate trade agreements, increase military spending, enforce immigration laws, and build a new wall along the border with Mexico to be funded by the Mexican government. Three televised debates were held between the two candidates in September and October in which Trump defended his most controversial statements and promised to jail Clinton, whom he frequently called "crooked."

Many of Trump's most controversial statements concerned women. He had a record of insulting women and making lewd comments. A large number of women came forward publicly accusing Trump of rape, unconsented groping and kissing, looking up their skirts and walking in on naked teenage contestants during pageants. Trump denied the allegations calling them "false smears." However, in October 2016, two days before the second presidential debate, a recording surfaced from 2005 in which Trump was heard privately boasting about kissing and groping women without their consent, saying: "When you're a star, they let you do it, you can do anything, grab them by the pussy." The comment caused widespread outrage and Trump was forced to make his first public apology of the campaign. Three months later, on the day after his inauguration, half a million demonstrators marched through the streets of Washington D.C. to protest against Trump's attitude towards women.

Polling showed Clinton leading Trump throughout the campaign as well as having an advantage in all the key states. However, the lead diminished as polling day approached. The level of Trump's support had been modestly underestimated and when the election was held, he won the majority states and votes in the electoral college. Trump won thirty states which gave him 304 electoral votes while Clinton won twenty states as well as the District of Columbia which gave her 227 electoral votes. Trump even won in states such as Michigan and Wisconsin which had a long tradition of voting for the Democrats. However, Trump received nearly three million popular votes less than Clinton, which made him the fifth person to be elected president while losing the popular vote. In addition to gaining the White

House, the Republicans also won a majority in both houses of Congress.

Presidential Election of 2016		
Candidate	Popular Votes	Electoral Votes
Donald J. Trump (Rep.)	62,984,828	304
Hilary R. Clinton (Dem.)	65,853,514	227

Trump's Administration 2017 – 2021

Trump was inaugurated on 20th January 2017. He appointed his son-in-law, Jared Kushner, as his senior advisor and his daughter, Ivanka, as his assistant. One of his first actions as President was to sign an executive order which repealed the Affordable Care Act. He also immediately began to plan the 1000-mile (1600km) border wall between the United States and Mexico. In 2018, Trump refused to extend government funding unless Congress allocated $5.6 billion in funds for the border wall,[329] resulting in the federal government partially shutting down for 35 days from December 2018 to January 2019, the longest U.S. government shutdown in history. Around 800,000 government employees were furloughed or worked without pay. Trump and Congress ended the shutdown by approving temporary funding that provided delayed payments to government workers but no funds for the wall. Very little of the wall had been completed by the time he left office in 2021.

Trump pledged to reduce illegal immigration and to deport illegal immigrants. This led to the separation of many children from their parents at the U.S. border. The administration ended the policy after condemnation by the public. In 2017Trump proposed on banning foreign Moslems from entering the United States until stronger vetting systems could be implemented. He later altered the proposed ban to apply to countries with a "proven history of terrorism". On January 27, 2017, Trump signed an Executive Order which suspended admission of refugees for 120 days and denied entry to citizens of Iraq, Iran, Libya, Somalia, Sudan, Syria, and Yemen for 90 days, citing security concerns. The order immediately took effect without warning, causing confusion and chaos at airports. The temporary order was replaced by a Presidential Proclamation on September 24, 2017, which restricted travel from the originally targeted countries except Iraq and Sudan, and further banned travelers from North Korea and Chad, along with certain Venezuelan officials. After lower courts partially blocked the new restrictions, the Supreme Court allowed the Proclamation to go into full effect on December 4, 2017, and ultimately upheld the travel ban in a June 2019 ruling.

When Trump took office the U.S. economy was in the middle of the longest period of expansion in its history. The economy began to grow in June 2009 and continued to increase in size until February 2020, when the COVID-19 pandemic caused it to contract. In October 2017, Trump signed the *Tax Cuts and Jobs Act 2017* which cut taxes permanently for businesses and until 2025 for individuals. It was argued that the tax cuts would lead to enhanced economic growth which would then pay for the cuts through increased revenues. However, together with an increase in government spending, the cuts led to an increase in the federal budget deficit. In 2020, he replaced the North American Free Trade Agreement (NAFTA) with the *United States-Mexico-Canada Agreement (USMCA)*. In 2020, the economy entered a recession due to the shutdown caused by the COVID-19 pandemic leading to widespread job losses. When he left office, the workforce was three million people lower than when he was elected.

In environmental policy, he attempted to boost the production and export of fossil fuels while reducing the budget for research into renewable energy. He withdrew the United States from the Paris Agreement which aimed at preventing global climate change by limiting increases in temperature. His social policies included reducing workplace protection against discrimination for LGBT people, advocating capital punishment, and appointing conservative justices to the Supreme Court. He took little action to improve gun control even though there were several mass-shootings during his term. He was accused of showing little sympathy for civil rights. When widespread civil unrest erupted across the nation following the murder of an African-American man called George Floyd by a policeman in Minneapolis in May 2020, Trump was accused of being more concerned with ending the protests than dealing with the cause.

In foreign policy, Trump often had a difficult relationship with America's European allies. He described NATO as "obsolete" and suggested that the U.S. should withdraw from the alliance. He also had difficulties with other countries. He launched a trade war with China by sharply increasing tariffs on 818 categories (worth $50 billion) of Chinese goods imported into the U.S. In July 2020, the Trump administration imposed sanctions and visa restrictions against senior Chinese officials, in response to expanded mass detention camps holding more than a million of the country's Uyghur Muslim ethnic minority. Trump actively supported the Saudi Arabian–led intervention in Yemen against the Houthis and in 2017 signed a $110 billion agreement to sell arms to Saudi Arabia. Under Trump, the U.S. recognized Jerusalem as the capital of Israel and Israeli sovereignty over the Golan Heights, leading to international condemnation including from the United Nations General Assembly, the European Union, and the Arab League. In August 2019 Trump withdrew the U.S. from the Intermediate-Range Nuclear Forces Treaty with Russia, citing alleged Russian non-compliance.

In *Afghanistan* troop numbers in Afghanistan increased from 8,500 in January 2017 to 14,000 a year later. In February 2020, the Trump administration signed a conditional peace agreement with the Taliban, which called for the withdrawal of foreign troops in 14 months "contingent on a guarantee from the Taliban that Afghan soil will not be used by terrorists with aims to attack the United States or its allies." By the end of Trump's term, U.S. troops had been reduced to 2,500. In April 2017 and April 2018, Trump ordered missile strikes against *Syria* after the regime of President Bashar al-Assad had used chemical weapons against civilians in Khan Shaykhun and Douma. Trump also inherited President Obama's troop commitment to Syria to defend the region against the Islamic State terrorist organization (ISIS). However, in December 2018, Trump ordered the U.S. troops to be withdrawn claiming that the battle against ISIS had been won. This contradicted an assessment made by the Department of Defense and the next day his Defense Secretary, James Mattis, resigned in protest, calling Trump's decision an abandonment of the U.S.'s Kurdish allies who had played a key role in fighting ISIS. In October 2019, U.S. troops in northern Syria were withdrawn from the area and Turkey invaded northern Syria, attacking and displacing American-allied Kurds in the area. Later that month, the U.S. House of Representatives, in a rare bipartisan vote of 354 to 60, condemned Trump's withdrawal of U.S. troops from Syria, for "abandoning U.S. allies, undermining the struggle against ISIS, and spurring a humanitarian catastrophe".

In May 2018, Trump withdrew the United States from the Joint Comprehensive Plan of Action (JCPOA), the 2015 agreement between *Iran*, the U.S., and five other countries that lifted most economic sanctions against Iran in return for Iran agreeing to restrictions on its nuclear program. Analysts have determined that Iran has moved closer to developing a nuclear weapon since the withdrawal. In January 2020, Trump ordered a U.S. airstrike that killed Iranian general Qasem Soleimani, who had planned nearly every significant operation by Iranian forces over the past two decades. Iran then retaliated with a ballistic missile strikes against two U.S. airbases in Iraq.

In 2017, when North Korea's nuclear weapons were increasingly seen as a serious threat, Trump escalated his rhetoric, warning that North Korean aggression would be met with "fire and fury like the world has never seen". In 2017, Trump declared that he wanted North Korea's "complete denuclearization", and engaged in name-calling with leader Kim Jong-un. After this period of tension, Trump and Kim exchanged at least 27 letters in which led to a warm personal friendship between the two men. Trump then met Kim three times: in Singapore in 2018, in Hanoi in 2019, and in the Korean Demilitarized Zone in 2019. Trump became the first sitting U.S. president to meet a North Korean leader or to set foot on North Korean soil. Trump also lifted some U.S. sanctions against North

Korea. However, no denuclearization agreement was reached, and in October 2019 talks broke down after just one day. While conducting no nuclear tests since 2017, North Korea has continued to build up its arsenal of nuclear weapons and ballistic missiles.

First Impeachment

In August 2019, a whistleblower filed a complaint with the Inspector General of the Intelligence Community about a telephone call made on 25th July between Trump and the President of Ukraine, Volodymyr Zelenskyy, during which Trump had pressured Zelenskyy to investigate alleged corruption by the Democratic presidential candidate Joe Biden and his son, Hunter, adding that the White House had attempted to cover-up the incident. House Speaker Nancy Pelosi initiated a formal impeachment inquiry on 24th September. Trump then confirmed that he withheld military aid from Ukraine, offering contradictory reasons for the decision. On 25th September, the Trump administration released a memorandum of the phone call which confirmed that, after Zelenskyy mentioned purchasing American anti-tank missiles, Trump asked him to discuss investigating Biden and his song. The testimony of multiple administration officials and former officials confirmed that this was part of a broader effort to further Trump's personal interests by giving him an advantage in the upcoming presidential election. On 13th December, the House Judiciary Committee voted along party lines to pass two articles of impeachment: one for abuse of power and one for obstruction of Congress. After debate, the House of Representatives impeached Trump on both articles on December 18. The impeachment trial began in the Senate on 16th January 2020. For three days, from the 22nd January 22nd to the 24th, the House impeachment managers presented their case to the Senate. They cited evidence to support charges of abuse of power and obstruction of Congress, and asserted that Trump's actions were exactly what the founding fathers had in mind when they created the Constitution's impeachment process. Responding over the next three days, Trump's lawyers did not deny the facts as presented in the charges but said Trump had not broken any laws or obstructed Congress. They argued that the impeachment was "constitutionally and legally invalid" because Trump was not charged with a crime and that abuse of power is not an impeachable offense. On the 5th February 2020, Trump was acquitted of both charges by the Republican Senate majority, 52–48 on abuse of power and 53–47 on obstruction of Congress. Following his acquittal, Trump fired impeachment witnesses and other political appointees and career officials he deemed insufficiently loyal.

COVID-19 Pandemic

In December 2019 the COVID-19 virus erupted in Wuhan, China, and quickly spread around the world. The first case in the United States was reported on 20th January 2020 and a public health emergency was declared eleven days later. Trump's initial response was criticized as he did not seem to appreciate the seriousness of the virus and was slow to address its spread. However, on 6th March he approved the *Coronavirus Preparedness and Response Supplemental Appropriations Act* which provided $8.3 billion in emergency funding for federal agencies. On 11th March the World Health Organization recognized the virus as a pandemic and two days later Trump declared a national emergency and introduced a partial ban on travel to and from infected countries. However, the number of infections and deaths continued to increase across America through the spring and into the summer. On 29th June 2020, Trump established the *White House Coronavirus Task Force*, but this also proved ineffective in reducing the spread of the virus. Trump provided daily briefings to guide and reassure the public, but often he used them as an opportunity to denounce his critics, China and the WHO. In July 2020, he accused the WHO of being under Chinese control and announced that the United States would withdraw from it. Critics later accused him of weakening his own administration's efforts to mitigate the pandemic by refusing to wear a facemask and attempting to reduce testing so that less cases were reported. They said that he seemed less concerned for the victims of the virus than its effect on his own popularity. In the fall of 2020, he insisted that schools should re-open even though the number of people infected was still increasing. On 2ⁿᵈ October, he notified the public that he, the First Lady and his son had all contracted the virus and he was admitted into hospital in Washington D.C. In what was obviously a severe case, it was later admitted that his blood had contained dangerously low levels of oxygen. Trump's handling of the virus became a key issue in the election that November and by the time Americans went to the polls the number of new cases had reached 100,000 per day. A vaccine was not approved and rolled out until December 2020, one month after the election.

2020 Presidential Election

The Democrats had taken control of the House of Representatives in the 2018 mid-term elections. However, the Republicans had increased their number of seats in the Senate which also increased their majority there. In August 2020, Trump formally became the Republican nominee for the 2020 presidential election, once again with Mike Pence as his running mate. The Democrats nominated former Vice-President Joe Biden with Senator Kamala Harris of California as his running mate. Trump focused his campaign on law and order and said that America's cities would descend into lawlessness if Biden became President. Biden attacked Trump's response to the COVID-19 pandemic which had already become one of the biggest tragedies in America's history. In the election Biden received 81.3 million votes (51.3 percent) to Trump's 74.2 million (46.8 percent) winning him 306 votes in the Electoral College votes to Trump's 232. However, at 2 a.m. in the morning after the election the results were still unclear and Trump declared victory. However, as the postal votes were counted, Biden emerged as the victor.

Throughout his campaign Trump had claimed that the widespread use of mail balloting would lead to massive election fraud and refused to say whether he would accept the result of the election. When Biden won the election, Trump alleged election fraud and refused to concede. Trump and his allies filed many legal challenges to the results, which were rejected by at least 86 judges in both the state and federal courts, including by federal judges appointed by

340

Trump himself. He did not provide any conclusive proof that his allegations were true. On December 11, the U.S. Supreme Court declined to hear a case from the Texas attorney general that asked the court to overturn the election results in four states won by Biden. In Georgia, Trump asked officials to "find" votes and announce a "recalculated" result. Trump did not attend Biden's inauguration in January 2021, leaving Washington for Florida hours before. He was the first President not to attend his successor's inauguration since 1869. On 10th February 2021, prosecutors in Georgia opened a criminal investigation into Trump's efforts to subvert the election in that state.

The Attack on the U.S. Capitol

After his defeat in the 2020 presidential election, there were fears that Trump would use a military coup to retain power. However, defense leaders said that the military had no role to play in the outcome of elections. On 6th January 2021, while congressional certification of the presidential election results was taking place in the United States Capitol, Trump held a rally at the Ellipse, Washington, D.C., where he called for the election result to be overturned. He urged his supporters to "take back our country" by marching to the Capitol to "show strength" and "fight like hell". Trump's speech started at noon. By 12:30 p.m., rally attendees had gathered outside the Capitol, and at 1 p.m., his supporters pushed past police barriers onto Capitol grounds. Trump's speech ended at 1:10 p.m., and many supporters marched to the Capitol as he had urged, joining the crowd already there. Around 2:15 p.m. the mob broke into the building, disrupting the certification and causing the evacuation of Congress. During the violence, Trump posted messages on Twitter and Facebook, eventually tweeting to the rioters at 6 p.m., "go home with love & in peace", but describing them as "great patriots" and "very special", while still complaining that the election was stolen. After the mob was removed from the Capitol, Congress reconvened and confirmed Joe Biden's election win in the early hours of the following morning. During the attack on the

Capitol, there were many injuries and five people died, including a Capitol Police officer and a woman shot by the police.

Second Impeachment

On 11th January 2021, an article of impeachment charging Trump with incitement of insurrection against the U.S. government was introduced to the House. On 13th January, the House voted 232–197 to impeach Trump making him the first U.S. president to be impeached twice. The impeachment, which was the most rapid in history, followed an unsuccessful bipartisan effort to strip Trump of his powers and duties via Section 4 of the 25th Amendment. Ten Republicans voted for impeachment—the most members of a party ever to vote to impeach a President of their own party. On 13th February, following a five-day trial in the Senate, Trump was acquitted when Senators voted 57–43 for conviction. This fell ten votes short of the two-thirds majority required to convict him. Seven Republicans joined every Democrat in voting to convict, the most bipartisan support in any Senate impeachment trial of a President or former President. Most Republican Senators voted to acquit Trump, although some held him responsible but felt the Senate did not have jurisdiction over former Presidents. Trump had already left office on 20th January.

Post-Presidency

At the end of his term, Trump went to live at his Mar-a-Lago club in Florida. As late as the summer of 2022, Trump was still pressuring state legislators to overturn the 2020 election by rescinding the state's electoral votes for Biden. Unlike other former presidents, Trump continued to dominate his party. When Trump left the White House in January 2021, he took government documents and material with him to Mar-a-Lago. When the National Archives and Records Administration (NARA) said that important documents had not been turned over to them at the end of his administration, the Department of Justice took action to recover them. On 3rd June, Justice

Department officials visited Mar-a-Lago and retrieved classified documents from Trump's lawyers. On 19th December 2022, the United States House Select Committee on the January 6 Attack recommended criminal charges be brought against Trump for obstructing an official proceeding, conspiracy to defraud the United States, and inciting or assisting an insurrection. On 15th November 2022, Trump announced his candidacy for the 2024 United States presidential election and set up a fundraising account. In March 2023, Trump was indicted by a court in New York accused of falsifying business records and in August 2023, he was indicted by a Grand Jury in Georgia accused of unlawfully trying to change the outcome of the 2020 presidential election. Following this indictment, Trump attended Fulton County Jail where his face was formally photographed for police records on 24th August. He was therefore the first President to provide a *mugshot*.

Summary

Opinion is divided as to whether Donald Trump was a good President or a bad one. To his opponents, he failed to effectively deal with the COVID pandemic and had an offensive attitude towards women and immigrants. To them, the way that he conducted himself in office was poor and "unpresidential." He was the first President to be impeached twice and he is accused of encouraging his supporters to storm the Capitol. He still faces criminal charges for actions connected with his time as President. To his supporters, however, Trump was such a good President that they would vote for him again. He showed a concern for the people of America that is sometimes said to be lacking from a rich and isolated political class.

CHAPTER 46 – JOE BIDEN

46th President of the United States 2021 to Present

Born: 20th November 1942, Scranton, Pennsylvania

Married: (1) Neilia Hunter (1942 – 1972), 27th August 1966 (2) Jill Jacobs (1951 –), 17th June 1977

Number of Children: Four (1) Two with Neilia (2) Two with Jill

Introduction

Joe Biden is an experienced U.S. Senator and former Vice-President that was elected the 46th President of the United States in 2020. Prior to entering the White House, Biden had spent 36 years serving in the U.S Senate and eight years as the Vice-President to Barack Obama. He has long been regarded as an expert on foreign policy. He became President when the country had 330 million people and was still the world's dominant power. He financed the rolling out of a vaccine that brought to an end the COVID pandemic and also provided the funds that then revived the nation's economy. He withdrew American troops from Afghanistan but continued to take a tough stance against the terrorists of Al Qaeda and Islamic State. He provided valuable support to Ukraine after their invasion by neighboring Russia in 2022, and then to Israel after a large-scale strike by terrorists from Hamas in 2023. Challenged by the growing power of China, Biden formed the AUKUS Pact with the United Kingdom and Australia and pledged to support Taiwan in the event of a Chinese attack. As the oldest man to be elected President, Biden's age has never ceased to be an issue for his opponents.

However, he has announced his intention to stand in the election of 2024.

Background

Joseph Robinette Biden was born on November 20th 1942 in Scranton, Pennsylvania, the eldest of four children of a businessman who later sold used cars. His ancestors had emigrated to America from Ireland and England and he was raised as a Roman Catholic. When he was ten his family moved to Delaware and he was educated at Archmere Academy in Claymont. He then entered the University of Delaware where he studied history, political science and English, graduating in 1965. He then studied law at the Syracuse University College of Law, graduating in 1968. While there he met student Neilia Hunter and married her 27th August 1966. They had three children. While studying at the universities in Delaware and Syracuse, Biden obtained five student draft deferments and therefore did not serve in the Vietnam War. He later received a medical deferment because he had suffered from asthma as a teenager. After leaving university, Biden worked as a clerk at a law firm in Wilmington. He was admitted to the Delaware bar in 1969 and later set up a law firm.

Entry into Politics

Biden first became interested in politics in 1969 when he registered as a Democrat. In 1970, Biden successfully ran for a seat on the New Castle County Council offering a liberal platform that included support for public housing in the suburbs. During his time on the council, Biden opposed large highway projects, which he argued might disrupt Wilmington neighborhoods. In 1972, Biden defeated Republican incumbent J. Caleb Boggs to become the U.S. Senator from Delaware. At the beginning of his election campaign, he had only limited funds and was given little chance of winning. However, members of his family managed and staffed the campaign, which relied on meeting voters face-to-face and hand-distributing position papers. He focused his campaign on the issues that mattered to voters which included civil rights, healthcare, taxation and withdrawal from the Vietnam war, and won with more than fifty percent of the vote. At the time of his election, he was 29 years old, but he reached the constitutionally required age of 30 before he was sworn in as Senator. At 30, he was the sixth-youngest senator in U.S. history. He was later re-elected in 1978, 1984, 1990, 1996, 2002, and 2008, becoming one of the longest serving senators in U.S. history.

On December 18, 1972, a few weeks after Biden was elected senator, his wife Neilia and one-year-old daughter Naomi were killed in an automobile accident while Christmas shopping in Hockessin, Delaware. Neilia's station wagon was hit by a semi-trailer truck as she pulled out from an intersection. Their sons Beau (aged 3) and Hunter (aged 2) were taken to the hospital in fair condition, Beau with a broken leg and other wounds and Hunter with a minor skull fracture and other head injuries. In 1975, Biden met teacher Jill Tacy Jacobs on a blind date and they married in the United Nations chapel in New York on 17th June 1977. Biden would later credit his second wife with renewing his interest in politics and life.

While in the Senate, Biden served on the Judiciary Committee, which he chaired from 1987 to 1995, and the Senate Foreign Relations Committee, which he chaired from 2001 to 2003 and 2007 to 2009. He made his first run for the presidency in 1988 but had to withdraw from the race after he was accused of plagiarizing a speech made by the leader of the British Labour Party, Neil Kinnock. He made his second run for the presidency in 2008 and focused on his experience in foreign policy and as chairman of the major Senate committees. However, he withdrew from the race after the first primary contest because Democrat voters clearly preferred Barack Obama and Senator Hillary Clinton.

Biden's candidacy did, however, raise his profile and stature in the political world and in August 2008 Barack Obama announced that Biden would be his running mate. Biden offered not only significant foreign policy experience but also appealed to working class voters. As part of the election campaign, Biden took part in a debate with the Republican candidate for Vice-President, Sarah Palin on Alaska.

A good performance created a favorable impression with the public. In the election that November, Obama and Biden won with 53% of the vote winning 365 votes in the electoral college to Senator John McCain's 173.

On January 20 he was sworn in as the 47th vice president of the United States. He was the first Vice-President from Delaware and the first Roman Catholic Vice-President. In November 2012, Obama and Biden won re-election defeating the Republican candidates Mitt Romney and Paul Ryan with 51% of the popular vote and winning 332 of the 538 votes in the Electoral College. During his time as Vice-President, Biden maintained his interest in foreign policy frequently visiting the Middle East and Latin America. In December 2012, Obama named Biden to head the Gun Violence Task Force, created to address the causes of school shootings such as the Sandy Hook Elementary School shooting. Biden never cast a tie-breaking vote in the Senate, making him the longest-serving vice president with this distinction.

Presidential Election 2020

Biden decided not to run for President in 2016. When he left the vice presidency, he became an honorary professor at the University of Pennsylvania and published his memoirs *Promise Me Dad* in 2017. In October 2018, he was unsuccessfully targeted by two pipe bombs sent through the mail. Then in April 2019 he announced his candidacy for the Presidential nomination in 2020. His campaign got off to a poor start when he came fourth in the Iowa caucuses and then fifth in the New Hampshire Primary. However, he then won the South Carolina primary as well as eighteen of the twenty-six contests on Super Tuesday to become the front runner. His main rival, Bernie Sanders, dropped out of the contest and endorsed Biden in April 2019. Former President Barack Obama endorsed Biden on 14th April. On August 11, he announced that Senator Kamala Harris of California would be his running mate, making her the first African-American and the first South Asian-American vice-presidential nominee on a major-party ticket. On August 18th 2020, Biden was officially nominated as the Democratic Party nominee at the 2020 Democratic national convention.

In the election, Biden faced the incumbent President Donald Trump. Biden made an issue of the way that Trump had handled the COVID-19 pandemic which led to thousands of infections and deaths. Trump said that the election of Biden would lead to a crime wave in American cities. In the election Biden won with 51.3 percent of the vote to Trump's 46.8 percent. Biden carried 25 states as well as Washington D.C. while Trump also carried 25 states. In the electoral college Biden won 306 votes to Trump's 232. He was the first candidate to defeat a sitting President since Bill Clinton had defeated George H.W. Bush in 1992.

Presidential Election of 2020		
Candidate	Popular Votes	Electoral Votes
Joe R. Biden (Dem.)	81,283,501	306
Donald J. Trump (Rep.)	74,223,975	232

However, Trump refused to concede the election claiming that it had been "stolen" through "voter fraud." He then attempted to overturn the election result in the courts. However, by the end of November, Biden had been recognized as the election's winner and the process of transition began between the Trump and Biden administrations. On January 6th 2021, when Congress convened to certify the election results, Trump encouraged his supporters to march on the Capitol and "take back our country." Shortly afterwards, demonstrators forced entry into the Capitol building in an attempt to disrupt the certification. Five people died, including a woman shot by the police, but the demonstrators were cleared from the building and the certification was completed. Biden addressed the nation, calling the events "an unprecedented assault unlike anything we've seen in modern times."

Biden's Administration 2021 to Present

Biden was inaugurated as the 46th President on 20th January 2021. At 78 years old, he was the oldest person to take the office. During his first weeks in the White House, the United States rejoined both the Paris Climate Agreement and the World Health Organization. His most immediate problem was to address the problems caused by the COVID-19 pandemic. A new vaccine was now available and Biden made funds available to roll it out across the country. He also attempted to launch a plan which he called "Build Back Better" to revive the economy by investing three trillion dollars in housing, education and clean energy. Although the plan was rejected in Congress, in March 2021 Biden signed a $1.9 billion COVID-19 relief bill that made direct relief payments of $1,400 to most adults in the U.S. Later in 2021, he signed a law that designated $1.2 trillion of funds to develop the country's infrastructure. In his first year in office, the economy grew strongly and unemployment fell as a record number of jobs were created. When the rate of inflation rose above seven percent, he signed the *Inflation Reduction Act* in August 2022 which made $ 740 billion of funds available to support healthcare and energy policies.

In *Afghanistan*, Biden inherited Trump's deal with the Taliban to completely withdraw U.S, forces by May 1st 2021. Biden delayed the final withdrawal until September 11th and most troops had withdrawn by July. In August the Afghan government fell and the Taliban took over the country. Biden sent 6,000 troops to Kabul to assist with the evacuation of American personnel and desperate Afghan allies. On 26th August, the Islamic State terrorist organization carried out a suicide bombing at the airport which killed at least 178 people including thirteen members of the U.S. services. The withdrawal was completed on 30th August but was criticized for being "chaotic" and "botched." Biden took responsibility for the situation telling a national television audience that the situation unfolded more quickly than he anticipated. After the withdrawal the United States kept up the pressure on Al Qaeda and Islamic State. In February 2022, Biden ordered a counter-terrorism raid in northern Syria that resulted in the death of Abu Ibrahim al-Hashimi al-

Qurashi, the second leader of the Islamic State. In July 2022, Biden approved the drone strike that killed Ayman al-Zawahiri, the second leader of Al-Qaeda, and an integral member in the planning of the September 11 attacks.

In February 2022, the Russian leader Vladimir Putin launched a full-scale invasion of the neighboring country of Ukraine. Biden led other western countries on providing military and economic assistance to the Ukraine that prevented the Russian army from taking control of their country. Biden made a trip to the Ukrainian capital of Kyiv where he met his counterpart, Volodymyr Zelenskyy. He also led a strong NATO response which prevented the war from spreading to other European countries and may have discouraged Putin from carrying out his threat to use nuclear weapons. In the wake of the invasion, two formerly neutral countries, Finland and Sweden, applied to join the alliance. In February 2023, Biden visited the Polish capital of Warsaw where he promised that America would never waver in her support of NATO or of Ukrainian independence. In October 2023, Biden visited Israel and pledged support after a large-scale attack by Hamas terrorists killed more than a thousand people.

Like Trump before him, Biden regarded China rather than Russia as America's most serious geopolitical challenge and there were lots of points of tension between the two countries. In September 2021, Biden hosted a summit of the leaders of the Quad alliance – the U.S., Australia, India and Japan – seen as a counter-weight to China in the Indo-Pacific region. That same month, the leaders of Australia, the United Kingdom and the United States agreed to a pact known as AUKUS to increase defense cooperation and supply nuclear submarines to Australia. In May 2022, China agreed a pact with the Solomon Islands which may lead to Chinese bases being constructed across the Pacific. In September 2022, Biden said that the U.S. would defend Taiwan if it was attacked by China. In February 2023, the U.S. shot down a Chinese weather balloon off the coast of South Carolina which they said was being used for spying. Biden repeatedly said that China posed challenges to America's security, prosperity and values and criticized human rights abuses conducted by the Communist Chinese government.

In September 2022, Biden represented the United States at the funeral of Queen Elizabeth II in Westminster Abbey. During in her seventy-year reign she had been the friend and ally of fourteen U.S. Presidents. In 2023, Biden returned to the UK where he me the newly crowned sovereign, King Charles III. He was the first U.S. President to meet two different reigning British monarchs.

Presidential Election 2024.

In the mid-term elections of 2022, the Democrats retained control of the Senate while the Republicans won a slim majority in the House of Representatives. In April 2023, Biden announced his candidacy for re-election once again with Kamala Harris as his running mate. He faced a brief challenge for the Democratic nomination from environmental lawyer, Robert Kennedy Jr. However, in October 2023, Kennedy announced that he would be dropping out of the primary race and standing as an independent candidate. One of the issues faced by Biden in his campaign is his age. If he is successful at being re-elected her will begin his second term at the age of 82 and would leave office at the age of 86. Since becoming President, Biden's age has never ceased to be an issue to his opponents. On several occasions they pointed to gaffes made by the President and said that his age and senility were responsible. Another issue may be the alleged inappropriate behavior, scandals and corruption of his son, Hunter.

Summary

It is too early to judge where Joe Biden ranks as a President. His term of office has not lacked achievements in either domestic or foreign affairs. The country and the economy have recovered from the pandemic and there has been considerable investment in infrastructure. Important support has been provided to Ukraine and Israel following external attacks on those countries. However, the withdrawal from Afghanistan was poorly conducted and there was little coordination and communication with America's friends and allies. The President's age looks as if it will be an important issue at the next presidential election.

APPENDIX – INTERESTING INFORMATION ABOUT THE PRESIDENTS

1. PRESIDENTIAL
RECORDS

Allll of the Presidents set a new record in some way. Here are the Presidents and the records they hold.

1. *George Washington* – was the first President of the United States and the only one to win one hundred percent of the votes in the Electoral College.
2. *John Adams* – was the first President to live in Washington D.C., and the White House.
3. *Thomas Jefferson* – was the first President whose election was decided by the House of Representatives and the first to be inaugurated in Washington D.C. He owned more slaves than any other President.
4. *James Madison* – was the first President to ask Congress to make a declaration of war (against Britain in the War of 1812).
5. *James Monroe* – was the first President to have a child marry while in the White House.
6. *John Quincy Adams* – was the most learned President and could speak seven languages. He was the first son of a President to also become a President and the first to be elected by a minority vote.

7. *Andrew Jackson* – was the first President to be born in a log cabin and the first Democrat to become President. He was the first to travel on a railroad.

8. *Martin Van Buren* – did not speak English as a first language and was the first President to lead America through a depression (the Panic of 1837).

9. *William Harrison* – was the first President to die in office and the first of two to die in the White House (the other being Zachary Taylor). His one month in office was the shortest of any President.

10. *John Tyler* – Had more children than any other President (15). He also had two First Ladies during his time in the White House.

11. *James Polk* – was the only President who had previously served as Speaker of the House.

12. *Zachary Taylor* – was the first President to use the term "First Lady."

13. Millard Fillmore – was the first President born in the 1800s and to install a library in the White House.

14. *Franklin Pierce* – was the first President born in the nineteenth century.

15. *James Buchanan* – was the only President who never married.

16. *Abraham Lincoln* – was the first Republican to become President and the first President to be assassinated.

17. *Andrew Johnson* – was the first President to be impeached by the House of Representatives.

18. *Ulysees S. Grant* – was the last President to own a slave and the first to approve the creation of a national park.

19. *Rutherford Hayes* – was the first President to use a telephone and a typewriter.

20. *James A. Garfield* – could write in two different languages at the same time using different hands. He was the first President to be directly elected by the House of Representatives.

21. *Chester Arthur* – took the oath of office in his own home and installed the first elevator in the White House.

22. *Grover Cleveland* (first presidency) – the first President to get married inside the White House.

23. *Benjamin Harrison* – was the only grandson of a President to also become a President.
24. *Grover Cleveland* (second presidency) – was the only President to serve two non-consecutive terms. He was the only President to have a child born in the White House (1893).
25. *William McKinley* – was the first President to ride in an automobile.
26. *Theodore Roosevelt* – was the first President to visit a foreign country while in office. He was also the first President to win a Nobel Prize.
27. *William H. Taft* – was the only President to become the Chief Justice of the United States and the first of two to be buried at Arlington National Cemetery (John F. Kennedy being the other).
28. *Woodrow Wilson* – was the first President to hold regular press conferences and the first to speak on radio. Like John Tyler, he also had two First Ladies during his time in the White House.
29. *Warren Harding* – was the first President to be elected after women gained the right to vote. He was also the first President to be elected while sitting in the U.S. Senate and the first to be broadcast on radio.
30. *Calvin Coolidge* – had the oath of office administered by his father. He was also the first President to deliver a radio address from the White House.
31. *Herbert Hoover* – was the first President to be born west of the Mississippi River. He was also the first to have a phone in his office.
32. *Franklin D. Roosevelt* – was the only President to win four terms in office. His term in office of 12 years, 1 month and 8 days was the longest of any President. He received more electoral votes than any other President (523 in 1936). He was the first President to speak on television.
33. *Harry S. Truman* – was the first and only President to authorize the use of nuclear weapons. His inauguration was the first to be shown on television across the nation.

34. *Dwight D. Eisenhower* – was the first President to preside over all fifty states of the U.S. He was the first to travel by a jet airplane and helicopter, the first to appear on color television and the first to be broadcast via a satellite in space.

35. *John F. Kennedy* – was the youngest President to be elected and the youngest to die (46 years old). He was the first President to be born in the twentieth century and the first of two Roman Catholics to become President (Joe Biden being the other). He took part in the first televised presidential debate (with Richard Nixon).

36. *Lyndon B. Johnson* – was the first President to be sworn in by a woman (Sarah T. Hughes). He was the first to appoint an African American to a Cabinet post (Robert C. Weaver) and to the Supreme Court (Thurgood Marshall).

37. *Richard Nixon* – was the first and only President to resign. He took part in the first televised presidential debate (with John F. Kennedy).

38. *Gerald Ford* – the only President never to be elected to the office of either President or Vice-President.

39. *Jimmy Carter* – was the oldest President and had the longest post-presidency. He was also the longest married President, being married to Rosalynn Smith Carter for 77 years and 135 days.

40. *Ronald Reagan* – was the oldest President to win an election being 73 years old when he was re-elected in 1984 (this record was later broken by Joe Biden). He was the first to appoint a woman to the Supreme Court (Sandra Day O'Connor).

41. *George H. W. Bush* – was the second President after John Adams who also had a son serve as President. He was the first President to have served as the U.S. Ambassador to the United Nations and as director of the Central Intelligence Agency (CIA).

42. *Bill Clinton* – was the first President with an official website and the first to send an email. He was also the first President to be married to a member of Congress (Hillary Clinton).

43. *George W. Bush* – was the second President (after John Quincy Adams) who also had a father serve as President. He

was the first President to appoint an African-American as Secretary of State (Colin Powell).

44. *Barack Obama* – was the first African-American to be President. He also was the first to appoint a former First Lady to be Secretary of State (Hillary Clinton).

45. *Donald Trump* – was the only President not to have previously served in a political or military office. He had more wives than any other President (three). He was the first President to be impeached twice by the House of Representatives and the first to be the subject of a mug shot (August 2023).

46. *Joe Biden* – was the oldest man to be elected President (he was 78 years old when elected in 2020) and the first to have a female Vice-President (Kamala Harris).

2. STATE OF BIRTH OF THE PRESIDENTS

Of the 45 men to be President, eight were born in Virginia, seven in Ohio, six in New York, four in Massachusetts, two in North Carolina, two in Texas, two in Pennsylvania and one each from fourteen other states. In all, the Presidents were born in twenty-one different states. Andrew Jackson was born on the border of North and South Carolina but considered himself to be from South Carolina.

Here are the Presidents, the years of their term of office and their state of birth.

1. George Washington - 1789 to 1797 - Virginia

2. John Adams - 1797 to 1801 - Massachusetts

3. Thomas Jefferson - 1801 to 1809 - Virginia

4. James Madison - 1809 to 1817 - Virginia

5. James Monroe - 1817 to 1825 - Virginia

6. John Quincy Adams 1825 to 1829 - Massachusetts

7. Andrew Jackson - 1929 to 1837 - South Carolina

8. Martin Van Buren - 1837 to 1841 - New York

9. William H. Harrison - 1841 - Virginia

10. John Tyler - 1841 to 1845 - Virginia

11. James Polk - 1845 to 1849 - North Carolina

12. Zachary Taylor -1849 to 1850 - Virginia

13. Millard Fillmore - 1850 to 1853 - New York

14. Franklin Pierce - 1853 to 1857 - New Hampshire

15. James Buchanan - 1857 to 1861 - Pennsylvania

16. Abraham Lincoln - 1861 to 1865 - Kentucky

17. Andrew Johnson - 1865 to 1869 - North Carolina

18. Ulysees S. Grant - 1869 to 1877 - Ohio

19. Rutherford Hayes - 1877 to 1881 - Ohio

20. James A. Garfield - 1881 - Ohio

21. Chester A. Arthur - 1881 to 1885 - New York

22. Grover Cleveland - 1885 to 1889 - New Jersey

23. Benjamin Harrison - 1889 to 1893 - Ohio

24. Grover Cleveland - 1893 to 1897 - New Jersey

25. William McKinley - 1897 to 1901 - Ohio

26. Theodore Roosevelt - 1901 to 1909 - New York

27. Willam H. Taft - 1909 to 1913 -Ohio

28. Woodrow Wilson - 1913 to 1921 - Virginia

29. Warren Harding - 1921 to 1923 - Ohio

30. Calvin Coolidge - 1923 to 1929 - Vermont

31. Herbert Hoover - 1929 to 1933 - Iowa

32. Franklin D. Roosevelt - 1933 to 1945 - New York

33. Harry S. Truman - 1945 to 1953 - Missouri

34. Dwight D. Eisenhower - 1953 to 1961 -Texas

35. John F. Kennedy - 1961 to 1963 -Massachusetts

36. Lyndon B. Johnson - 1963 to 1969 -Texas

37. Richard Nixon - 1969 to 1974 - California

38. Gerald Ford - 1974 to 1977 - Nebraska

39. Jimmy Carter - 1977 to 1981 -Georgia

40. Ronald Reagan - 1981 to 1989 - Illinois

41. George H. W. Bush - 1989 to 1993 - Massachusetts

42. Bill Clinton - 1993 to 2001 - Arkansas

43. George W. Bush 2001 to 2009 - Connecticut

44. Barack Obama - 2009 to 2017 - Hawaii

45. Donald Trump - 2017 to 2021 - New York

46. Joe Biden - 2021 to present - Pennsylvania

3. PRESIDENTS BORN IN
A LOG CABIN

Seven Presidents were born in a log cabin and rose from their humble origins to take the highest office in the land.

No.	President	Date of Birth	Place of Birth
7	Andrew Jackson	15th March 1767	Waxhaw Settlement, South Carolina
11	James Polk	2nd November 1795	Pineville, North Carolina
13	Millard Fillmore	7th January 1800	Locke, New York
14	Franklin Pierce	23rd November 1804	Hillsborough, New Hampshire
15	James Buchanan	23rd April 1791	Cove Gap, Pennsylvania
16	Abraham Lincoln	12th February 1809	Hardin, near Hodgenville, Kentucky
20	James A. Garfield	19th November 1831	Orange Township, Ohio

4. PRESIDENTS' WIVES AND FIRST LADIES

T he White House recognizes the following 47 women as having been the First Lady of the United States. Please note that Frances Folsom had two spells as First Lady. She was married to Grover Cleveland who had two non-consecutive terms as President.

1. Martha Dandridge Custis was married to George Washington from 1759 until his death in 1799 and was the nation's first ever First Lady between 1789 and 1787.

2. Abigail Smith was married to John Adams from 1764 until 1818 and was the nation's First Lady between 1797 and 1801. She was the mother of the sixth President, John Quincy Adams.

3. Martha Wayles Skelton was married to Thomas Jefferson from 1772 until her death in 1782. She died nine years before he was inaugurated as President.

4. Dolley Todd was married to James Madison from 1794 to 1836 and as the nation's First Lady between 1809 and 1817.

5. Elizabeth Kortright was married to James Monroe from 1786 to 1830 and served as the nation's First Lady between 1817 and 1825.

6. Louisa Johnson was married to John Quincy Adams from 1797 to 1848 and was the nation's First Lady between 1825 and 1829. She was the first (of two) First Lady to be born in a foreign country.

7. Rachel Donelson Robards was married to Andrew Jackson from 1791 to 1828. She died shortly after his victory in the 1828 presidential election and three months before his inauguration as President.

8. Hannah Hoes was married to Martin Van Buren from 1807 until her death in 1819. She died eighteen years before he was elected President.

9. Anna Symmes was married to William H. Harrison between 1795 and 1841, when he died in office. She was the nation's First Lady for one month in 1841 and was the shortest serving First Lady. She was the grandmother of the 23rd President, Benjamin Harrison.
10. Letitia Christian was married to John Tyler between 1813 and 1842. She was the nation's First Lady between 1841 and 1842.

11. Julia Gardiner was married to John Tyler from 1844 to 1862 and was the nation's First Lady between 1844 and 1845.

12. Sarah Childress was married to James Polk from 1824 to 1849 and was the nation's First Lady between 1845 and 1849.

13. Margaret Mackall Smith was married to Zachary Taylor between 1810 and 1850. She was the nation's First Lady between 1849 and 1850.

14. Abigail Powers was married to Millard Fillmore between 1826 and 1853. She was the nation's First Lady between 1850 and 1853.

15. Jane Appleton was married to Franklin Pierce from 1834 to 1863. She was the nation's First Lady between 1853 and 1857.

16. Harriet Lane is the only woman recognized as a First Lady by the White House who was not married to a President. She was the niece

of the only bachelor to be President, James Buchanan, and performed the functions of the First Lady between 1857 and 1861.

17. Mary Todd was married to Abraham Lincoln between 1832 and 1865 and was the nation's First Lady between 1861 and 1865.

18. Eliza McArdle was married to Andrew Johnson between 1827 and 1875 and was the nation's First Lady between 1865 and 1869.

19. Julia Dent was married to Ulysees S. Grant between 1848 and 1885 and was the nation's First Lady between 1869 and 1877.

20. Lucy Ware Webb was married to Rutherford Hayes between 1852 and 1889 and was the nation's First Lady between 1877 and 1881.

21. Lucretia Rudolph was married to James A. Garfield from 1858 to 1881 and was the nation's First Lady in 1881.

22. Frances Folsom was married to Grover Cleveland from 1886 to 1908 and had two spells as the nation's First Lady. Her first one was between 1886 and 1889. She was the youngest person to become First Lady and was just 21 when she married Cleveland in 1886.

23. Caroline Lavinia Scott was married to Benjamin Harrison from 1853 to 1892 and served as the nation's First Lady between 1889 to 1892.

24. Frances Folsom had her second spell as First Lady between 1893 and 1897, when Grover Cleveland served his second term.

25. Ida Saxton was married to William McKinley from 1871 to 1901 and was the nation's First Lady from 1897 to 1901.

26. Edith Carrow was married to Theodore Roosevelt from 1886 to 1919 and was the nation's First Ladt between 1901 and 1909.

27. Helen "Nellie" Herron was married to William Howard Taft from 1886 to 1930 and was the nation's First Lady from 1909 to 1913.

28. Ellen Louise Axson was married to Woodrow Wilson from 1885 to 1914 and was the nation's First Lady from 1913 to 1914.

29. Edith Bolling Galt was married to Woodrow Wilson from 1915 to 1924 and was the nation's First Lady between 1915 and 1921.

30. Florence Kling DeWolfe was married to Warren Harding from 1891 to 1923 and was the nation's First Lady between 1921 and 1923.

31. Grace Anna Goodhue was married to Calvin Coolidge from 1905 to 1933 and was the nation's First Lady between 1923 and 1929.

32. Lou Henry was married to Herbert Hoover from 1899 to 1944 and was the nation's First Lady between 1929 and 1933.

33. Anna Eleanor Roosevelt was married to Franklin D. Roosevelt from 1905 to 1945 and was the nation's longest serving First Lady for twelve years between 1933 and 1945.

34. Elizabeth "Bess" Wallace was married to Harry S. Truman from 1919 to 1972 and was the nation's First Lady between 1945 and 1953. She lived longer than any other First Lady and died in 1982 aged 97 years and 247 days.

35. Mary "Mamie" Dowd was married to Dwight D. Eisenhower from 1916 to 1969 and was the nation's first lady from 1953 to 1961.

36. Jacqueline Lee Bouvier was married to John F. Kennedy from 1953 to 1963 and was the nation's First Lady from 1961 until 1963.

37. Claudia Lady Bird Taylor was married to Lyndon Baines Johnson from 1934 to 1973 and was the nation's First Lady from 1963 to 1969.

38. Thelma Catherine "Pat" Ryan was married to Richard Nixon from 1940 to 1993 and was the nation's First Lady from 1969 to 1974.

39. Elizabeth "Betty" Bloomer was married to Gerald Ford from 1948 to 2006 and was the nation's First Lady between 1974 and 1977.

40. Rosalynn Smith was married to Jimmy Carter from 1946 to 2023 and was the nation's First Lady between 1977 and 1981. She was married longer than any other First Lady. When she died on 19th November 2023, she had been married to Jimmy Carter for 77 years and 135 days.

41. Nancy Davis was married to Ronald Reagan from 1952 to 2004 and was the nation's First Lady between 1981 and 1989.

42. Barbara Pierce was married to George H. W. Bush from 1945 to 2018 and was the nation's First Lady between 1989 and 1993. She was the mother of the 43rd President, George W. Bush.

43. Hillary Rodham has been married to Bill Clinton since 1975 and served as the nation's First Lady between 1993and 2001. She ran for President in 2008 and 2016.

44. Laura Welch has been married to George W. Bush since 1977 and was the nation's First Lady between 2001 and 2009.

45. Michelle LaVaughn Robinson has been married to Barack Obama since 1992 and was the nation's First Lady between 2009 and 2017.

46. Melania Knauss has been married to Donald Trump since 2005 and was the nation's First Lady between 2017 and 2021.

47. Jill Jacobs has been married to Joe Biden since 1977 and has been the nation's First Lady since 2021. She was the oldest person to become First Lady and was 69 years old when her husband was inaugurated as the 46th President of the United States.

Not every woman who married a President became the First Lady. Six wives died before their husbands took office and two woman married Presidents who had already left office. In addition, three women were divorced from their husbands before they became President.

The six wives that died before their husbands became President were as .

1. Martha Wayles Skelton married Thomas Jefferson in 1772 but died in 1782, nineteen years before he was inaugurated as President.

2. Rachel Donelson Robards married Andrew Jackson in 1791 but died in 1828, four months before he was inaugurated as President.

3. Hannah Hoes married Martin Van Buren in 1807 but died in 1819, eighteen years before he was inaugurated as President.

4. Ellen Lewis Herndon married Chester Arthus in 1859 but died in 1880, the year before he was inaugurated as President.

5. Alice Hathaway Lee married Theodore Roosevelt in 1884 and died the same year, seventeen years before he was inaugurated as President.

6. Neila Hunter married Joe Biden in 1966 but died in 1972, forty-nine years before he was inaugurated as President.
Theodore Roosevelt and Joe Biden were the only two widowed Presidents to later remarry.

The two women that married Presidents that had already left office were as follows.

1. Caroline McIntosh married Millard Fillmore in 1858, five years after he left office.

2. Mary Lord Dimmick married Benjamin Harrison in 1896, three years after he left office.

The three women who divorced their husbands before they became President were as follows.

1. Jane Wyman married Ronald Reagan in 1941 but divorced him in 1948, thirty-three years before he was inaugurated as President in 1981.

2. Ivana Marie Zelnickova married Donald Trump in 1977 but divorced him in 1992, twenty-five years before he was inaugurated in 2017.

3. Marla Maples married Donald Trump in 1993 but divorced him in 1999, eighteen years before he was inaugurated in 2017.
Donald Trump has had more wives than any other President and is also the only President to be divorced twice.

5. VICE-PRESIDENTS WHO BECAME PRESIDENTS

F ifteen Vice-Presidents went on to become President of the United States. Of these fifteen, eight succeeded to the Presidency upon the death of the incumbent, six were elected to office and one took over from a President that had resigned.

Vice-Presidents that became President Upon the Death of the Incumbent

The eight Vice-President that became Presidents upon the death of the incumbent were as follows:

1. 1841 - John Tyler, upon the death of William Henry Harrison.

2. 1850 - Millard Fillmore, upon the death of Zachary Taylor.

3. 1865 - Andrew Johnson, upon the assassination of Abraham Lincoln.

4. 1881 - Chester Arthur, upon the assassination of James A. Garfield.

5. 1901 - Theodore Roosevelt, upon the assassination of William McKinley.

6. 1923 - Calvin Coolidge, upon the death of Warren Harding.

7. 1945 - Harry S. Truman, upon the death of Franklin D. Roosevelt.

8. 1963 - Lyndon B. Johnson, upon the assassination of John F. Kennedy.

Vice-Presidents that became President Upon the Resignation of the Incumbent

The one Vice-President that became President when the incumbent resigned was as follows:

1. 1974 - Gerald Ford, upon the resignation of Richard Nixon.

Vice-Presidents that became President after Winning an Election

The six Vice-Presidents who subsequently became President after winning elections were as follows:

1. 1796 - John Adams

2. 1800 - Thomas Jefferson

3. 1836 - Martin Van Buren

4. 1968 - Richard Nixon

5. 1988 - George Bush

6. 2020 - Joe Biden

John Adams , Thomas Jefferson, Martin Van Buren and George H. W. Bush were all sitting Vice-Presidents when they were elected President.

6. PRESIDENTS THAT SERVED IN THE U.S. SENATE

Seventeen Presidents have also served in the U.S. Senate.

1. James Monroe served as a Senator for Virginia from 1790 to 1794 and as President from 1817 to 1825.

2. John Quincy Adams served as a Senator for Massachuseets from 1803 to 1808 and as President from 1825 to 1829.

3. Andrew Jackson served as a Senator for Tennessee from 1797 to 1798 and from 1823 to 1825, and as President from 1829 to 1837.

4. Martin Van Buren served as a Senator for New York from1821 to 1828 and as President from 1829 to 1837.

5. William Harrison served as a Senator for Ohio from 1825 to 1828 and as President in 1841.

6. John Tyler served as a Senator for Virginia from 1827 to 1836 and as President from 1841 to 1845.

7. Franklin Pierce served as a Senaot for New Hampshire from 1837 to 1842 and as President from 1853 to 1857.

8. James Buchanan served as a Senator for Pennsylvania from 1834 to 1845 and as President from 1857 to 1861.

9. Andrew Johnson served as a Senator for Tennessee from 1857 to 1862 and in 1875, and as President from 1865 to 1869.

10. Benjamin Harrison served as a Senator for Indiana from 1881 to 1887 and as President from 1889 to 1893.

11. Warren Harding served as a Senator for Ohio from 1915 to 1921 and as President from 1921 to 1923.

12. Harry S. Truman served as a Senator for Missouri and as President from 1945 to 1953.

13. John F. Kennedy served as a Senator for Massachusetts from 1953 to 1960 and as President from 1961 to 1963.

14. Lyndon B. Johnson served as a Senator for Texas from 1949 to 1961 and as President from 1963 to 1969.

15. Richard Nixon served as a Senator from California from 1950 to 1953 and as President from 1969 to 1974.

16. Barack Obama served as a Senator for Illinois from 2005 to 2008 and as President from 2009 to 2017.

17. Joe Biden served as a Senator for Delaware from 1973 to 2009 and as the since 2021.

7. PRESIDENTS THAT SERVED IN THE U.S. HOUSE OF REPRESENTATIVES

Nineteen Presidents have also served in the U.S. House of Representatives.

1. James Madison served as a representative for Virginia from 1789 to 1797 and as President from 1809 to 1817.

2. John Quincy Adams served as a representative for Massachusetts from 1831 to 1848, and as President from 1825 to 1829.

3. Andrew Jackson served as a representative for Tennessee from 1796 to 1797, and as President from 1829 to 1837.

4. William H. Harrison served as the representative of Northwest Territory from 1799 to 1800 and as the representative of Ohio from 1816 to 1819, and as President in 1841.

5. John Tyler served as the representative of Virginia from 1816 to 1821 andas President from 1841 to 1845.

6. James Polk served as the representative of Tennessee from 1825 to 1829 and as President from 1845 to 1849.

7. Millard Fillmore served as the representative of New York from 1833 to 1835 and from 1837 to 1843, and as President from 1850 to 1853.

8. Franklin Pierce served as the representative of New Hampshire from 1833 to 1837 and as President from 1853 to 1857.

9. James Buchanan served as the representative of New Hampshire from 1821 to 1831 and as President from 1857 to 1861.

10. Abraham Lincoln served as the representative of Illinois from 1847 to 1849 and as President from 1861 to 1865.

11. Andrew Johnson served as the representative of Tennessee from 1843 to 1853, and as President from 1865 to 1869.

12. Rutherford Hayes served as the representative of Ohio from 1865 to 1867 and as President from 1877 to 1881.

13. James A. Garfield served as the representative of Ohio from 1863 to 1880 and as President in 1881.

14. William McKinley served as the representative of Ohio from 1877 to 1883 and from 1885 to 1891, and as President from 1897 to 1901.

15. John F. Kennedy served as the representative of Massachusetts from 1947 to 1953 and as President from 1961 to 1963.

16. Lyndon B. Johnson served as the representative of Texas from 1937 to 1945 and as President from 1963 to 1969.

17. Richard Nixon served as the representative of California from 1947 to 1950 and as President from 1969 to 1974.

18. Gerald Ford served as the representative of Michigan from 1949 to 1973 and as President from 1974 to 1977.

19. George H. W. Bush served as the representative of Texas from 1967 to 1971 and as President from 1989 to 1993.

8. PRESIDENTS THAT SERVED AS STATE GOVERNORS

Seventeen Presidents have also served as State Governors.

1. Thomas Jefferson served as the Governor for Virginia from 1779 to 1781 and as President from 1801 to 1809.

2. James Monroe served as the Governor of Virginia from1799 to 1802 and again in 1811 and as President from 1817 to 1825.

3. Martin Van Buren served as the Governor of New York in 1829 and as President from1837 to 1841.

4. John Tyler served as the Governor of Virginia from 1825 to 1827 and as President from 1841 to 1845.

5. James Polk served as the Governor of Tennessee from 1839 to 1841 and as President from 1845 to 1849.

6. Andrew Johnson served as the Governor of Tennessee from 1853 to 1857 and as President from 1865 to 1869.

7. Rutherford Hayes served as the Governor of Ohio from 1868 to 1872 and from 1876 to 1877, and as President from 1877 to 1881.

8. Grover Cleveland served as the Governor of New York from 1883 to 1885 and as the 22nd and 24th Presidents from 1885 to 1889 and from 1893 to 1897.

9. William McKinley served as the Governor of Ohio from 1892 to 1896 and as President from 1897 to 1901.

10. Theodore Roosevelt served as the Governor of New York from 1899 to 1900 and as President from 1901 to 1909.

11. Woodrow Wilson served as the Governor of New Jersey from 1911 to 1913 and as President from 1913 to 1921.

12. Calvin Coolidge served as the Governor of Massachuseets from 1919 to 1921 and as President from 1923 to 1929.

13. Franklin D. Roosevelt served as The Governor of New York from1929 to 1932 and as President form 1933 to 1945.

14. Jimmy Carter served the Governor of Georgia from 1971 to 1975 and as President from 1977 to 1981.

15. Ronald Reagan served as the Governor of California from 1967 to1975 and as the President from 1977 to 1981.

16. Bill Clinton served as the Governor of Arkansas from 1979 to 1981 and from 1983 to 1992, and as President from 1993 to 2001.

17. George W. Bush served as the Governor of Texas from 1995 to 2000 and as President from 2001 to 2009.

9. PRESIDENTIAL ELECTION RECORDS

Here are some of the most important election records.

1. 1840 - William Henry Harrison and Martin Van Buren became the first candidates to win more than one million votes

2. 1920 - Warren Harding became the first candidate to win more than ten million votes.

3. 1928 - Herbert Hoover became the first candidate to win more than twenty million votes.

4. 1952 - Dwight D. Eisenhower became the first candidate to win more than thirty million votes.

5. 1964 - Lyndon B. Johnson became the first candidate to win more than forty million votes.

6. 1984 - Ronald Reagan became the first candidate to win more than fifty million votes.

7. 2004 - George W. Bush became the first candidate to win more than sixty million votes.

8. 2020 - Joe Biden became the first candidate to win more than seventy million votes and the first candidate to win more than eighty million votes.

10. PRESIDENTS THAT LOST THE POPULAR VOTE

F ive Presidents were elected to office even though they lost the

popular vote.

1. 1824 - The sixth President, John Quincy Adams, was elected with 32 percent of the vote.

2. 1876 - The nineteenth President, Rutherford Hayes, was elected with 48 percent of the vote.

3. 1888 - The twenty-third President, Benjamin Harrison, was elected with 48 percent of the vote.

4. 2000 - The forty-third President, George W. Bush, was elected with 48 percent of the vote.

5. 2016 - The forty-fifth President, Donald Trump, was elected with 46 percent of the vote.

11. PRESIDENTS IN A CHANGING WORLD

T

he world has changed a great deal since George Washington was inaugurated as the first President. Here as some of the key presidential "firsts."

1. 1833 - Andrew Jackson became the first President to ride on a train.

2. 1847 - George Washington became the first President to appear on a postage stamp.

3. 1849 - James Polk became the first President to appear in a photograph while in office.

4. 1877 - Rutherford Hayes became the first President to speak on a telephone.

5. 1889 - Benjamin Harrison became the first President to have his voice recorded.

6. 1897 - William McKinley became the first President to appear in a film.

7. 1899 - George Washington became the first President to appear on a coin.

8. 1901 - William McKinley became the first President to ride in a car.

9. 1905 - Theodoree Roosevelt became the first President to travel on a submarine.

10. 1910 - Theodore Roosevelt became the first President to fly in a plane.

11. 1922 Warren Harding became the first President to be broadcast on the radio.

12. 1929 - 1933 - Herbert Hoover became the first President to appear in a color film. The precise date has not been determined.

13. 1939 - Franklin D. Roosevelt became the first President to appear on TV.

14. 1944 - Franklin D. Roosevelt became the first President to appear in a color photograph.

15. 1956 - Dwight D. Eisenhower became the first President to appear on color TV.

16. 1957 - Dwight D. Eisenhower became the first President to fly in a helicopter.

17. 1958 - Dwight D Eisenhower became the first President to be broadcast via satellite.

18. 1961 - John F.Kennedy became the first President to meet an astronaut when he met Alan Shepard.

19. 1969 - Richard Nixon became first President to speak to someone on another world when he spoke to the Apollo 11 astronauts while they were on the surface of the moon.

20. 1994 - Bill Clinton became the first President to send an email.

21. 1994 - Bill Clinton became the first President to have a website.

12. INTERNATIONAL VISITS MADE BY PRESIDENTS

H

ere is the date of the first visit made by a serving President for a selection of countries.

1. Australia - 1966 - Lyndon Baines Johnson

2. Brazil - 1928 - Herbert Hoover

3. Canada - 1923 - Warren Harding

4. China - 1972- Richard Nixon

5. Cuba - 1928 - Calvin Coolidge

6. Egypt - 1943 - Franklin D. Roosevelt

7. France - 1918 - Woodrow Wilson

8. Germany - 1945- Harry S. Truman

9. India - 1959 - Dwight D. Eisenhower

10. Ireland - 1963 - John F. Kennedy

11. Israel - 1974 - Richard Nixon

12. Italy - 1919 - Woodrow Wilson

13. Japan - 1974 - Gerald Ford

14. Mexico - 1909 - William Howard Taft

15. North Korea - 2019 - Donald Trump

16. Panama - 1906 - Theodore Roosevelt

17. Saudi Arabia - 1974 - Richard Nixon

18. South Africa - 1998 - Bill Clinton

19. South Korea - 1960 - Dwight D. Eisenhower

20. Soviet Union/Russia - 1945 - Franklin D. Roosevelt

21. United Kingdom - 1918 - Woodrow Wilson

22. Vatican - 1919 - Woodrow Wilson

23. Vietnam - 1966 - Lyndon B. Johnson

The first President to visit another country while in office was Theodore Roosevelt when he visited Panama in 1906. A hundred years later, George

W. Bush visited 73 different countries during his time in the White House, a record for any President.

On his visit to Europe in 1918-19, Woodrow Wilson became the first serving U.S. President to meet a reigning King of England and a Pope.

Eisenhower also visited South Korea as President-Elect in December 1952.

13. PRESIDENTS WHO OWNED SLAVES

A total of twelve Presidents owned slaves during their lifetime. Eight Presidents owned slaves while they were in office while four had owned slaves before they entered the White House.

The eight Presidents that owned slaves while they were in office were:

No. President

1 George Washington 1789 – 1797

3 Thomas Jefferson 1801 – 1809

4 James Madison 1809 – 1817

5 James Monroe 1817 – 1825

7 Andrew Jackson 1829 – 1837

10 John Tyler 1841 – 1845

11 James Polk 1845 – 1849

12 Zachary Taylor 1849 – 1850

Jefferson owned more slaves than any other President.

The four Presidents that owned slaves before entering office were as follows:

No. President

8Martin Van Buren 1837 – 1841

9William Henry Harrison 1841

17Andrew Johnson 1865 – 1869

18Ulysees Grant 1869 – 1877

Ulysees Grant was presented with a slave by a member of his family but he granted the man his freedom shortly afterwards.

14. PRESIDENTS THAT DIED IN OFFICE

Eight Presidents have died in office, four of whom were assassinated.

1. William Henry Harrison, the ninth President, died from illness on 4th April 1841.

2. Zachary Taylor, the twelfth President President, died from illness on 9th July 1850.

3. Abraham Lincoln, the sixteenth President, died on 15th April 1865. He shot in the head by John Wilkes Booth the night before.

4. James A. Garfield, the twentieth President, died on 19th September 1881. He was shot by Charles. J. Guiteau on 2nd July 1881.

5. William McKinley, the twenty-fifth President, died on 14th September 1901. He was shot by Leon F. Czolgosz on 6th September 1901.

6. Warren Harding, the twenty-ninth President, died from illness on 2nd August 1923. It has also been alleged that he was poisoned by his wife. Please see chapter 29.

7. Franklin D. Roosevelt, the thirty-second President, died from illness on 12th April 1945.

8. John F. Kennedy, the thirty-fifth President, was shot and killed by Lee Harvey Oswald on 22nd November 1963.

15. THE PRESIDENTIAL SUCCESSION

If the President dies, resigns or is removed from office then the Vice-President will become President. This has happened on nine occasions. The Vice-President will also take over temporarily if the President becomes unable to perform his duties. When a Vice-President replaces a President in office then he may nominate a new Vice-President who will then take office once approval has been obtained from Congress.

After the Vice-President, the following government officials are the next in line to the Presidency:

1. Speaker of the House of Representatives
2. President *Pro Tempore* of the Senate
3. Secretary of the State
4. Secretary of the Treasury
5. Secretary of Defense
6. Attorney General
7. Secretary of the Interior
8. Secretary of Agriculture
9. Secretary of Commerce
10. Secretary of Labor
11. Secretary of Health and Human Services
12. Secretary of Housing and Urban Development

13. Secretary of Transportation
14. Secretary of Energy
15. Secretary of Education

A NOTE ON SOURCES

T his book was researched over many years from wide range of sources including history books, biographies, diaries, newspapers, speeches, letters, and official documents. Sources are quoted in the text when appropriate.

The cover photograph shows a portrait of George Washington painted by Gilbert Stuart in 1796. Known as the *Lansdowne Portrait*, it used to belong to the British Prime Minister, the 1st Marquess of Lansdowne, and shows the first President of the United States during his last year in office. In 2001, the original portrait was purchased by the National Portrait Gallery in Washington D.C. for $20 million. The image for this book was provided under license from Getty Images.

ABOUT THE AUTHOR

Andrew W. Martin

Andrew W. Martin is a graduate of the widely respected School of History at the University of Leeds in Yorkshire, England. He is interested in American, British, European and world history across all periods of time and tries to write well-researched books that will appeal to both general readers who wish to know more about a subject as well as students undertaking courses at school and college. "A New and Concise History of the Presidents of the United States of America" is the first title that he has published on Amazon.

Made in the USA
Columbia, SC
16 September 2024

42069531R00222